Wealth Inequality in America

Causes, Consequences, and Solutions

THE DESTRUCTION OF THE AMERICAN MIDDLE CLASS

DR. JAMES GLENN
Foreword by Miles Hamby, Ph.D.

Pensiero Press

Wealth Inequality in America: Causes, Consequences, and Solutions: The Destruction of the American Middle Class

P Pensiero Press

Websites: www.ThePensieroPress.com | www.LentzLeadership.com
Twitter: https://twitter.com/drcheryllentz
Facebook: https://www.facebook.com/Dr.Cheryl.Lentz

Books are available through Pensiero Press at special discounts for bulk purchases for the purpose of sales promotion, seminar attendance, or educational purposes. Special volumes can be created for specific purposes and to organizational specifications. Please contact us for further details.

Volume ISBN: 978-1-7329382-9-8
LAW009000 LAW / Business & Financial
*Kindle and electronic versions available

Cover design & production: Gary Rosenberg • www.garyarosenberg.com

Volume 1

CONTENTS

I would like to thank my wife Arleen Scott whose humor, love, and patience made this book possible. I'd also like to thank my friend and colleague, Miles Hamby PhD who was instrumental in making this book possible by offering his ideas and energy towards the completion of this book. I would also like to thank my editor, Dr. Cheryl Lentz whose guidance, patience, and support were critical in bringing this book to fruition.

REVIEWS

Linda F. Patten

Leadership Trainer for Women Entrepreneurs and Changemakers—President & CEO, Dare2Lead With Linda

Website: www.dare2leadwithlinda.com

email: linda@dare2leadwithlinda.com

Being solidly placed in the middle class, my parents saw the economic growth of the post-World War II era. They also lived through the Depression, and both worked at a time when women did not work outside the home, providing financial security for the family and through to the ends of their lives.

Growing up, I was blissfully ignorant of the mechanics of money, and even into my college years as an economics major.

Dr. Glenn has expertly and definitively called out what has happened to our money since the FED was formed and the policies of Reaganomics have played out. I for one watched it happen in my own bank account, through short-selling our home in 2012, through the devastation of our retirement accounts (and we aren't even retired yet). This process is laid out for us by Dr. Glenn with shocking clarity at how ignorant we all are. We have been fooled for so many years into thinking it will be all right—and it definitely won't be.

After reading this insightful book, I am now convinced that after Covid-19 the world, and especially the United States, needs to step into a new normal which does not include the FED and the other entities that create a divide between the uber-rich and the rest of the country. This is our call to take action, to eliminate the disparity, and to create a monetary system that supports equality.

Jeanne Alford

Executive Director, Sudden Cardiac Arrest Association
Co-author in six anthologies, including the best-selling *Experts and Influencers: Women's Empowerment Edition*
Award-winning Communications and Media expert
www.suddencardiacarrest.org

Understanding contemporary economics is often a heroic journey—until you read this book. In the hands of Dr. Jim, it's as easy as following the money, literally. If you've ever questioned why, at the heart of this free economy, we have a small group controlling interest rates and the money supply, or why the wealth gap seemingly grows on its own, this book is for you. Dr. Jim draws you in with the birth of the FED system and keeps you enthralled through the deleterious predictions and effects of the military-industrial complex to the potential for a "sustainable economic renaissance."

FOREWORD

In the late 19th Century, the distance between the *haves* and *have nots* in America was extreme. Don't fall for the Hollywood portrayal of a "happier, simpler time." The Robber-Barons had it all! Around the turn of the century, we started making some progress toward a more just society with "trust-busting," consumer protection, fair labor legislation, a progressive income tax, and other legislation. The robber-barons, panicked by the thought of losing their fortunes, would fix that in 1913—they created the Federal Reserve! And the wealth gap, once again, slowly started increasing. As you will see in this book, the wealth gap has become a metaphoric Titanic taking America toward an iceberg of financial devastation—except for the wealthy!

Ten years ago, I began a collegial association with the author of this book, Dr. James Glenn, that has evolved into a high, mutual regard. Dr. Jim's extensive background in finance and economics, both as a practitioner and educator, was readily apparent from the beginning. To paraphrase an old TV commercial for a well-known financial advisor group, when Dr. Jim spoke, I listened! Finally my insistence that he "write it down" has paid off. *Wealth Inequality in America* is an erudite but readable polemic of where the last 100 years of greed and ignorance has brought us as a country.

As you will see in *Wealth Inequality in America*, there are many stories of how greed and ignorance drive the wealth gap.

The cover image tells most of it—the unjustly "legal" transfer of wealth from the middle class to the hands of the super wealthy. Every statement Dr. Jim writes in this book is substantiated by facts and data, punctuated with charts and images illustrating his points. As we both like to say, don't take my word for it—look at the data and decide for yourself.

As you read *Wealth Inequality in America*, keep in mind that you cannot look honestly at the perniciously increasing wealth gap and financial bubbles without being political. There is indeed a partisan motivation to the gap. As you will see, the evidence is overwhelming. And as you read, keep asking yourself "so what can I do about it!?" This book is not meant to turn you into an economic scholar, politician, or political activist, but it is meant to help you become an enlightened voter! Look behind the effects and delve into the legislation—make up your own mind—and vote!

Miles M. Hamby, PhD
www.MilesFlight.com

Miles M. Hamby, PhD

PERSONAL NOTE

I began writing this book in 2017, alarmed at the vitriol and divisiveness between political parties, communities, corporations, and the public, and extremist groups fulminating at the ideas of racial and gender equality. I finished writing the book in January 2020, well before the tidal wave of the recent health crisis crashed upon our shores.

This pandemic exacerbated the fragility of our financial system, and laid bare the false notions, perpetrated by generations of politicians and bankers, that a country can borrow its way to prosperity, an ideology promoted by these same self-serving bankers and politicians, to extend their own power, wealth, and prosperity at the expense of our once great middle class. I discuss this at length and in all humility (I hope), throughout this book, and recent events just provide more anecdotal evidence to corroborate my assertions, that our political and economic systems are in urgent need of a serious overhaul.

As events unfold in April 2020 as this book is being readied for publication, I need to note to my readers that I, and many others have been warning and waiting on a major market correction. Interest rates have been artificially suppressed for over a decade by central banks around the world, distorting the free market pricing mechanism for the cost of money (interest charged), leading to a massive build up in government, corporate, and personal debt worldwide. This debt overhang is soon to bury Western economies in an avalanche of bank closings, government and municipal defaults, and foreclosures and personal bankruptcies. Once again, central banks and their proxies have created an enormous asset bubble in corporate and government bonds, and of course a stock market bubble, creating heretofore unimaginable malinvestment, speculation, and tremendous profits for them and their member banks, at the expense of the majority of Americans. I detail how this bank profiteering was created, abetted, and used over the centuries in the pages to follow.

Another idea discussed at length in the following pages is the idea that our financial system must be highly regulated and not allowed to create money out of thin air through the fractional reserve banking system currently in place in this country. It is this excessive money and credit creation allowed through fractional reserve banking that needs to end, and is at the center of the country's financial problems. I discuss possible solutions and alternatives to such a system in the last chapter.

With any luck, the economic ramifications and dislocations caused by the recent health crisis will be short lived. I am not nearly as sanguine about the outlook for our political system and economy if we continue to allow bankers and corporations to run our country.

P.S. The amount that I now quote in the book as the national debt, $30 trillion dollars, is not a mistake. As of January 2020, the Federal Reserve (FED) has added another $3–7 trillion dollars to our national debt by funding the CARES Act recently passed by the U.S. Congress in March 2020. This and other legislation designed to ease the economic burden on our businesses and our unemployed was necessary in my opinion but will add to an already enormous bill owed by our children and grand-children. In January 2020, the national debt stood at $23.5 trillion dollars. Add another $3–7 trillion to that and you are close to, or over $30 trillion dollars. All of this money is borrowed. You might ask, "Where did all that money come from?" Read on to find out.

James Glenn, August 2020

PREFACE

Like many Americans, I have become increasingly alarmed at the divisiveness in our country, the vitriol that now passes for political discourse, the twisting of fiction into fact, and the rise and repetition of revisionist history from demagogues and political opportunists. We live in a country where the disingenuous editorials on both sides of the aisle, are taken as fact, because many American's and journalists do not take the time to check for facts. Most disturbingly, I see a wealth transfer from the lower and middle class to the top 5% of the population perpetuated by a corrupt tax code, central bank, and political and economic elites.

Predictably, this has led to the well documented demise of our once great middle class.

Sadly, we as a nation have allowed a myriad of vested interests, the central bank, Wall Street, K Street, the military-industrial complex, politicians, corporatists, and plutocrats to corrupt our economy and usurp the political process. With the recent passing of Citizens United (January, 2010), corporations are now legally enshrined as individuals, with all the rights of individuals, but none of the responsibilities. As a result of this questionably legal largesse, and a growing plutocracy, wealth disparity has grown enormously, and our middle class has shrunk dramatically over the last 40 years.

This wealth gap is very well documented. The rich are getting much richer and the poor, poorer. The process of how this happens exactly is not so well documented. That is the point of this book.

It appears extremely complicated to see how all of these interests are interwoven because of the very deliberate obfuscation by our central bank, politicians, and economic elites. But not really. All one needs to do is to follow the money, which is why I start my book with the founding of the Federal Reserve. For it is this central banking entity and cadres of associated elites who prefer working in the shadows, rather than the transparency of democracy that perpetuate the billionaire's club and the *corporatocracy* that are at the very heart of the wealth disparity problem in my opinion.

The central bank and its member banks have controlled the destiny of our country since the industrial revolution and will continue to do so, unless we the people, put a stop to their machinations and mismanagement, once and for all. It is these entities responsible for the demise of the middle class.

As Andrew Jackson said about central banks over 150 years ago,

> The bold effort the present (central) bank has made to control the government . . . are but premonitions of the fate that await the American people should they be deluded into a perpetuation of this institution or the establishment of another like it. (Jackson, 1832, p. 2)

Indeed, our founding fathers—Jefferson, Madison, Adams, Franklin, and Washington—were all adamantly opposed to the creation of a central bank because they understood the pernicious effects they ultimately have on the economy, the destructive mal-investment and speculation they encourage, and the boom-bust cycles they choreograph for their own profit.

George Washington said in 1787 in a letter to J. Bowen in Rhode Island that, "Paper money has had the effect in your state that it will ever have, to ruin commerce, oppress the honest, and open the door to every species of fraud and injustice" (Washington, 1787, para. 3).

Thomas Jefferson was appalled at the thought of a central bank and said,

> If the American people ever allow private banks to control the issue of their money, first by inflation and then by deflation, the banks and corporations that will grow up around them (around the banks) will deprive the people of property until their children will wake up homeless on the continent their father conquered. (Jefferson, 1816, p. 1)

Jefferson was obviously very prescient.

Barry Goldwater wrote in his book *With No Apologies*,

> Does it not seem strange to you that these men just happened to be on the Council on Foreign Relations (CFR) and just happened to be on the Board of Governors of the Federal Reserve that absolutely controls the money and interest rates of this country? A privately owned organization . . . which has absolutely nothing to do with the United States of America. (Goldwater, 1953, p. 4)

Yes, fellow citizens, our country has been stolen, but not by the people most often cited in the press or by demagogues in politics. It has been stolen by our so called Federal Reserve (which is not Federal), plutocrats, Congresspeople, and the military industrial complex which Eisenhower warned us about as he was leaving office many years ago. As Dwight Eisenhower so ominously noted in his farewell speech to the nation on January 17, 1961,

> This conjunction of an immense military establishment and a large arms industry is new in the American experience. The total influence—economic, political, even spiritual—is felt in every city, every statehouse, every office of the federal government. We recognize the imperative need for this development. Yet we must not fail to comprehend its grave implications. Our toil, resources and livelihood are all involved; so is the very structure of our society. In the councils of government, **we must guard against the acquisition of unwarranted influence, whether sought or unsought, by the military—industrial complex.** The potential for the disastrous rise of misplaced power exists, and will persist. We must never let the weight of this combination endanger our liberties or democratic processes. We should take nothing for granted. Only an alert and knowledgeable citizenry can compel the proper meshing of the huge industrial and military machinery of defense with our peaceful methods and goals so that security and liberty may prosper together. (Eisenhower, 1961, p. 1)

Finally, as a citizen I simply ask myself and you this question: Does it not seem odd to you that at the very heart of an alleged free market economy we have a monopoly that controls interest rates and the money supply of our great nation? A monopoly more powerful than the President or U.S. Congress? A monopoly that is run by non-elected bureaucrats?

We do not need a central bank to set interest rates. We have the most efficient free market mechanism that does so on a daily basis—it is called the bond market. Likewise, we have the U.S. Treasury Department which can issue money as needed for additional economic growth.

So why, I ask myself, did the Federal Reserve Act mysteriously find its way to the U.S. Congress in 1913 after nearly 100 years without one? Is this situation not an anathema to all we know and love as Americans and believers in the free market?

I have spent a lifetime pondering this as an educator, financial manager, history buff, and citizen. The following book is my look at those who truly control our country and how they are perpetuating the demise of the middle class, which is so vital to our democracy. I consider myself a child of the once great American middle class and it saddens me deeply to see it disappearing like the polar ice caps, only faster.

This book is not a political diatribe. It is a look at our country, what is, and more importantly, what could be. The quotes above and throughout this book come from all parties and pundits, left, right, and center. I am not as sanguine or as hopeful as many about the course of our country. I am very worried for my country, which is why I share the following with you.

CHAPTER 1.
The Problem:
The Ever-Widening Wealth Gap

"Paper money eventually returns to
its intrinsic value-zero."

—VOLTAIRE, 1729

Why should you read this book? In the summer of 2017, I was at an event at Eisenhower Farm National Park in Gettysburg, PA, in the heart of Republican country. I met a local man and something prompted one of us to mention the approaching tax *reform* bill the Republicans were hurriedly trying to get passed before the year's end after their failure to repeal the Affordable Care Act (ACA). He said "Things will be much better if the middle class gets a tax cut. I won't be so stretched." I said, "I hope you realize that it will be mainly a huge tax cut for the wealthy." He responded "I don't care about that. There will always be rich people. Just as long as I get a tax cut, I don't care."

I was struck by the realization that *this* is how the rich keep getting richer! The rich, over the last century, have allowed the middle class to have just enough to keep the middle class from seeing how poor they really are by perpetuating the myth that upward economic mobility is in everyone's grasp. And this is the problem—it isn't! Upward economic mobility is only for the rich, for only the rich can afford to manipulate and take advantage of the tax laws that allow their wealth to grow, a bifurcated educational system where equal opportunity is a myth, and a financial system designed by the rich, for the rich. And, as this book will demonstrate, that is exactly what the *rich*, euphemistically called *the investing class*, want—to keep the middle class in the illusion of wealth while they transfer middle class money to the top. It is not trickle down; it is wealth transfer from the bottom and middle to the top.

The problem most people cannot see is not that there are rich people or even that there is a large gap between the wealth of the rich and the middle class, but that the rich are getting richer at the expense of the middle class. Wealth redistribution from the bottom and middle up, not from the top down aided and abetted by central banking and monetary policy is how the rich get richer year-after-year, decade-after-decade. This regressive wealth redistribution, when pointed out to conservatives for what it is, a social travesty, often draws a knee jerk visceral reaction from most of the wealthy and conservatives. Anyone questioning the financial system as it is currently configured is a pariah, and more often than not, immediately marginalized by the right as a communist or socialist.

The perception of that man in my anecdote is that there is an unlimited supply of money and therefore the rich can continue to get richer because the middle class will continue to get richer. That is simply not true. He does not realize that investing is a zero sum game that for every winner, there must be a loser. He is blinded by the illusion of wealth and a financial system that favors debt and consumption over a more prudent one favoring savings and investment. So, he keeps voting for the people who perpetuate the myth that rich people (the investing class) *trickle down* their money into investing in American jobs (they don't), that his tax cut for the middle class is proportional and equitable to that for the rich and the large corporations (it is not), that poor people do not want to work (they do, but they cannot), and that the Republican party has his best interests at heart (they don't).

It is pretty simple when one considers the philosophical underpinnings of our two political parties. Generally, Republicans feel that money and wealth is best left in the hands of the wealthy, and that it is they that will create economic prosperity through more business investment which will eventually benefit all by increasing jobs, wages, and incomes. Anecdotal, as well as mountains of empirical evidence over the last 40 years, simply does not corroborate this belief. Democrats, on the other hand, generally believe that by improving the economic lot of the great middle class and generating economic, social, and tax policy that favors the working class, that the middle class will grow and prosper, making all in society better off by creating a higher standard of living for all in the process.

But redistribution does not necessarily mean from the top down. Defined by the Stanford Encyclopedia of Philosophy, redistribution is "The social mechanism, such as a change in tax laws, monetary policies, or tort law, that engenders the redistribution of goods and services among these subjects" (Stanford Encyclopedia of Philosophy, 2004, p. 1). Economists call this the wealth transfer mechanism. Over the last century and well into the 21st century, wealth in American has been, and continues to be, redistributed much more from the bottom up than the top down (trickle down).

Princeton sociologist Douglas Massey (2007), writing about the inequality of wealth in America, noted that legislation passed in the 1930s designed to limit stratification and promote economic equality have been dismantled over the last 40 years and replace by fiscal, monetary and trade legislation from the 1970s onward, specifically designed to institutionalize economic exploitation of the middle and lower classes

The rules of the American political economy have been steadily transformed since Reagan, to favor the rich at the expense of the middle and lower classes. This is well documented in study after study. Starting with the Reagan administration in the 1980s, unions have been steadily weakened, entry-level wages have been reduced and have stagnated for the vast majority, access to social protections and a broader social safety net curtailed, anti-poverty spending cut back, and taxes on lower-income families have been raised while those on upper-income families were reduced, yielding a sharp and well publicized reduction in the size of the welfare state starting with Reagan's Tax Reform Act of 1986 and continuing with the Republican sponsored *Welfare Reform* under Clinton and a Republican House and Senate in the late 1990s.

Robert Reich, Chancellor's Professor of Public Policy at the University of California who also served as Secretary of Labor under the Clinton administration (1993–2001), wrote that President Donald Trump's 2017 tax act was proposing the largest redistribution of wealth from the poor and middle class to the rich in modern history. The Republican Congress has already embarked on it with the passage of the Tax Reform Act of 2017. More tax cuts for those that least need them, the Fortune 500 and top 1% of the income scale. This tax cut was done, I might add, during an expansion, precisely the time when it is not needed. You cut taxes and increase government spending, exactly what President Trump and the Republicans have done in 2017, in a recession to spur consumption and generate economic growth. All the 2017 tax cuts did was promote the largest stock buyback binge in stock market history, and make the wealthy, even wealthier.

The wealth gap continues to increase at an accelerating rate driving many social ills that will ultimately lead to a major economic collapse and massive social unrest in our country. The problem is immediate —not for me (I will likely be dead), but it will be for that man in Pennsylvania, his family, and my nephews, nieces, and their children. Why the man in my anecdote does not care if the rich get richer is because he does not currently see himself as truly poor or even *strapped*. He sees himself as just not able to buy all the consumer goodies he wants. He cannot envision what truly hard times will mean for him and his family. Like my cousin, he thinks *just getting by* means putting off buying new skis for this coming season as he has done for every ski season of his adult life. He cannot see that it will mean no more new skis, no new car for the remainder of his life, buying clothes from second-hand stores, no more going out to dinner, no cable TV, no new laptop computer or cell phone every year, no concert tickets, no football game tickets, etc., etc., etc. The current poor will be better off; they have already adapted their lives to truly just getting by. He remains blinded to his own unfortunate economic reality by the illusion of wealth.

According to the National Bureau of Economic Research in 2008, the United States holds 25.4% of the world's wealth yet ranks near the top as the *industrialized world's most unequal distribution of wealth*. In a list of distribution of wealth of all the world's countries by **Gini coefficient** (named after statistician Corrado Gini (1884—1965), who measured wealth inequality by an index with 1.00 being perfect inequality and 0.00 being prefect equality), the United States scored .801, with Japan being the most *equally* distributed with a coefficient of .547, and Namibia being the most unequally distributed with a coefficient of .847. It is interesting to note that all the countries in the world scored more equal in wealth distribution (lower Gini coefficient) than the United States, except for Switzerland (.803), Zimbabwe (.845), and Namibia (.847).

As Robert Reich (2007) pointed out in *Supercapitalism*, *if* real median household income has gone nowhere since 1980, while the overall economy has been tepid for most Americans with wage growth stagnating and incomes flat lining for the majority of Americans, the costs of everything, notably education and health care, have risen inexorably. In short, capitalism has failed the vast majority of Americans. Where has all the wealth gone? Mostly to the very top obviously. It is ironic to note that those who create wealth, which is in in its simplest form is excess production, the working class, have not enjoyed the fruits of their own labor. Productivity continues to rise much faster than wages, yet wages, in inflation adjusted terms, have stagnated since 1975.

Professor Emmanuel Saez of the University of California at Berkley and Thomas Pikkety of the E'cole Normal Sup'erieure in Paris examined U.S. tax records and found America's top 1% of earners received 16% of the nation's total income—double their 8% share in 1980. The share going to the top 1% more than tripled since 1980 to 7% (Saez & Pikkety, 2018).

These are sobering statistics indeed, and as noted earlier, this trend in inequality has only accelerated since 2006 with Reich

(2007) in *Supercapitalism* noting that wealth inequality has exploded since Reagan.

The Effects of the Wealth Gap

Disparity in wealth has extremely negative consequences from a public policy and social welfare standpoint. Major negative effects of a widening wealth gap are asset inflation making housing less affordable, speculation in all asset markets, mal-investment, and increased and unbridled spending by the U.S. Congress, much of it on borrowed money that results in decreased national saving and an exploding national debt. As the rich get richer, they, and their proxies, lobbyists, politicians, and multinationals, write and enact fiscal legislation favorable to themselves, their industries, or their states. This newly created tax legislation enacted and perpetuated by economic elites (the top 15% of income earners) exacerbates an already corrupt and regressive tax code, inexorably shifting more of the tax burden from corporations and the wealthy, to the middle class. This progressively regressive tax code puts the tax burden on working Americans who rely on earned income and typically favors those with unearned income, the wealthiest among us.

Why the Emphasis on the Federal Reserve?

Our central bank, The Federal Reserve (FED), was created in 1913 by economic elites of the industrial age, to control U.S. money, credit, and interest rates to perpetuate their own wealth and influence, and to gain total control of the economic levers of our economy. Through its member banks, the FED expands and contracts money supply and controls interest rates to create asset bubbles making them wealthier still. The *fractional reserve* banking system, borrowed from the Bank of England, whose model in turn originated in Switzerland in the 1600s, is diabolically clever and beautiful in its simplicity, and yet another tool used by central banks to exacerbate an already disgraceful wealth gap in the United States (more on this later).

Suffice it to say here that in such a system *money* is literally created out of thin air. In such a system, money is loaned into existence by a bank loan, that is,

debt = money and money = debt

Money is only created when a bank loan is made. In a fractional reserve system such as ours, a dollar in reserves magically turns into $9 in loans. The excessive use of leverage in such a system, combined with the application of interest, leads ultimately to a situation of too much money chasing too few goods and assets, a situation economists call too much money chasing too few goods (stocks, bonds, and real estate). That is, excess liquidity created through fractional reserve banking must, and does lead to inflation. Inexorable, relentless inflation, a speculator's best friend, and a saver's worst enemy. For inflation is the most pernicious, some would say evil, tax of all. It is a stealth tax. Completely regressive, for simply put, if you do not have the credit or the capital necessary to take advantage of the asset inflation created by central banks (bond, stock, and real estate bubbles), then you are left behind, economically speaking. Wage earners, and pensioners incomes are destroyed in such a system, for wages never rise as fast as inflation. The wealthy of course are delighted with such a system, for they have the means to take advantage of these asset bubbles generated by excess liquidity, enriching themselves further still.

It is this boom bust asset cycle which is largely responsible for the ever-widening wealth gap and destruction of our middle class. Health care and education, two vital components of becoming successful in a system such as ours are growing at close to 5%-10% a year (doubling every 10–15 years), while wages, as noted earlier, have remained flat for 40 years (since 1980).

In conjunction with the increasingly inequitable banking system and the regressive tax code mentioned above, the military industrial complex that President Eisenhower warned us about in 1960, is controlled primarily by the investing class, which deliberately fosters armed conflict around the world to enrich themselves through war profiteering. Their incessant fear mongering in turn keeps the public feeling the need for increased military spending by perpetuating the fear that we are unprotected, and need to spend even more on "defense." As Gore Vidal famously said, the United States has perpetual wars for perpetual profit. This large, and ever-expanding military footprint worldwide (U.S. troops in 70 countries around the world-that we know of) has been accompanied of course, by an exploding national debt Most of these needless military misadventures since WWII must be paid for, and much of the money needed is borrowed, compounding a national debt now approaching $30 trillion dollars (Vidal, 2002).

By the early 1970s, the illusion of prosperity created by the central bank had all but disappeared as the United States went into a long period of stagflation, from which we have never really recovered. As noted in a remarkably erudite paper by Servaas Storm (2017) *secular economic stagnation* is now the new normal, with our economy characterized by a rapid slowdown of *aggregate economic growth* with a concomitant increase in wealth inequalities and a commensurate decrease in upward socio-economic mobility (Storm, 2017). These findings, supported by studies by Fernald (2014; International Monetary Fund [IMF], 2015), as well as studies by Foster and Magdoff (2009), and Palley (2012), noting the steady decline in the American economy.

Storm's (2017) discussion of these disappointing findings corroborate the facts which are also consistent with the recent Gini coefficient results noted earlier that show the United States slipping steadily further behind all our major competitors when it comes to social mobility and wealth equality.

Sadly, other academics such as Eberstadt (2017) noted that the worst hit by the economic slowdown of the last decade have been the U.S. middle and lower classes who have had to cope with higher education and health care costs, rising economic inequality, flat wages, and job insecurity. Eberstadt succinctly summarized the dilemma facing the average U.S. worker. Job insecurity, falling wages, slow growth, and an inability to *keep up* economically, lead inevitably to the recent heightened political populism, class angst, and eventually, *class warfare* that are the likely results of these growing and persistent socio-economic disparities.

More than 8 years after the Great Financial Crisis, U.S. growth remains anemic, even after interest rates hit the *zero lower bound* and the unconventional monetary policy arsenal of the Federal Reserve has been all but exhausted. Output growth has not returned to its prerecession trend and this has led some commentators, including Foster and Magdoff (2009), Palley (2012), and Summers (2013, 2015), to suggest that this lopsided and uninspiring recovery reflects a *new economic normal,* characterized by *secular economic stagnation,* which had set in *already well before* the global banking crisis of 2008 (Fernald, 2014, 2016; IMF, 2015). If true, it means that the extraordinary policy measures taken in response to the 2008 crisis merely stabilized an otherwise already comatose U.S. economy. This *new normal* is characterized not just by this slowdown of *aggregate* economic growth, but also by a concurrent heightening of income and wealth inequalities and a growing polarization of employment and earnings into high-skill, high-wage and low-skill, low-wage jobs—at the expense of *middle-wage* jobs (Autor & Dorn, 2013; Temin 2017; Weil, 2014).

What Do the Facts Say?

According to a study by Wolff (2017), the top 1% own 40% of the country's wealth, the highest level it has been since 1962. Wolff noted that from 2013 the percentage shot up by 3% alone, and notes further that today as many pundits, observers, and academics, have noted recently the top 1% of households own more wealth than the bottom 90% combined. That gap between the rich upper class and poor has only increased in the last 10 years and became wider still in the past several decades. These figures come from the survey of consumer finances (Wolfe, 2017).

Financial inequality was greater than inequality in total wealth, with the top 1% of the population owning 42.7%, the next 19% of Americans owning 50.3%, and the bottom 80% owning 7%. However, according to the Federal Reserve,

> For most households, pensions and Social Security are the most important sources of income during retirement, and the promised benefit stream constitutes a sizable fraction

of household wealth, including pensions and Social Security in net worth makes the distribution more even. When including household wealth from pensions and social security, the richest 1% of the American population in 1992 owned 16% of the country's total wealth, as opposed to 32% when excluding pensions and social security. (Federal Reserve, 2018, para. 12)

After *The Great Recession*, which started in 2007, the share of total wealth owned by the top 1% of the population grew from 34.6% to 37.1%, and that owned by the top 20% of Americans grew from 85% to 87.7%. The Great Recession also caused a drop of 36.1% in median household wealth but a drop of only 11.1% for the top 1%.

According to the Congressional Budget Office (CBO) (2010), between 1979 and 2007, incomes of the top 1% of Americans grew by an average of 275%. During the same time period, the 60% of Americans in the middle of the income scale saw their income rise by 40%. From 1992–2007, the top 400 income earners in the United States saw their income increase 392% and their average tax rate reduced by 37%. In 2009, the average income of the top 1% was $960,000 with a minimum income of $343,927 (Congressional Budget Office [CBO], 2010).

During the economic expansion between 2002 and 2007, the income of the top 1% grew 10 times faster than the income of the bottom 90%. In this period, 66% of total income gains went to the 1%, who in 2007 had a larger share of total income than at any time since 1928. According to PolitiFact (2019), the top 400 wealthiest Americans have combined wealth greater than half of all Americans, going on to note that much of this wealth is inherited, giving the wealthy a giant head start on the rest of us. Depressingly, they observe that if a family has a positive net worth, that is, more assets than liabilities, they have more wealth than over 30 million American families, because the bottom 25% of Americans have a negative net worth (Stone, Trisi, Sherman, & Taylor, 2019).

Alarmingly, also according to PolitiFact, the wealthiest three families in the country own more assets than the bottom 50% of the country (Kertcher, 2019). This is an astounding revelation and an outrageous development in one of the wealthiest countries in the world.

Pareto Analysis

One cannot discuss wealth distribution without mentioning Pareto Analysis. Italian engineer, sociologist, economist, political scientist, and philosopher Vilfredo Federico Damaso Pareto (1848—1923) was fascinated by problems of power and wealth and especially how it was distributed. His research included tax records from around Europe and South America covering three centuries of tax data which looked at contemporary rental income and personal income. Plotting the data on graph paper (no computers in those days), a startling consistency emerged—20% of the people owned 80% of the wealth (the 80–20 Rule)-everywhere! Wealth, as Pareto demonstrated, was not remotely a bell-shaped normal distribution—it is highly skewed. He referred to it as a *social law* and something *in the nature of man* (Jha, 2011).

The distribution of wealth in the United States today in 2016 is no different. In fact, it is even more skewed. Figure 1—Distribution of Wealth in America, *2016,* depicts that the upper 10% of American households own 73% of the wealth while the next 50% of American families own only 27%. Even more shocking is that the bottom 40% of American households own only 0.2% of the wealth—i.e., 40% of American families are in official poverty status. (see Figure 1).

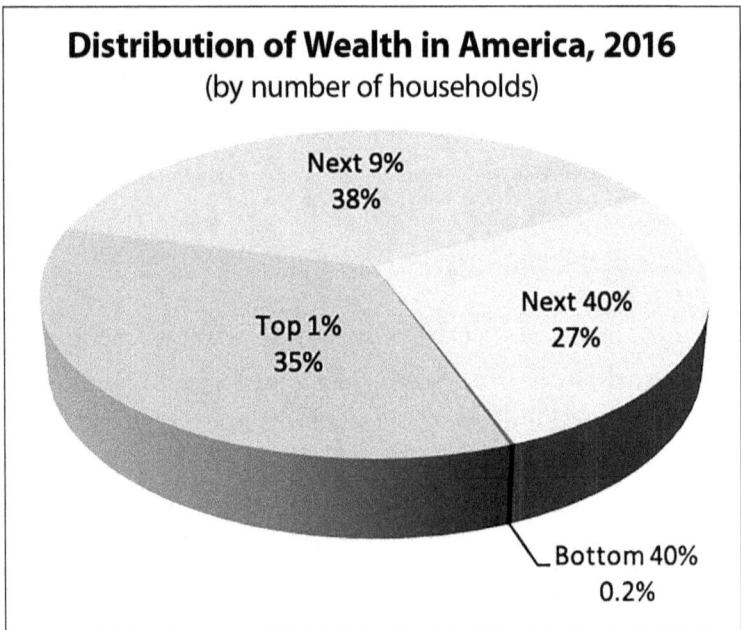

Figure 1: Distribution of Wealth in America by Households

Note: Reprinted with permission from The Washington Center for Equitable Growth.

Consider that in 2007, the total value of U.S. household wealth was $65.9 trillion. Very soon after, the total value plunged to $48.5 trillion during the first quarter of 2009 but rebounded to $54.2 trillion in the fourth quarter of 2009 (Distribution of Wealth, 2016).

In a rigorous and definitive study to estimate the trends in wealth in America, Saez and Zucman (2014) found that wealth followed a U-shaped evolution from 1913 to 2012.

Wealth Gap
Difference between Top 10% and Bottom 90%

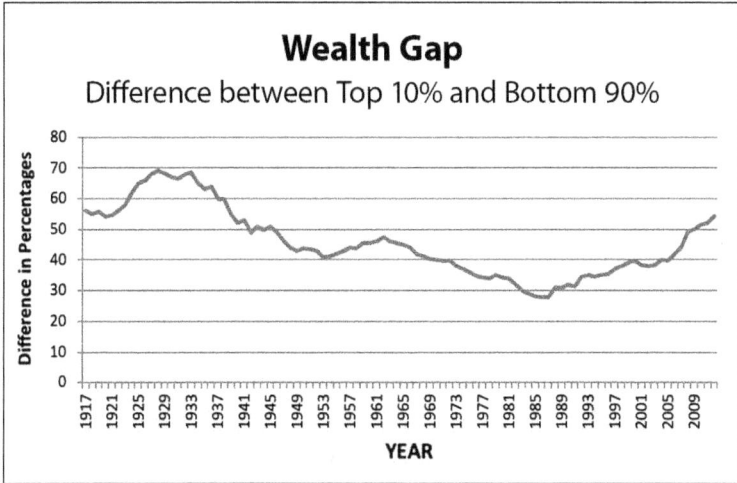

Figure 2: The Top 10% vs. the Bottom 90%

Note: Reprinted with permission from Miles Hamby, PhD, 2019. Alexandria, VA, 2019.

Notes: The figure plots the top 10% wealth share in the United States from 1917 to 2012 using the capitalization method. The unit is the family (single adult person with or without children dependents or married couple with or without dependents).

As depicted in Figure 2, the percent share of total wealth owned by the top 10% income is U-shaped. They (the wealthy) were both high in the beginning of the twentieth century (1920–1929), but fell from 1929 to 1978, but has continuously increased since then. As I will point out later in book, this can be mostly explained by the equity legislation such as Social Security and social spending following World War II and in the 1960s, and then the increase in Republican-led legislation favoring the big banks and corporations, beginning with Nixon and especially under Reagan (S & L deregulation) in the 1980s.

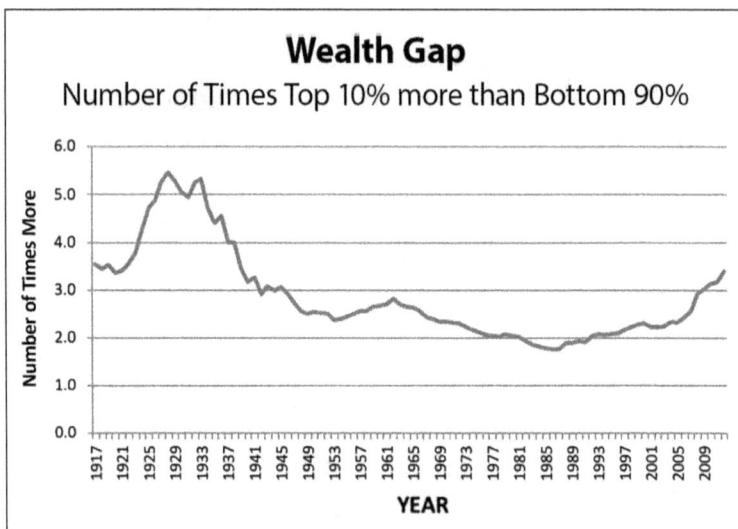

Figure 3: The Top 10% vs. the Bottom 90%.

Note: Reprinted with permission from Miles Hamby, PhD, Alexandria, VA, 2019.

As noted in Figure 3, the top 10% owns more than the bottom 90% in terms of wealth. Note, the number of times more wealth accruing to the top 10% which owned more than bottom 90%. For example, in 1917, the Top 10% owned 3.6 times more wealth than the bottom 90% (i.e., 78% / 22% = 3.55), reaching a peak in 1928 of 5.5 times, to a low in 1985 of 1.8 times as much, then increasing steadily to 3.4 times more in 2012.

Figure 3: Wealth Gap depicts the difference between the percentage of wealth owned by the Top 10% and the bottom

90%. For example, in 1917, the Top 10% owned 78% of the wealth in America and the Bottom 90% owned 22% of the wealth resulting in a difference of 56% (78%-22%). The slope of the line indicates that as the Top 10% owns a bigger share of the wealth, the bottom 90% owns a lesser share and the difference in percentages increases. This is the wealth gap. Thus, an increasing slope of the line indicates a widening wealth gap, i.e. the share of the Top 10% getting larger while the share of the Bottom 90% is shrinking. From 1917 (4 years after the 16th Amendment to the U.S. Constitution allowing federal income tax), the wealth gap was approximately 56% and widened to its widest in 1928 (approximately 69%, coincident with the stock market crash the following year), then closed steadily through World War II, then widened in the late 1950s (coincidently with the Eisenhower Republican era), then closed during the 1960s (coincidently with LBJ and the increase in social spending), then began a steady widening (coincident with Reagan and so-called *trickle-down* economics), until 2012, where it reached 54.4%, almost where it started in 1917.

In Figure 3, the number of times more wealth the top 10% owns than the bottom 90% depicts the wealth gap in terms of how much more wealth the Top 10% owns than the bottom 90%. For example, in 1917, the Top 10% owned 3.6 times more wealth than the bottom 90% (i.e., 78% / 22% = 3.55), reaching a peak in 1928 of 5.5 times, to a low in 1985 of 1.8 times as much, then increasing

The Ever Widening Wealth Gap

This ever-widening wealth gap and concomitant erosion of the middle class has been well documented over the last four decades (1980–2020) by academics, pundits, and anecdotal evidence, as well as mountains of empirical evidence. In a recent working paper by Servaas Storm (2017) on the subject of wealth inequality, it was noted that the *American Dream* is increasingly elusive for a majority of Americans, with the prospects of today's children earning more than their parents 45% less likely. According to Temin (2017), America is no longer *great* and its faltering economy is now a dual economy- two very different economies, with totally different economic realities, resources, and potentials. As George Carlin (2010) once quipped, "they call it the American Dream because you have to be asleep to believe it" (2013 PBS Newshour).

In line with all of this, recent evidence suggests that the American dream of inter-generational progress has begun to fade with children's prospects today of earning more than their parents has fallen from 95% for children born in 1940 to less than 50% for children born in the early 1980s (Chety et al., 2016). America can no longer be considered the lynchpin to the global economy it once was (75% of world gross domestic product (GDP) after WWII) and is no longer great, as its economic growth slows, partly because of generalized secular stagnation but more importantly, because it is becoming a caste economy, that is two countries, each with very different possibilities, potentials, expectations and resources. available to each, with the top 10% garnering the majority of tax benefits, and the bottom 90% struggling to stay in the same economic position. In brief, the middle class is vanishing (Temin 2017).

This obvious duality between the very wealthy and rest of us, has been clearly evident since Senator John Edwards first ran for President in 2004, when he ran on a platform of a divided

America, a dual economy, and pointed out the glaring social and economic inequalities between the haves and the have nots. Since then, the wealth transfer mechanism called fractional reserve banking, in conjunction with an increasingly regressive tax code, has worked brilliantly for the rich, even better than even they could have hoped for, as the statistics noted above demonstrate. This gross income inequality leaves more and more Americans behind economically, polarizing the country, and making it much more difficult for our children to achieve the living standards their parents have enjoyed. This is a national travesty and the end of the middle class unless reversed immediately.

CHAPTER 2.
The Structure of the Federal Reserve Bank

*The last duty of a central banker is
to tell the public the truth.*

—ALAN BLINDER, VICE-CHAIRMAN OF THE FEDERAL RESERVE,
ON PBS'S NIGHTLY BUSINESS REPORT IN 1994

*I am a most unhappy man. I have unwittingly ruined
my country. A great industrial nation is controlled by
its system of credit. Our system of credit is concentrated.
The growth of the nation, therefore, and all our
activities are in the hands of a few men. We have
come to be one of the worst ruled, one of the most
completely controlled and dominated Governments
in the civilized world no longer a Government by free
opinion, no longer a Government by conviction and
the vote of the majority, but a Government by the
opinion and duress of a small group of dominant men.*

—WOODROW WILSON, AFTER SIGNING THE FEDERAL RESERVE
INTO EXISTENCE, 1913

This book intends to demonstrate how America's third central bank—the Federal Reserve (FED) plays a pivotal role in the destruction of the American middle class and the rise of the biggest *wealth gap* in American history. As one who has worked in financial services and banking, and now as an academic, I have followed the machinations of our central bank with a mixture of curiosity, dread, and disgust for four decades. Although much has been written on the FED's nefarious activities and opaque origins, little has been written that specifically ties FED's monetary policy and banking activity to the continued erosion of our middle class.

The idea of granting a private entity—i.e., the Federal Reserve—the right to issue privately issued debt instruments (currency) is not a new one. The idea has been around for centuries and began primarily as a means for monarchs to pay for wars and other foreign misadventures they could not afford (why the Bank of England was created), and of course, domestic programs to ensure domestic tranquility. Sound familiar?

To understand how a central bank and its minions can transfer wealth from the middle and lower class to the upper class requires an understanding of how a fractional reserve banking system works, for that is what we are stuck with today. Understanding how money is created in a fractional reserve banking system (i.e., it is literally *loaned* into existence: **money = debt**), how inflation is baked and built into the system, and finally who the primary beneficiaries of such a system are, is critical for an understanding of why the American middle class is rapidly disappearing.

In the United States, we have a central bank called the Federal Reserve (FED) modeled on European counterparts, which is actually our third central bank since 1789. The first lasted from 1789–1811 and was created to help pay for the Revolutionary War. The second was created in 1816 and was abolished in 1832 by Andrew Jackson who ran on a platform of closing the hated institution and won! The third was created in 1913, ostensibly as a result of the Wall Street Panic of 1907, which evidence suggests, was deliberately created to sow the seeds of fear among the populace to allow the very wealthy to create our third central bank. Many historians suggest the panic was deliberately created by the same people responsible for creating the Federal Reserve, the Morgans, Warburgs, Rothschilds, Carnegies, and other wealthy industrialists of the time. The FED was created by the rich, for the rich, and run by the rich ever since.

Who Was There?

A group spear-headed by these wealthy industrialists, their agents, and Wall Street bankers, met in secrecy at Jekyll Island off the coast of Georgia in 1911, and conspired to use the 1907 financial panic as an excuse to create our third central bank. Many historians believe they deliberately created the financial panic of 1907 as a means to justify the establishment of our third central bank. At this meeting, these bankers and industrialists disingenuously dubbed their new bank the Federal Reserve. I say it was disingenuous because the name was intended to deliberately fool the American people into believing that the bank was part of the U.S. government—it is not. It is owned by its member banks.

From this meeting, the seeds of greed germinated into a full-fledged plan to create a Federal Reserve System, owned by its member banks and agents, run by non-elected officials and bureaucrats who would control the money supply and interest rates of the largest economy on earth at that time. The *FED* would also control interest rates, and, through the fractional reserve banking system described below, expand and contract that money supply with tools such as reserve requirements, interest rates, and open market operations, in turn very deliberately creating the boom bust economic cycles and asset bubbles that we have become all too familiar with.

Other luminaries of the time attending this meeting at Jekyll island included Abram Piatt Andrew, assistant secretary of the Treasury; Henry P. Davison, a business partner of Morgan's, Charles D. Norton, President of the First National Bank of New York; Benjamin Strong, another Morgan friend and the head of Bankers Trust; Frank A. Vanderlip, President of the National City Bank, and Paul M. Warburg, a partner in Kuhn, Loeb, & Co. and a German citizen.

An enterprising opportunist and Senator of the time (early 1900s), Nelson Aldrich seized upon the financial Panic of 1907 as a means to create a monetary system primarily for the bankers, by the bankers, and of the bankers. As Rham Emmanuel, former President William Clinton's Chief of Staff, quipped not so long ago, "Never let a serious crisis go to waste" (as cited in Elynsky, 1971, p. 89). Bankers seized on this Crisis of 1907 as the imperative for a third central bank of the United States.

Aldrich wasted no time in turning the fabricated panic of 1907 to his advantage, and thus the Aldrich-Vreeland Act was passed in 1908, and the National Monetary Commission was born, a precursor to the Federal Reserve established in 1913. Senator Aldrich, a Rhode Island Republican and sponsor of the act, uncertain of how to mold a uniquely *American* form of fractional reserve banking, promptly embarked on a trip to

Europe to meet with European bankers, ministers, and businesspeople who could provide guidance in the formation of a uniquely American banking system.

Senator Aldrich was a child of the *gilded age* (ca. 1890s and the Robber Barons) and may have been the person responsible for the word *crony* in *crony capitalism*. He was a personal friend of J.P. Morgan, and his daughter was married to John D. Rockefeller Jr. Aldrich saw, in the European banks that he visited, useful templates for the American model he helped create which would eventually become known as the Federal Reserve Bank (FED). The models he found in Europe proved to be more effective and efficient at creating and controlling credit and the money supply than anything in the United States at that time.

As noted in *Empire of Debt* by Bonner and Wiggin (2006), legislation eventually emerged from this fact finding tour of Europe known variously as the Owen-Glass Act or Currency Bill, which eventually merged into the Federal Reserve Act of 1913. The bill provided for the creation of a dozen regional reserve banks, with monetary policy coordinated and choreographed by a chairman appointed by the president. It would be this new entity, a private institution, controlled by an unelected chairman, that would now have the power to control interest rates and money and credit in the United States. Thus, for the first time in the nation's history privately issued currency would be issued by a privately held institution but backed by the full faith and credit of the United States government.

This was, in retrospect, a diabolically clever move on the part of the *money trust* and bankers. It would allow a private organization to control the economic and financial destiny of the United States, the greatest economy on earth at the time, creating the opportunity for fractional reserve banking system (creating money out of thin air) where

debt would = money, and **more debt would = more money**

leading ultimately to inflation and the asset bubble economy I speak of in the following pages. Legislation, variously called the Currency Bill and Owen-Glass Act, emerged as the Federal Reserve Act of 1913. It created a dozen regional Reserve Banks to be coordinated by a chairman who would be appointed by the U.S. President. While the U.S. Constitution grants the U.S. Congress the right to print money, under the Federal Reserve Act of 1913, Congress approved a plan to delegate the right to the FED, which is not part of Congress or the U.S. government. The U.S. dollar is not issued by the U.S. Treasury but by a privately owned organization which also influences bank interest rates, the amount of currency in circulation, and even the levels of inflation in the United States. It bears repeating, that for the first time, privately issued debt instruments (currency) would be issued by a private institution but guaranteed by the full faith and credit of the United States (our tax dollars).

Fractional Reserve Banking

Yes, you read that last quote correctly. The FED was authorized by the U.S. Congress to issue currency (look at the bills in your pocket—the bill says, *Federal Reserve* Note, **not** *Treasury* Note). More insidious to note is that currency does not have to be backed by anything because the FED is allowed to create the money out of thin air by simply putting numbers in an account; in accounting terms, creating a bookkeeping entry.

Even more concerning, under its charter, 90% of each dollar created by the FED may be loaned out leaving a 10% *reserve*. So, the FED creates $100 for JM Bank to borrow (a loan-because they asked to borrow it and are a *member* bank) and deposits it in JM Bank's account that it created with the FED. JM Bank then lends $90 to another bank (i.e., 10% of $100) keeping a 10% reserve, by law. Then that bank lends out $81 (10% of $90) to a smaller bank (like a mortgage lender). Then that smaller bank lends $72.90 to a borrower who wants to buy a house. Thus, from the original $100 the FED created, there is now $343.90 of loans outstanding (100 + 90 + 81 + 72.90) that is not backed by even the numbers the FED originally put into JM Banks account (i.e., $100). This scheme is called *fractional reserve banking*. As the expression goes, it's FM! (*Funny* Money!). With a 10% (currently) *reserve requirement* a bank can lend out nine times what it has in reserves, loans with money created out of thin air! An accounting bookkeeping entry. The *loan* is their asset and your debt.

This may seem harmless at first, but consider the implications. This system allows other banks to also create money out of thin air, thereby de-basing the existing money supply, predictably leading to inflation and often hyperinflation.

As noted in *The Economics of Money* (1930), central banking came into existence before governmental monetary authorities existed, when bankers realized that not all depositors would withdraw their money at the same time. This fact allowed bankers to only keep a fraction of depositor's money on hand at any point in time, just enough to meet the day to day needs of depositors. Gold owners looking to keep their gold safe would leave it with banks and receive a note in return. These *notes* over time, became negotiable allowing their holders to use them for goods and services and major asset purchases. This is the earliest form of a checking account.

And so, fractional reserve lending was born. This system worked well enough as long as depositors had confidence in the depository. That is, that the notes would and could be, redeemable on demand. If depositors lost faith in the depository (bank) however, a bank run could be expected. This was the case with many early banks in Europe (1600s-see Bank of Amsterdam). Fractional reserve banking is thus a two edged sword. On the one hand, it allows for expansion of the money supply, allowing faster GDP growth, but on the other hand, it also increases the risk that a bank may not be able to meet demand for withdrawals, leading to financial upheaval and social calamity.

As noted in *Money Facts* (1964), the creation of central banks reduced the probability of bank runs which are inherent in a fractional reserve banking system. The *system* as originally configured in Switzerland, has changed little and continues to this day in much the same form as it did in the 1600s (Money Facts, 1964).

So what is the harm with fractional reserve banking I hear some of you asking? The process of fractional reserve banking and the potential harm that such a system has on individuals, and society at large, are well documented throughout history. With a 10% *reserve requirement* for each dollar a bank holds as reserves, can be loaned out 9 times over. The money is literally created out of thin air, so $1 becomes $9 in circulation in the economy. This additional *money* is only created when a debt with a bank is generated. Their bookkeeping entry (your debt) becomes their asset and your liability. As the amount of debt expands in the economy, the economy and supply of money must grow commensurately (equally). Thus, if one does not have a commensurate rise in the creation of goods and services, inflation must be the final result (either in financial assets and goods and services or both) and is. The price level doubles in the United States about every 10 to 15 years, because the value of your currency is constantly debased in such a system.

What's wrong with inflation you ask? My Uncle Joe from Pennsylvania may have noticed at the local diner that the price of a dinner of meatloaf and mashed potatoes has doubled in the last 10 years. Is this because the prices of the ingredients went up over that time OR because the value of the currency was devalued over that time?

Increasing Inflation = Falling Standard of Living

Intuitively my uncle at Joe's Diner knows that inflation destroys the purchasing power of currency. As goes your currency, so goes your standard of living.

A depreciating dollar = falling standard of living.

This is a major reason for the demise of the middle class. Unlike the top 20%, most of America, much of the middle class do not have the savings to invest in the inflation hedges like real estate, stocks, and precious metals that will rise with the overall price level created by the inflation generated under a fractional reserve banking system. Wages seldom (never) rise as fast as inflation, with the end result being that there is a slow painful economic decline for most Americans who simply cannot keep up with the inflation created under such a banking system. For Uncle Joe, it means eating out once a week, instead of twice a week. The excess money created through this fractional reserve banking system ultimately also finds its way into assets like stocks and real estate, creating asset bubbles that make those that take advantage of them, much wealthier, but leaving most Americans without the wherewithal to purchase such assets (about 80% of the population), financially poorer in relative terms. The top 20% of Americans who own most of this wealth revel in such asset bubbles, get much richer, and the bottom 80% get much poorer.

A Little History

The Swedish Riksbank was the world's first central bank, created in 1668. Many nations followed suit in the late 1600s to establish central banks which were given the legal power to set the reserve requirement, and to specify the form in which such assets (called the monetary base) are required to be held. To mitigate the impact of bank failures and financial crises, central banks were also granted the authority to centralize banks' storage of precious metal reserves, thereby facilitating transfer of gold in the event of bank runs, to regulate commercial banks, impose reserve requirements, and to act as lender-of-last-resort if any bank faced a bank run. The emergence of central banks reduced the risk of bank runs which is inherent in fractional-reserve banking, allowing the practice to continue as it does to this very day.

It works like this. Let's take the example mentioned earlier. The FED creates $100 for X bank to borrow (because X bank asked to borrow it) and deposits it in XX Bank's account with the FED. X bank agrees to pay the FED's discount rate of 1% interest (for example, as it changes all the time). X bank then lends $90 to Farmers Bank of Nebraska (a fictitious name) at 2% interest, charging more because the whole reason X bank borrowed the money, knowing it had to pay it back (because it was a loan, after all) was to lend it out to make money. Then that bank lends out $81 to a Savings & Loan for 3% interest. That S & L lends $72.90 to a home buyer at 4% interest as a mortgage. So, the FED makes $1 in interest, X bank makes $1.80, Framer's Bank makes $2.43, and the S & L makes $2.91 for a total of $8.15 in interest on a virtual $343.90 that emanated from an initial "virtual" $100. If all the principle were paid back, that would still leave $8.15 of virtual money after the FED zeroed out its $100 liability for having created it out of the air. The point is, before the FED created that $100, the economy was balanced—now there is $8.15 of money in the economy with nothing backing it. Multiply that by billions! And today, trillions! And, as wryly ascribed by the late Republican Senator Everett Dirksen of Illinois, "a billion here, a billion there; pretty soon you're talking real money!" (Dirkson, 1965, p. 2).

The Principle of a Central Bank: Pulling Money Out of the Air

America's central bank is the Federal Reserve, often referred to as *the lender of last resort*. This is an appropriate moniker because, as we will see, if the government cannot get real money that it needs to borrow for deficit spending from elsewhere, it goes to the FED, which literally, creates it out of the air, i.e., from nothing. The underlying principle of a central bank is to allow a government to borrow money from itself, for itself. Often, the initial reaction is probably one of surprise, if not horror, and it should be. Essentially, when a government overspends, it needs to get money to cover that spending. This has occurred innumerable times throughout history, especially during times of war, in order to finance those wars. It is happening today with the United States in two wars it cannot afford, Afghanistan and Iraq. There are not enough domestic savings to cover the governments annual spending needs and these wars, and foreigners are increasingly unwilling to lend money to the world's largest debtor country, leaving a funding shortfall (deficit), and increasing borrowing, thereby increasing the national debt.

This annual deficit compounds year-after-year and is referred to as our national debt which is now nearly $30 trillion dollars. Where does the money for deficit spending come from if the government cannot borrow it from its citizens or foreign investors and central banks? As the lender of last resort, it comes from the FED who creates the electronic credits necessary which get deposited into government operating accounts, and the FED in return receives a stack of I.O.U.s called U.S. government securities for the amount loaned which we, the taxpayers, pay the interest on.

How much interest you might ask? The interest on the national debt is, as of this writing in late 2019, now $479 billion and growing every year. It is now the third largest item in the U.S. budget behind Social Security and military spending. How does this impact U.S. citizens? Economist use a term called *crowding out* to describe a situation in which government deficit spending immediately reduces the money available for other government discretionary spending and business. Funds that could be used for productive investment go to pay for interest on an exploding national debt. In short, we are mortgaging our children's future to borrow and spend beyond our means today.

In the longer run, as an economist would say, an increasing national debt burden becomes a major problem for everyone. According to the World Bank (2018), when a country's debt to GDP (national debt / GDP) reaches or exceeds 77%, the country reaches an economic tipping point and risks the very real possibility of a currency and financial crisis. By the second half of 2019, the United States had a debt to GDP ratio of 103% (Amadeo, 2019).

So, this is how creating money out of thin air works.

Step 1. The U.S. Congress decides on a budget of spending that includes social programs, defense programs, infrastructure, Social Security, Medicare, ad infinitum ad nauseum. Since 1970, that spending budget has been in a deficit, that is, the budget calls for more money than the government takes in (usually in revenues such as income tax and corporation tax). This is called deficit-spending. The Congress then authorizes (by a simple majority vote of the House of Representatives and the Senate) the U.S. Treasury to *borrow* money to cover the shortfall in the budget, i.e. the deficit (Beers, 2019).

Step 2. The Treasury acquires the needed money by selling a T-Bill (Treasury Bill). A T-Bill is a short-term debt obligation backed by the U.S. Treasury Department. They are usually sold in denominations of $1,000 up to a maximum purchase of $5 million and mature (i.e., are paid back to the buyer with a specified interest) at various periods usually within 1 year. These T-Bills are also called *government securities* and *Treasury notes*. They are essentially an IOU from the U.S. government to pay back the buyer the amount of the note sold with the specified interest accrued over the specified period. In September

2014, foreigners owned $6.06 trillion of these T-Bills (26% of America's total debt of $23 trillion). The largest holders were China, Japan, Belgium, the Caribbean banking centers, and oil exporters.

Step 3. Now this is the interesting part. Other nations, companies, people, and all banks other than the FED must pay for the T-Bill with money they actually have, or at least profess to have. (More on that later). But the FED pays for it, as former Federal Reserve Chairman Ben Bernanke said in his fourth lecture at George Washington University on March 29, 2012, "by crediting the bank accounts of the people who sold them [government securities] to us" (Bernanke, 2012, p. 3). They do not explain what *crediting the bank accounts* means. It truly means the FED creates an account for the U.S. Treasury and, into it, digitally places the purchase price—no actual money changes hands. The obvious question is: where did the FED get the money to put into the Treasury's account? And the answer is —it pulled in out of the air. Truly!

Step 4. The Balance Sheet. As a corporation under U.S. Corporate laws and regulations, the FED cannot justify giving a sum of money that it never had to anyone UNLESS it shows a liability on a balance sheet. The FED did not have the money they give to the Treasury, so it *borrowed it from itself* to give to the FED to buy the T-Bill. Thus, as a loan from itself, it accounts for that loan by entering the amount of the *credit* it gave to the Treasury's account on the FED's balance sheet as a liability, meaning it was now obligated to pay for it at some point. How did it *borrow* it from itself? By pulling it out of the air—i.e., it very simply digitally entered a liability on its balance sheet for the purchase price it credited to the Treasury. There was nothing backing it—there was no promise from anyone else to cover it—there was no paper, such as currency, representing it—it was very truly numbers entered on a page, i.e. the liability side of the balance sheet ledger. These are simply bookkeeping entries. At the beginning of 2018, the FED itself held $2.38 trillion of the national debt, (Nearly $7 trillion now in 2020) i.e., T-Bills, up from only $492 billion at the beginning of 2009, an increase of $2.366 trillion (Fred, 2019). This should tell you something—that we can't get other nations to buy our T-Bills, so we are borrowing it from ourselves.

Step 5. The Treasury takes the *virtual money* credited to its account and spends it, that is, it goes into the operating account of the U.S. government. But eventually, that T-Bill has to be repaid. How does it do that? By borrowing more money! If the Treasury still does not have enough real money from tax revenues, etc., then, it has no alternative but to borrow it once again. That is what we have been doing each year since 2001. Each year shows the highest debt in American history—nearly $23 trillion on April 11, 2018, according to the USDebtClock. org, with $900 billion in Treasury Securities to be paid. Total net interest on the debt was $291 billion. (Keep in mind that the interest on the debt is supposed to go back to the FED from whence the Treasury borrowed it and remember, the FED just pulled that out of the air!)

The Federal operating budget for 2018 was $4.45 trillion while revenues received (taxes) equaled approximately $3.8 trillion it for 2018 (about a $700 billion shortfall / deficit) which was a 3.8% increase from the year before. Three and a half trillion was taken in by the Internal Revenue Service in

2018 with total outlays equaling that year with $467 billion paid out in tax refunds and 7.4% of it was marked to pay just the interest on the debt (i.e., the interest on the T-Bills it has to pay back). Total federal tax revenues were only $3.654 trillion, with actual operating budget coming in at $4.094 billion. And the Republican sponsored tax *reform* bill passed in 2017 just added at least another $1.5 trillion to the debt over the next 10 years. As they say, *do the math*. There is no way out!

Step 6. The U.S. Treasury pays off the outstanding T-Bills. Ideally, this would be done with *real* money obtained from government revenues (mainly taxes). The only way that can be done is for the government to take in more money in revenues than the money it gives out in expenditures (spending). (By the way, that is the main difference between government and private enterprise accounting terms —governments have *revenues* and *expenditures* while private enterprise has *income* and *expenses*. The difference is subtle but essentially it implies that government revenues are not freely offered to the government in exchange for goods or services as private income is offered to a business and that government *spends* money, not as a cost of those goods and services or of doing business as it is with private *expenses*, but as a requirement to fulfill the will of the people.) The last time this was done was in 2001 when the debt was paid off, i.e., there were no outstanding T-Bills. (But paying off the T-Bills also has deleterious consequences—more on that later.)

Step 7. The FED, after receiving money from the Treasury to pay off the T-Bills it holds, credits itself with the money and zeroes out the liability it had put in its balance sheet. But it also received interest for that T-Bill which it credits in its assets. In essence, the FED got back more money than the *virtual* money it gave out, money it never had in the first place. Even worse, if the Treasury paid back the T-Bill with *virtual* money it borrowed from the FED initially, then, the FED can only zero out the initial $100, but still has another $101 dollars of virtual money in its liabilities (i.e., another $100 loan to the Treasury to pay off the first $100 loan plus an additional $1 so the Treasury can pay the interest that was part of the original T-Bill offering). So, unless the Treasury can get *real* money from a source other than the FED, the FED just keeps making the economy more and more dependent on *nothing.*) That is called rolling over the debt.

Your Uncle and the Lawnmower

Now, imagine doing this yourself. Your uncle comes to you and begs you to lend him $100 to buy a lawnmower.

> "Not for long," he says, "just long enough to get me through. I promise you, Fred, I will pay it back in 2 weeks."

You say that you are absolutely broke, but you will lend it to him anyway. So, you pull out a piece of paper, write **Balance Sheet** on the top and put the labels **Assets** on the left and **Liabilities** on the right. You then write out a piece of paper that says "$100" and hand it to him.

> He says, "Wow! I now have $100!" and he writes you out an IOU for $100 to be paid back in 2 weeks which you write in on the left under **Assets** as "$100—IOU from my uncle."

But, you think,

"That's not really right—I don't really have $100."

"Ah!" you say.

But if my uncle gives me back that piece of paper I gave him that said $100, then it becomes a wash. And if he actually pays it back with real money, then I am actually $100 ahead! So, you simply write "$100" on the right side under **Liabilities** as a reminder that if your uncle is able to actually *spend* that piece of paper, it will eventually come back to you with a demand for $100 worth of real money and you will have to cover it with real money! (Or get that piece of paper back from him.)

Now your uncle tries to spend it. But no one will take it because it does not show up in a legitimate bank account he owns (with no money in it, as he has told you), so he has two options: (a) he can try to get a legitimate bank to give him a $100 bill (which is actually a Federal Reserve Note that is also based on *virtual money*, but accepted by the public as legal tender) or (b) he can ask the seller from whom he wishes to buy the lawnmower to accept your piece of paper in exchange. The bank will not give him legal tender, but the seller says,

"Well, I have faith in you and your credit is good with me, so I will accept your piece of paper."

Your uncle is happy because not only does he get the lawn mower he wanted, he got rid of that piece of paper which he knows cannot come back to him. So he thinks!

Now, the week after he *bought* the lawnmower, your uncle wants to erect a wall around his property and comes once again to you for another $100.

You say "Sure if you will take another piece of paper. But you still owe me $100. He says, don't worry, I still have another week to pay it back."

So you, once again, write out a piece of paper that says "$100" to give to him, record it in your assets column as "$100—loan #2 to Uncle," and record $100 in the liabilities. Now you have $200 of money you never had, but in the form of an IOU and $200 as liabilities with only two promises from your uncle to pay you back to cover it.

Now your uncle goes to the wall manufacturer and says,

"You know me, Chin! Will you take this piece of paper marked "$100" and let me have the wall materials?"

Chin says,

"Sorry, Uncle Sam, you have been doing this for so long, and I already have so many of your pieces of paper, and no one else will buy them from me, so I no longer have full faith in you and you no longer have credit with me!"

So, eventually your uncle finds someone else to give him the materials in exchange for that piece of paper.

Now another week passes, and you go to your uncle and say,

"Where is the first $100 you promised to pay back?"

And your uncle says,

"Gosh, I'm really sorry Fred, but I don't have it. Could you loan me another $100 to pay you?"

And, because he is your uncle, you say,

"Well, I have already loaned you $200, but you are my uncle, so I guess I have to."

Now you have $300 in bogus assets (which are just promises from your uncle to pay it back) and $300 in liabilities. So your uncle says,

"Thanks!"

and immediately gives you back that piece of paper as payment for the first IOU, which you subtract from the $300 liability, leaving you with $200 in liabilities and $200 in IOUs. You have gained nothing, and your uncle has given himself another 2 weeks to find the money to pay off IOU #2 and #3.

But now, your uncle's friends come to him saying,

"You have borrowed so much money from us that we now want "real" money as payment or real goods and services, and if we don't get it, you will get nothing from us and you will have to start giving us real goods and service free until you pay off your debt!"

And your uncle thinks,

"Oh no! I really need my coffee in the morning and I really love shrimp and lamb and Gucci shoes."

Eventually, this is what is going to happen—the seller says,

"I don't want any more pieces of paper from you, Fred. I have to eat! From now on, your credit is no good with me.

So, I am going to start taking real things you own from you to cover what you owe me."

So, being flat broke, as you were in the beginning, with only liabilities in the right column of the balance sheet and no *real* assets in the left, you now no longer have anyone who will extend you credit. Your liabilities start coming due, you cannot pay them back with real money, you are evicted, and your house is auctioned off to pay for some of your liabilities, and you start walking the street looking for handouts.

If you haven't guessed it by now, your uncle's name is Sam and the seller he gave your piece of paper to is named Publius, AKA the American people. And this is where we are—government expenditures are being *covered* by IOUs (T-Bills) that are bought with *virtual* money from the FED, with no real money coming in to the FED to cover its liabilities. And this is the insidious nature of a national, central bank—to obfuscate the fact that the U.S. government is spending *virtual* money by convincing its people that the government is not creating the money—the bank is—and banks, as the people have come to believe, only deal with real money. In other words, the government can say,

"We are not printing money! So, don't worry! The debt is covered."

So why does the U.S. Government need the Federal Reserve? Because, as noted in the story above, when other nations stop believing in us, the government has to get the money, real or virtual, from somewhere and if it borrowed it directly from itself, i.e., the U.S. Treasury, the voters probably would not

THE STRUCTURE OF THE FEDERAL RESERVE BANK

accept it because taxes would have to be raised. *So, the govern-ment needs to distance itself from its own financing arm, albeit thinly veiled as The Federal Reserve so as not to be seen as political.* The irony is that the FED is obscenely political being started by the rich, for the rich and run by the rich—and who are the rich? They are mostly Republicans, for as we all know, the party of big business is the Republican party.

Do They Really Pull Money Out of the Air?

Ben Bernanke openly confessed that the FED pulls money out of the air using a printing press, a euphemism in his speech to the National Economists Club, Washington, DC, November 21, 2002, entitled Deflation: *Making Sure "It" Doesn't Happen Here,* Bernanke stated:

> But the U.S. government has a technology, called a print-ing press, or, today, its electronic equivalent, that allows it to produce as many U.S. dollars as it wishes at essentially no cost. By increasing the number of U.S. dollars in cir-culation or even by credibly threatening to do so, the U.S. government can also reduce the value of a dollar in terms of goods and services, which is equivalent to raising the prices in dollars of those goods and services. (Bernanke, 2002, p. 2)

So here it is Uncle Joe! The reason that meatloaf and mashed potatoes doubled in 10 years!. We have it straight from the horse's mouth, as they say in Pennsylvania. Bernanke just admitted in front of a room full of economists, in the nation's capital no less, that the FED could, and would create inflation at all costs by *creating* money out of thin air. Creating electronic *credits* for its member banks to reduce the value of the dollar and raise the prices of goods and services! Unabashedly, he's confessed to us all that the FED will do whatever they have to create inflation. This begs the question, what is wrong with prices staying the same or better still, going lower?

This is deflation, and heaven forbid, a central bankers worst enemy! Falling prices? Great for consumers but not for bankers. Why not I hear my uncle asking. Because friends, we have a debt and consumption based economy meaning that without more debt (loans) there is no *expansion* (of bank profits in particular). The U.S. economy is now a consumption based economy meaning that debt (loans) must expand continuously to generate economic growth. *Consumption* is now over 70% of U.S. GDP because we don't produce much anymore, we *consume.*

No consumption = No to low growth = Falling banking and corporate profits

Importantly Uncle Joe asks, how is the government going to tax falling prices? It's easy to calculate what taxes should be in a period of rising incomes (expansion) but how do you tax consumers on savings from lower prices for goods and services? They cannot of course, so government tax revenues would fall precipitously in such a scenario (deflation). The FED MUST have inflation.

Bernanke (2012) back peddled on the notion that the FED would increase inflation at all costs in his fourth lecture at George Washington University on March 29, 2012, Bernanke tries to obfuscate the notion that FED pulls money out of the air by saying:

Sometimes you hear that the FED is printing money in order to pay for the securities we acquire . . . But as a literal fact, the FED is not printing money to acquire these securities, and you can see it from the balance sheet here, the light blue line [pointing to Federal Reserve currency notes] is basically flat. The amount of currency in circulation has not been affected by these activities. (Bernanke, 2012, p. 1)

Evasion! Bernanke chose to interpret *printing money* literally, as in using printing presses to print more Federal Reserve notes, rather than interpreting it as the euphemism for unsubstantiated entry of numbers (i.e., "pulling money out of the air") that he himself used in his earlier speech in 2002. Bernanke continued,

So the FED is a bank for the banks. Banks can hold deposit accounts with the FED, essentially, and those are called reserve accounts. And so as the purchases of securities [T-Bills] occurred, the way we paid for them was basically by increasing the amount of reserves that banks had in their accounts with the FED. So you can see this, here, [pointing to an image of the FED's balance sheet] this is the liabilities side of the FED's balance sheet. Of course, assets and liabilities have to be equal. So the liabilities side had also to rise near $3 trillion, as you can see. Now, you might ask the question, well, the FED is going out and buying $2 trillion of securities—how did we pay for that? And the answer is that we paid for those securities by crediting the bank accounts of the people who sold them to us and those accounts, at the banks, showed up as reserves that the banks would hold with the FED. (Bernanke, 2002, p. 2)

He is of course really saying that the FED simply creates money out of the air whenever it feels like it, and, through fractional reserve banking, even more money is created out of thin air. Most of his speech, if you read the whole thing, contains euphemisms and phrases to obfuscate this fact by trying to justify it as "preventing deflation," [and to] "preserve a buffer zone for the inflation rate" [and] "asset purchases," [and] "assets and liabilities have to be equal," [and the] "liabilities side had to rise," [and] "crediting accounts" (Bernanke, 2002, p. 2).

CHAPTER 3.

How Inflation Is Created for the Middle Class and Asset Bubbles Are Created for the Rich— Trickle Up Economics

The world is increasingly alarmed by America's profligacy. It's not just the staff of the International Monetary Fund who lecture us as if we were a banana republic. Global leaders at the Davos World Economic Forum and other venues speculate openly about how long the dollar will remain the world's reserve currency and about whether the U.S. financial system will take down the global economy when it implodes.

—PETER G. PETERSON, FORMER CHAIRMAN OF THE COUNCIL ON FOREIGN RELATIONS AND FORMER CHAIRMAN OF THE FEDERAL RESERVE BANK OF NEW YORK, 2004

Before getting too deep into the machinations of how the FED creates and manipulates money and what the effects of these monetary machinations are, a little background to the structure of the Federal Reserve might help. The official website of the Federal Reserve (www.federalreserve.gov 2019) states:

The Federal Reserve System is the central bank of the United

States. It performs five general functions to promote the effective operation of the U.S. economy and, more generally, the public interest.

These five functions are ostensibly to conduct the nations monetary policy while simultaneously attempting to maintain price stability and "moderate" interest rates in the U.S. economy. They are also responsible for promoting the stability of the financial system while attempting to mitigate systemic risks through "active monitoring" and "engagement" in the U.S. and abroad (?? What are they doing abroad

Other actions they are responsible for is promoting the "safety and soundness" of individual member banks and the banking system, while promoting consumer protection through "consumer focused supervision and analysis of consumer issues and trends. ("About The FED," 2019, p. 1)

The official website notes the framers of the Federal Reserve Act purposely rejected the concept of a single central bank. Instead, they provided for a central banking *system* with three salient features: (1) a central governing board, (2) a decentralized operating structure of 12 Reserve Banks, and (3) a combination of public and private characteristics . . . Although parts of the Federal Reserve System share some characteristics with private-sector entities, the Federal Reserve was established to serve the public interest. ("About the FED", 2019, para. 6)

As I will reveal throughout this book, the above statement that the FED "purposefully rejected the concept of a single central bank" is a blatant obfuscation of the truth—it really is and has always been intended to be a central bank.

There are three components to the Federal Reserve System: the Board of Governors, the Federal Reserve Banks (Reserve Banks), and the Federal Open Market Committee (FOMC).

The Board of Governors is an agency of the U.S. federal government that reports to and is directly accountable to the U.S. Congress which is supposed to be diligent in its oversight of the FED, as well as providing general guidance for the system and oversees the 12 regional Reserve Banks. In this system, there are basic responsibilities shared between the Board of Governors in Washington, DC whose members are appointed by the President with the advice and consent of the Senate and the Federal Reserve Banks and Branches, which constitute the System's operating presence around the country. Ostensibly, the Federal Reserve has frequent communication with the executive branch and congressional officials, but ultimately its decisions are made independently ("About the FED," 2019, para. 1–7).

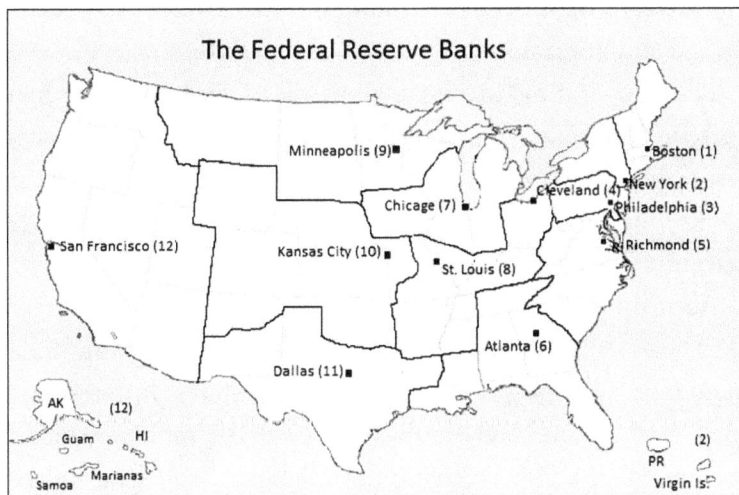

Figure 4: The Structure of the Federal Reserve System in the United States
Note: Reprinted from the official Federal Reserve site.

*Note: Retrieved April 13, 2018, from www.federalreserve.gov/aboutthefed/section7.htm) Federal Reserve Official Website: About the FED, 2019, para. 1–7) www.federalreserve.gov/aboutthefed/structure-federal-reserve-system.htm.

There are 12 banks in the Federal Reserve system as depicted in Figure 5—Federal Reserve Banks. If you look on any $1 dollar bill of U.S. currency, you will see at the top of the *portrait* side (George Washington) the words *Federal Reserve Note*. (Currency notes used to say *Silver Certificate* between 1878 and 1964 and they were redeemable for their face value in silver coins (which no longer exist) until the practice was phased out, and stopped completely in 1964.) The seal on the right says, *Department of the Treasury*. The outer band of the seal on the left indicates *Federal Reserve* and inner band will say *Bank of Atlanta Georgia* or *Bank of* . . . (any one of the 12 banks of the Federal Reserve system to which that particular note was assigned by the Treasury for release into the economy). To release the notes into the economy for circulation, that Federal Reserve Bank sends that note to other banks, all privately owned and operated.

Banks operating in one region (of 12) receive their hard currency from the respective Federal Reserve Bank in their respective geographic region. As currency wears out, private banks send it back to the respective Federal Reserve Bank who accounts for the note and replaces it with new notes.

According to the official website of the Federal Reserve (FED, 2019), originally, the 12 banks were to operate independently, offering their own discount rates (interest rate they charge commercial banks). Eventually, monetary policy required increased coordination throughout the Federal Reserve System and The Federal Reserve Act was revised in 1933 and 1935, with these revisions together creating the modern-day Federal Open Market Committee (FOMC). Further coordination was enacted with the Depository Institutions Deregulation and Monetary Control Act of 1980 (Monetary Control Act) dealing mostly with the pricing of financial services offered to depository institutions.

Dividend amount. *After all necessary expenses of a Federal reserve bank have been paid or provided for,* **the stockholders of the bank (member banks boards of directors***) are entitled to receive an annual dividend on paid-in capital stock of—in the case of a stockholder with total consolidated assets of more than $10,000,000,000, the smaller of the rate equal to the high yield of the 10-year Treasury note auctioned at the last auction held prior to the payment of such dividend and 6%; and in the case of a stockholder with total consolidated assets of $10,000,000,000 or less 6%.*

Dividend cumulative. *The entitlement to dividends under subparagraph (A) shall be cumulative.*

Inflation adjustment. *The Board of Governors of the Federal Reserve System shall annually adjust the dollar amounts of total consolidated assets specified under subparagraph (A) to reflect the change in the Consumer Price Index, published by the Bureau of Economic Analysis. Please take note here, dear reader that there are* **stockholders** *of the* **FED.** *The FED is owned by its member banks and those sitting on its board of directors.*

But, I hear Uncle Joe ask,

"Isn't the FED owned and operated and or an agency of the U.S. Federal Government?"

Shaking my head sadly I say,

"I'm sorry Uncle Joe, but their name was deliberately picked to confuse most Americans into believing they *were run* by the U.S. government. They are not, Uncle Joe. They are ostensibly an agency of the Federal Government but are actually run independently. To learn more about how they operate and who actually owns them, you should go do some more research on them. You may be shocked. In fact, we (American population) don't even know what the FED is doing most of the time. Getting an annual audit of the FED has been as difficult as getting a peek at the President's tax returns."

The FED's Balance Sheet

Traditionally, the FED's assets have mainly consisted of U.S. government securities and loans extended to member banks. When the FED buys government securities, it pays for them by electronic credit through member banks, thus increasing the bank's reserves, and expanding the potential money supply. This is what the FED does through its member banks when it is following an expansionary monetary policy. It SELLS government securities to member banks when it wants to reduce reserves (banks must use their capital to buy government securities) and this occurs when it wants to CONTRACT THE MONEY SUPPLY (reduce loan availability).

When the FED loans money to a member bank, it is crediting the reserve account of the member banks through a book entry becoming an asset. In case member banks wish to convert their reserve balances into hard cash, the FED issues them dollar bills or extends loans through their discount window where member banks can borrow money if needed.

If the FED is buying junk scraps by paying money, that

would become its asset. The Federal Reserve, like any bank, can acquire / create an asset simply by crediting a bank account. As Ben Bernanke explained as head of the Federal Reserve in 2012 and in innumerable speeches during his "tenure as head of the Federal Reserve, the FED has an unlimited capacity to spend U.S. dollars. It can and does, create trillions of dollars with a simple keystroke creating a book keeping entry. (more on this later). As he said in 2012,

> Now, you might ask the question. Well, if the FED is going out and buying $2 trillion dollars of securities—how did we pay for that? And the answer is that we paid for those securities by crediting the bank accounts of the people who sold them to us, and those accounts, at the banks, showed up as reserves that the banks would hold with the FED. (Bernanke, 2012, p. 3)

IF the FED can create trillions of dollars with a simple keystroke, then why do many politicians say we are out of money?

The answer is simple. Most of us don't understand the monetary system or, as Warren Mosler (2012) said, "Because we fear becoming the next Greece, we're turning ourselves into the next Japan" (as cited in Kelton, 2012, p. 1). Japan, as many of you know, has been in a stagnating economy since their real estate and stock market bubbles burst simultaneously in the 1980s. The country has never recovered from the reckless and yes, feckless monetary creation and liquidity fueled bubbles created by the Bank of Japan (BOJ) in that decade (1980s). Are we headed in exactly the same direction?

There is an alternative to this destructive boom bust asset bubble economy that has existed since the FED's founding.

End fractional reserve banking. And this begins with an understanding of the U.S. monetary system. The cat is already out of the bag. Chairman Bernanke confirms it. Money is no object.

Who Pays the Taxes?

According to data collected by individual income taxes are the U.S. federal government's single biggest revenue source. In fiscal year 2017, which ended Sept. 30, the individual income tax was expected to bring in nearly $1.66 trillion or about 48% of all federal revenues, according to the Office of Management and Budget (OMB). The corporate income tax was estimated to raise another $324 billion or 9% of total federal revenue. (see Figure 5 and 6).

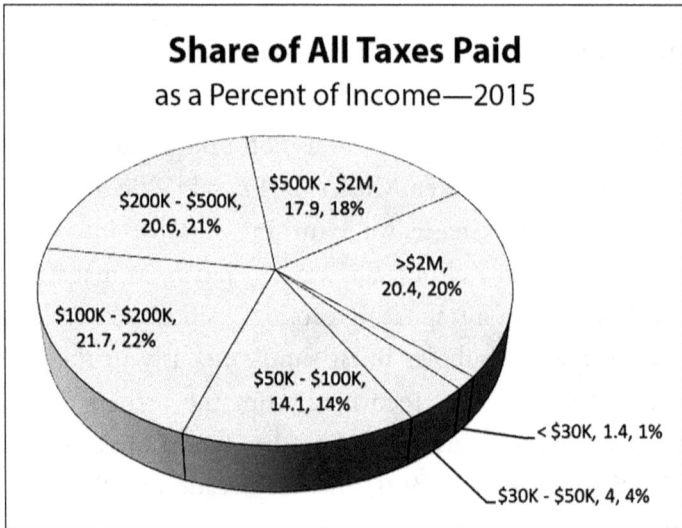

Figure 5: Share of All Taxes Paid as a Percent of Income

Note: Figures from Internal Revenue Service: Chart put together by the Pew Research Center, Washington, DC, 2019.

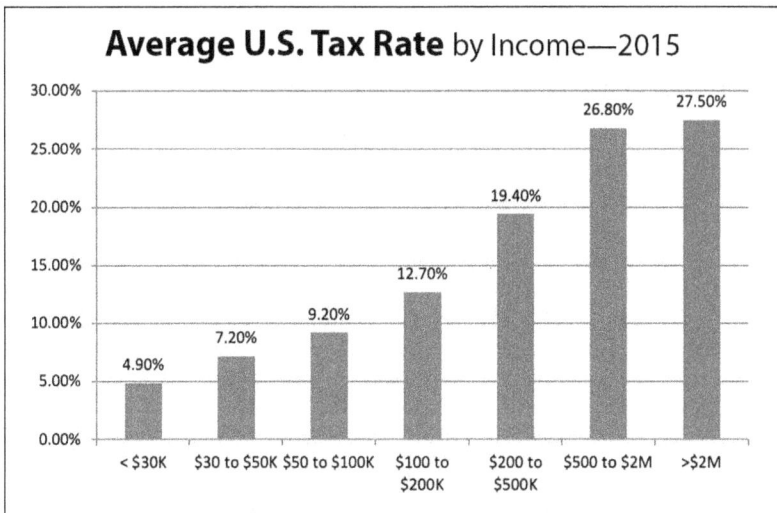

Figure 6: Average U.S. Tax Rate by Income

Note: Reprinted with permission from the Pew Research Center, Washington, DC.

*Note: Effective tax rate is total income tax due as a percentage of total adjusted gross income on returns with tax liablity

More Debt = More Money = More Inflation = More Debt = More Money = More Inflation = Currency Devaluation

Now that you have an idea why central banks were created and are allowed to exist, as well as how fractional reserve banking works, you need to know how inflation is built into a fractional reserve banking system. As we've seen, money in a fractional reserve system is only created when a loan (debt) is incurred by a consumer. Your debt becomes the bank's asset (like your mortgage), even though the bank created the money (debt instrument / loan agreement) out of thin air. It was money that was never theirs in the first place—**simply and only,** an accounting bookkeeping entry!

As new debt is created, there is more money in circulation, but the supply of goods and services stays the same. This outcome ultimately creates a situation economists call "too much money chasing too few foods." That is, inflation and destruction of the purchasing power of your dollar. As the debt rises, so must the rate of inflation. As the money supply increases while the total output of goods and services remains the same, prices must go up. And they do! Prices double every 10–15 years, thanks to the inflation created under such a system.

More money = More inflation in consumer prices or assets (housing, stocks, etc.)

Generally speaking, it is not really the price of things going up, it is the value of your currency going down. This is the legacy of the FED and its member banks—destruction of our currency and unending inflation, the most pernicious tax of all.

More money in circulation = More inflation = More depreciation of the currency

Those with the wealth or credit to buy inflation hedges like stocks, precious metals, and real estate, flourish in such a system. Those without inflation hedges are left behind, economically speaking.

Inflation naturally follows debt creation. CPI (essentially the cost of goods), as demonstrated in 1913, a good costing $10 because of inflation costs $14 (41% increase from 1913) in 1940 (before World War II), and costs $41 in 1971 (just before going off the gold standard, a 309% increase from 1913), and costs $100 in 1983 (first year of Reagan's administration, a 906% increase from 1913), and costs $216 in 2009 (first year of Obama's administration, a 2,076% increase from 1913), and today (2018) costs $252, a 2,415% increase from 1913.

Incrementally, buying that same good at the inflated respective price for that year, inflation increased 41% from 1913 to 1940, 189% from 1940 to 1971, 146% from 1971 to 1983, 115% from 1983 to 2009, and 16% from 2009 to 2018 (U.S. Inflation Calculator, 2019).

So, as debt grows, so must money, because debt is money in a fractional reserve banking system. Depicted in Figure 7 (below) depicts the national debt rising simultaneously and at virtually the same rate as the money supply (M3) and the consumer price index (CPI). As we now know, they must.

More debt = More money
More money = More debt = More
inflation=Rising Prices (CPI)

Note also how the slope (rate of increase) of the true money supply (M3) depicted in Figure 7: True Money Supply parallels and virtually equals the rate of increase in debt. Debt and money supply ran steadily and almost equally under $200 billion until after World War II in 1946, then a slow rise until 1971 when President Nixon took the nation off the gold standard, **then skyrockets from about $300 billion in 1970 to over $13.6 trillion in 2016, and $22.7 trillion as of this writing (2019) and is now approaching 30 trillion in 2020 (U.S. debt clock, 2019).**

U.S. National Debt & Money Supply vs. Consumer Price Index (CPI)

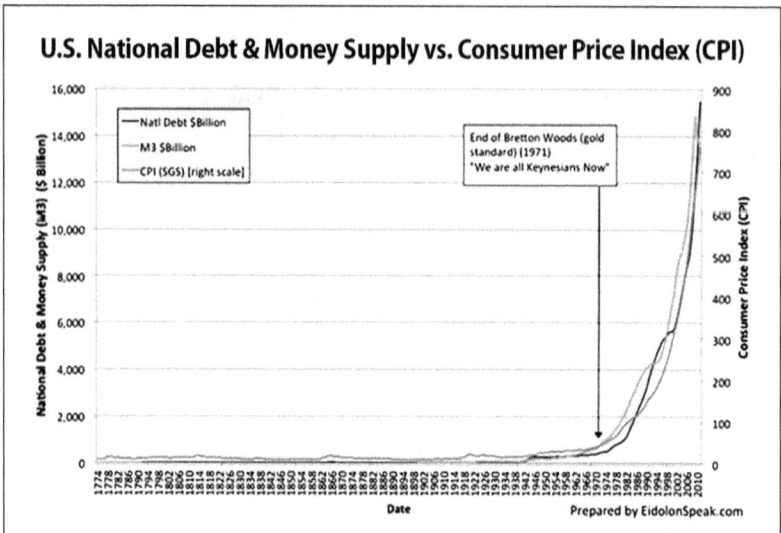

Figure 7: National Debt and Money Supply Growth

Note: Reprinted with permission from www.Eidolonspeak.com, Dr. Susanne Lomatch.

Note: Please take note of the parabolic rise of consumer prices, as debt and money supply move in tandem, starting in 1971 when the United States went off the gold standard.

Please note also in Figure 7, as the national debt grows, so does the money supply. A greater money supply equals more money in circulation which leads to inflation, of course, which leads to higher consumer prices or asset bubbles or both. More money in circulation, as my Uncle Joe realizes, equals more inflation, which depreciates your currency leading to loss of consumer purchasing power and a lower standard of living. Growing the money supply faster than the economy results in consumer price inflation or asset bubbles (great for banks and the rich) or both, simultaneously.

Or more simply put, when the Standard and Poor's index

rises nearly 30% in a year (2019) and wages in the same year rise less than 3%, the rich who own most of the stocks in the S & P 500 grow their wealth (unearned income) 10 times faster than wage earners (earned income). This is the crux of the wealth inequality problem. How is the stock bubble blown up? With excess liquidity being created by the FED.

As goes the currency, so goes your standard of living, which is why we should all be so concerned with the current banking system as gains from loans are privatized and bank losses become socialized, (bank bailouts by the taxpayer) i.e., the taxpayer's responsibility. As the average Joe (Uncle Joe) may understand, inflation is not the price of things going up, it is your currency going down in value through too much credit and money creation by the FED and the banking system.

Historically, the U.S. price level has doubled every 10–15 years from fractional reserve banking and excessive money supply growth. It is important to realize that this inflation puts a real economic squeeze on the middle and lower classes who do not own the inflation hedges like housing, stocks, bonds, and collectibles required to conserve or increase their wealth under such a system. Their wages and cost of living increases (COLAs) simply do not nor cannot keep pace with the rise in the overall price level. This ultimately leaves many pensioners and working people in poverty.

Please note above how money creation and debt rise simultaneously and at the same rate.

Money = Debt
Debt = Money

More money with no commensurate increase in goods and services = more inflation in assets, goods, and services, or both, which is particularly destructive to wage earners, (those on fixed incomes) and pensioners, and the most vulnerable in our society (the working poor).

The Mandrake Mechanism— Creating Something Out of Nothing

In his fascinating and very well researched read on the history of central banking in Europe and the United States, G. Edward Griffin in *The Creature from Jekyll Island* (1994) introduced his readership to the Mandrake Mechanism, a moniker taken from the 1940s cartoon called *Mandrake the Magician.* Mandrake's specialty was creating something out of nothing like the FED. In the cartoon, Griffin noted that money in a fractional reserve banking system such as ours, is not created until the moment it is borrowed! Most Americans have a very difficult time wrapping their heads around this fact. Remember,

Debt = Money
Money = Debt
More money and debt = More inflation

It is difficult to wrap one's head around but our total money supply is backed by nothing but debt! If all debt were repaid then, there would be no money in circulation. All money would disappear!

CHAPTER 4.

The Federal Reserve (FED) and Their Role in the Demise of the American Middle Class

"The first panacea for a mismanaged nation is inflation of the currency; the second is war. Both bring a temporary prosperity; both bring a permanent ruin. Both are the refuge of political and economic opportunists."

—Ernest Hemingway

The U.S. government, through well intended notions like the Federal Deposit Insurance Corporation (FDIC) created in the 1930s to bolster consumer confidence and to end bank runs, has yet again, created moral hazard in the banking sector with FDIC insurance, encouraging reckless lending and speculative lending behavior which is rewarded through higher profits and bonuses. Bankers, knowing they will be bailed out by the FDIC for poor lending decisions, all too often behave and invest recklessly. Of course—it is not their money! Crazy, isn't it?! It makes you wonder why we, the people, can't get bail-outs too, when these bankers make bad investment decisions decade-after-decade, leading to very questionable bailouts like the Resolution Trust Corporation (RTC) and the Troubled Asset Relief Program TARP, which fly in the face of capitalist theory (You make bad decisions as a business, you go out of business!) THAT is capitalism—you do not bail companies out.

This reckless behavior of which I speak is well documented and anyone over 50 years of age is familiar with the results of such reckless and irresponsible lending behavior by banks. The recession of 1980–81, the stock market Crash of 1987, the S & L disaster of the late 1980s, the recession of 1990–1991, the bond bubble of the mid 1990s, the Peso, Ruble, and Baht currency collapses in the late 1990s, Long-Term Capital Managements (LTCM) collapse in 1997 (the first hedge fund), the tech bubble and collapse of 2000, and of course the mother of all bubbles, the housing collapse of 2007–2008.

And these are just the financial calamities brought on by the likes of Lehman Brothers et al. and the FED in just 40 years! Hmmm, 40 years divided by 10 bubbles / recessions equals a financial disaster and subsequent financial and social and economic dislocation and social pain about every 4 years. It appears we are many years overdue for a major financial calamity! All kidding aside, because this is not really funny, it is a large part of the problem of why our middle class has been eviscerated by a deregulated financial services industry which has spawned one financial disaster after the next and robbed an entire generation of their savings through asset bubbles and their subsequent collapses.

Laughably, our present day Federal Reserve allegedly has two primary mandates: (a) to create price stability and (b) to maximize employment (full employment). Even a cursory review of the financial history of the United States makes it painfully clear, even to the FED's most ardent supporters (mostly on Wall Street, the investing class, and the banking sector) that the FED has been an abject failure at doing both. As a matter of fact, ironically and painfully, it should be abundantly clear that the FED IS the institution primarily responsible for most of the financial carnage in our economy since their creation in 1913. A dollar from 1913 is now worth .03 cents. Price stability? Destruction of our currency and therefore our purchasing power is the sad reality.

And here is the real rub . . . inflation, perhaps the greatest and most pernicious tax of all, robs us all—*slowly!* It is called a debtor's best friend and a saver's worst enemy for a reason. Why? Because debtors pay back loans in depreciated currency and savers are robbed because the *interest* they earn on their savings seldom keeps up with inflation under a fractional reserve banking system. Their savings depreciate year-after-year. We are like the proverbial frog in boiling water under such a system—we do not know we are being robbed (i.e. boiled to death) because it (being robbed) happens slowly. Usually, unless you live in Venezuela, Zimbabwe, Mexico, Thailand, or Argentina, where currency devaluations of 20–50% often occur overnight.

As we have seen, inflation is nearly always a monetary phenomenon. That is, it is nearly always created automatically under a fractional reserve banking system, and very deliberately when central banks grow money and credit far faster than the economy (GDP), in turn generating inflation in goods and services, and creating asset bubbles for their constituents, the banks, and the investing class. We've seen that inflation is literally baked into a fractional reserve banking system.

How Fast Should Money Supply Grow?

An economy growing at a 3% rate should have its money supply also grow at 3%. If the FED injects more money into the economy, say 12%, where does the extra 9% of created money go? There is now 9% more money and credit sloshing around the economy than needed for actual GDP growth.

Answer: It goes into asset bubbles or higher prices for goods and services or both simultaneously, because as the economist would say, you now have created a situation where you have too much money chasing too few goods.

And here is another kicker—the FED can create money and lots of excess liquidity and credit at the touch of a button and does so routinely for reasons discussed above and below. But there is a catch, a caveat if you will. It can seldom control where all that extra cash / liquidity will go. So, that extra 9% of money may end up in the stock market, becoming a stock bubble; in real estate, becoming a real estate bubble; in the bond market, becoming a bond bubble; or collectibles becoming an art and collectibles bubble. Or it may show up in higher prices for goods and services across the board in everything from milk to attorney's fees.

The point is the excess money (excess liquidity/credit) has to go somewhere and it does. Those who often proclaim that there is no inflation by saying, just look at the CPI, its only up 2% are being disingenuous about inflation. There is plenty of inflation, but it is in asset prices (like the stock market now) or increased spending on imports, not the CPI. For this reason, most economists will agree the CPI is a poor measure of overall inflation because of *hedonic adjustments* and other massaging by economists and U.S. government statisticians (Palmer, 2019).

All this inflation is great for people who own assets that will rise with inflation like real estate, stocks, collectibles etc. as noted earlier.

But what about those who cannot afford such inflation hedges? They, of course, by an accident of birth or because they are living on a fixed income, are left in the financial dust, becoming more impoverished while prices double every 10–15 years. Savers, pensioners, and wage earners are financially annihilated under such a system. Inflation created by reckless monetary policy is an ugly truth that those who have managed to stay ahead of such inflation often refuse to look at, much less acknowledge as a truth. It is one of the primary causes of the evisceration of the middle class over the last 40 years (since 1980).

The FED Surrogates

As a citizen, there are other very disturbing things about the FED to which I object. First, the head of the FED (i.e., the Chairman of the Board of Directors of the Federal Reserve) has more power than anyone in the country, including the President; yet he or she is not elected; he or she is *appointed by the President.* The chief FED head (Federal Reserve head) is appointed by the President and basically controls monetary policy for the country, i.e., creating money and credit, and controlling interest rates. As the Lord Mayer Rothschild (1815) noted hundreds of years ago, "Permit me to issue and control the money of the nation and I care not who makes its laws" (p. 1). The FED is all powerful, possibly one of the most powerful institutions on earth, full of non-elected bureaucrats working for a privately owned organization.

Second, again as a VERY concerned citizen, I find it very ironic, not to mention the height of hypocrisy, that at the very heart of our supposed free market economy there is a monopoly! Republicans routinely remind us that we have the greatest *free market economy on earth* without ever acknowledging the notion that we are as controlled an economy as any *planned* socialist economy, perhaps worse. Our alleged *free markets* are routinely managed by the FED and its myriad of minions, and proxies including Goldman Sachs and JP Morgan, two of the largest. Subsidies, tax breaks, a corrupted tax code weighted toward the upper one-percent, a regressive tax system, and plutocrats at the highest levels of government perpetuate this system designed over the decades to enrich the few at the expense of the many. And this is a fundamental point that so few, except the rich, understand, that the rich get their money from the middle class. Money all goes up and very little *trickles* down, as the term so ironically implies! (i.e., trickledown economics).

Third, this monopoly (i.e., the FED) controls the price and availability of money and credit through its member banks that represent about 75% of the banks in the country. Additionally, the FED historically has favored capital over labor, so I have yet another reason to want to see them strictly regulated or abolished. This is exactly the opposite of what should exist in a Democracy. The FED, as we have learned, was not brought into existence for some egalitarian, altruistic reason for the working man's benefit (please!). They were formed to be the banker's bank! The very font of money and credit creation in the United States! Those first in line for FED largesse are its member banks! And what do they do with FED funds they can borrow for virtually (pun intended) nothing? They are supposed to be lending it out to us, as in U.S. citizens, but more often than not, they just speculate with it or leave it on account with the FED where they earn risk free interest on it. Incredibly galling. Banks like Goldman Sacks are particularly adept at speculating with other people's money as noted by Taibbi (2010) in *The Great American Bubble Machine*, where he noted sadly, that Goldman Sachs and other investment banks have become the masters of economic disasters by picking the American middle class carcass clean for decades, nay, centuries using the tired old trick of pump and dump, that is, artificially inflating the price of an asset through blatantly false and misleading statements.

This often rampant speculation by investment banks is an extremely unfortunate loophole in the system of Western democratic capitalism, which was never designed to defeat organized greed. How could such a thing happen? That is, where a system of free markets (allegedly) and ostensibly free elections, that our country, and particularly the middle class, would be ravaged routinely by its own banking sector and financial and investing elites? As noted throughout this book, America is now a financialized economy, where consumer banking profits override any democratic agenda or concern for the average American. My Uncle Joe may not understand intellectually that his country is being run by mega-privately owned and operated institutions and banks, but he knows it intuitively. Hence the steady decline in trust by the American people in their institutions, politics, and banking system.

Investment banks routine financial machinations and financial re-engineering for profit, and their adroit ability to stay two steps ahead of any regulators, are great examples of institutionalized speculation, often bordering on fraud, if not outright illegality, their tactics now legendary. The general modus operand (MO) of these "investment banks" is to find some depression-era bill and either get it killed through lobbying as was done with the Glass-Stegall Act (overturned in 1999), which eliminated the depression-era firewall between investment banking and consumer banking, thus providing "investment banks" and other questionable financial intermediaries the opportunities to create toxic mortgage backed securities and sell them through wholly owned banks and or affiliated third parties in the United States and worldwide. Or the opportunity to pump up asset prices and sell or short them (the dump) before the inevitable collapse.

As Matt Taibbe (2010) so eruditely points out in *The Great American Bubble Machine*, Goldman and other euphemistically titled, *investment banks* along with the big consumer banking giants, have turned American finance into a giant *pump and dump* machine. The trick is as old as it is tawdry and has been used by banks for centuries to defraud the public to line their own coffers.

It is relatively straight forward, and goes like this. First the investment bank finds a piece of depression era legislation, or government guaranteed programs (like government guaranteed mortgages or now, the student loan program) that can be gutted or can be financially reengineered to meet the needs of the bank, not the public. (like the Glass Stegall Act). Then, with an accommodating central bank (FED), investment banks like Goldman, provide liquidity to the sector through easy credit terms and rapid money supply expansion while also generating media excitement through every media channel possible, (PUMP). As asset prices begin to rise these investment banks, now positioned as the market makers or intermediary between the asset and the public, make more of the asset available for an increasingly enthusiastic and gullible investing public (Think swelling of initial public offerings (IPOs) leading up to the technology bubble of the late 1990s and *Teck wreck of 2000* or the housing surge of 2002–2007). (PUMP).

And now comes the really creative part. Investment banks create *derivatives* and related financial instruments to provide enormous leverage and speculative opportunities in both buying and selling the asset(s). (Think CDOs in housing for example). These derivative creations allow financial intermediaries to leverage the asset at a10–1 ratio. (PUMP). Then of course the banks must make themselves the intermediary (as noted above) for trading the asset. That is, you become the market maker. (PUMP) As prices begin to rise in the asset you go full bore with a media blitz to heighten public excitement and increase your asset position du jour. (PUMP)

Eventually the public's appetite for the asset wanes, as the reality of how overpriced the asset is sets in, and now, being the market maker in the asset, you will know when demand begins to slacken. At this point you DUMP. As the public becomes increasingly aware of the asset price(s) falling, they begin to sell en mass with a selling panic ensuing. Here, as the market maker in the asset, you make still more money. (DUMP). Finally, when the selling is exhausted, you move in and pick up the pieces at rock bottom prices, and begin again.

It Is a Zero Sum Game

This is the MO of GS Bank and many others in the investment banking game and is how they rob the middle class decade-after-decade. Pump and dump. Unfortunately, it is a zero sum game. For every winner like GS Bank there must be, and is, a loser. The losers are the middle class and their pensions. This is yet another key for understanding why the rich get richer and the poor get poorer. For the average American their *investments* in stocks and real estate have been systematically robbed by *investment banks* using this formula decade-after-decade.

This trick of pumping and then dumping assets is as old as banking itself, now enshrined as an art form in Western Democracies with populations too ignorant or gullible to put their banking and financial services sectors on a very short leash. GS Bank and other *successful* investment banks are as ruthless, as they are relentless, very complex machines built to mercilessly take the savings of society (a lot of it middle class savings) and converting them into profits for GS Bank and its shareholders through this tried and true pump and dump scheme. This scheme, pumping and dumping, is what I like to call *trickle up* economics,, and has been deployed and artfully perfected by investment banks in the United States for many years.

Again? Really?

GS Bank and their brethren investment banks through financial re-engineering, and disgraceful profiteering have used this pump and dump playbook over and over again. In summary as noted above, but worth repeating, it is relatively simple: GS Bank positions itself in the middle of a speculative bubble created by the excess liquidity provided by the Federal Reserve, selling investments they know are of poor quality (junk bonds for example) and with the assistance of the aforementioned corrupt financial, political, and socio-economic systems rewrite the legislation protecting the investing public or eliminating it (legislation) altogether, as they did with Glass-Stegall in 1999. With the help of an often accommodating central bank, an often corrupted political system, and yes, very cooperative financial elites, they then create an asset bubble, with them as middle men, running up asset prices, and then selling them to a gullible, and now unprotected public that is left holding the worthless paper when GS Bank and friends sell. This is the MO for the stock market collapse of 2000 (The Tech Wreck) and the housing bubble of 2001–2008 (The Housing Bubble). Trillions were made by the banking system and ancillary businesses, but the middle and lower classes were decimated. **The gains were privatized while the booms lasted, and the losses socialized through taxpayer "bail outs" like the Resolution Trust Corporation (RTC / late 1980s), and the Troubled Asset Relief Program (TARP / 2010).**

Then, after the dust has settled after the crash du jour, ever so quietly, the cartel (Goldman and friends) start buying the assets back for pennies on the dollar and they start the whole ungodly process over again. These *bankers* or *banksters* as my Uncle Joe calls them, have been doing this over and over again since the 1920s.

Yes fellow citizens, simply **follow the money**. Banks like GS Bank and others have been pulling these financial stunts for centuries. The sad truth is that it is these banks and their unbridled greed and malfeasance that are a big reason for the disappearance of the middle class in the United States, over the last four decades since 1980. How? Because the middle class has been systematically robbed and defrauded by their own banking system. Painfully ironic, isn't it?

Taibbe (2010) and others including myself have noted that investment banks like GS Bank (what a euphemism-Investment bank) were directly or indirectly responsible for the housing bailout (2008), the Tech Wreck of 2000, the oil and gas bubble in the early 1970s, and of course, the mother of all crashes, the crash of 1929.

Of course this list is only the tip of the iceberg. One might reasonably ask, where were the regulators? Sadly, the situation in banking and the financial services industry now is something akin to the fox guarding the hen house. The primary responsibility for regulating and monitoring banking activities falls to . . . you guessed it! . . . the Federal Reserve! For S & Ls, it is the Office of Thrift Supervision, and in the realm of publicly traded securities like mortgage backed securities (MBSs), it is the Securities and Exchange Commission (SEC). Where were they during the *Tech Wreck of 2000* or the housing bubble? The MBSs and credit default obligations (CDOs), and credit default swaps (CDSs) were publicly traded. Where on earth were those created to protect us, the middle class? There were none, as we so painfully realized after the fact, and the fall, and the inevitable U.S. Congressional hearings and subsequent legislation like Sarbanes Oxley and Dodd-Frank passed in an attempt to placate and assuage an outraged and stripped down public. Where was the SEC? Where was the FED while GS Bank and others made their trillions on the backs of the middle class and poor worldwide? They were there, but as we all know, are lap dogs for the industry they were created to regulate. As long as the American middle class remains politically complacent, the wealthy will have their way, and the middle class will continue to suffer financially.

The Housing Bubble

The housing bubble, our most recent financial fiasco, provides a compelling example of how the FED under Chairman Alan

Greenspan was conveniently absent while the underwriting guidelines used for 70 years to ensure solid lending practices were thrown out the window between 2001 and 2008, resulting in the calamity known as the *housing crisis*. To enable this bubble to inflate our central bank threw bank underwriting guidelines out the window, and pumped trillions of excess money and credit into the economy creating the FED fueled liquidity-housing speculation, now known as the housing bubble. My Uncle Joe has asked me why was it primarily the FED's fault and not the people and businesses speculating in real estate?

My short answer to Uncle Joe is that the Federal Reserve has a set of mortgage underwriting guidelines that their member banks are supposed to adhere to and that the FED is supposed to enforce. IF these underwriting guidelines had been adhered to, I tell Uncle Joe, the bubble could not have occurred because most of the people buying homes would not have qualified for the loan in the first place.

Added to this fact is the fact that if the excessive credit were not made available through our central bank, the funds (money) would not have been available to make these mortgage loans. The FED's member banks had the reserves to lend ONLY because the FED created them. No excess reserves, not as much lending possible. No lending, no housing bubble.

In summary then, this massive amount of excess liquidity grossly inflated housing prices. Remember, the FED can and does often create excessive money and credit (more than that needed for economic growth) but cannot control where all the extra money goes most of the time. With the stock market crash still fresh in their minds American investors were not about to pile into the stock market. What was the next best alternative? Real estate! Of course!! It is obvious at a glance that money supply (money created by the FED) peaked with housing in 2008 (see Figure 8). **No excess money and credit creation = no bubble trouble** Uncle Joe.

Figure 8: Annual U.S. Money Supply Growth.

Note: Reprinted with permission from John Williams of Shadowstats.com: www. shadowstats.com.

Note: As one can clearly see, M3-Broad Money Supply, peaked in 2008–2009, followed by a peak in M1 and M2 coinciding exactly with the top of the housing bubble, and then collapsed in late 2009–2010.

This housing bubble, indeed, any bubble, cannot occur without excess liquidity created by the FED. That is, by the FED creating money and credit at a faster rate than the growth of the economy. No excess liquidity, no bubble trouble! But then, how would its member banks make money? That is not just a vacuous statement of disgust, it is the very heart of my argument against the FED. That is, to make money (i.e., un-earned income), you have to have excess liquidity (credit grown in excess of GDP).

Again, please note in the Figure 8, the very high correlation between the surge in money supply growth (excess liquidity created by the FED) and the peak in the housing bubble (nothing coincidental). The *housing bubble* could not have happened if the excessive liquidity for expansion was not provided by the FED and its member banks OR if the FED had been enforcing its own real estate underwriting guidelines with its member banks.

The FED also brought interest rates down to 50-year lows and held them there for the duration of the bubble. Greenspan, not so coincidentally, vacated his office in 2008, just before it all hit the fan (i.e., he literally walked out the door as then President George W. Bush pleaded for funds from the U.S. Congress). A somnambulant and complacent FED sat idly by while GS Bank and their brethren robbed the country.

So what else is new, you ask? As Taibbe (2010) noted, most of the blame for the bubble goes to, you guessed it, the FED, who threw their own underwriting guidelines out the window, to allow their member banks to speculate with, and to profit enormously from the real estate bubble. The MO was the same, only the vehicles used to strip the public varied. Instead of an inflated stock market and initial public offerings (IPOs) as was the case in the tech wreck of 2000, it was a willful disregard for real estate underwriting guidelines in the housing bubble (2002–2008). As Uncle Joe now understands, because there was little enforcement of existing mortgage underwriting standards by the FED, combined with the FED leaving interest rates at historically low levels for a long period of time, and excessive credit created by the FED, the housing bubble was allowed to germinate, and then blossom into the catastrophe that was. That bubble or any asset bubble for that matter, cannot grow without excessive credit creation, and an accommodating, often tainted, banking and financial services sector. There are two other major reasons for this mother of all bubbles happening which Taibbe (2010) failed to mention in his article—the rise of securitization and the gutting of banking regulations.

CHAPTER 5.

The Rise of Securitization and the Bubble Economy

This struggle may be a moral one, or it may be a physical one, and it may be both moral and physical, but it must be a struggle. Power concedes nothing without a demand. It never did and it never will. Find out just what any people will quietly submit to and you have found out the exact measure of injustice and wrong which will be imposed upon them, and these will continue till they are resisted with either words or blows, or with both. The limits of tyrants are prescribed by the endurance of those whom they oppress.

—FREDERICK DOUGLASS, 1857

The first reason and foremost reason for the housing bubble was the rise and popularity of *securitization in the financial services and banking sector*. Securitization is the process of taking an illiquid asset and transforming it into a security. Credit card receivables, car loans, and mortgages all began to be securitized in the late 1980s. Mortgage backed securities were popularized as an investment vehicle in the early 2000's leading ultimately to the buildup, and inevitable collapse of the housing market in 2008–2009. These mortgage backed securities (MBS's) were *bundled* and resold to investors, insurance companies, and pension funds worldwide during the housing bubble.

Securitizing (bundling of an asset class for resale to investors) and then bundling mortgages for resale to investors worldwide, was a brilliant, albeit dangerous development because it took all of the credit risk off the bank and placed it squarely in the investor's lap (surprise). How? Before securitization (BS), when a loan was originated and underwritten, the bank had to live with the loan on its balance sheet for the life of the loan. It stayed on its balance sheet until the homeowner sold the home or paid it off. Thus, *the bank was very careful about to whom they provided credit.* By the time the banks were done evaluating the credit risk of a potential borrower, you might say, they knew them better than their own mother!

With securitization, things in the mortgage industry changed rather dramatically, to say the least. Banks could now underwrite a mortgage loan and resell it to Goldman or other investment banks that would package and resell them to investors, insurance companies, mutual funds, etc., worldwide in the form of mortgage backed securities (MBSs). Voila! Relieved of the onerous and pesky burden of having to determine the credit quality of potential borrowers, consumer banks began underwriting, and quickly re-selling mortgages to investment banks like Goldman, who packaged and resold them willy-nilly, in the late 1990s, to insurance companies, pension funds, mutual funds, and the public. Credit quality was no longer a concern. The only thing the banks worried about at this point was their *origination fee* of 1–2% of the loan value on each mortgage sold. When the asset (mortgage) was sold, the bank was no longer responsible for it.

Thus, a new boom was born. With easy money provided by the FED, record low interest rates, and, alas, no underwriting standards, the banks went berserk! A whole new class of borrower was born—the "sub-prime" borrower—people who, under prior circumstances, would never have qualified for a mortgage, could now buy homes 10 to 20 times more than their annual income.

New types of home loans were created to fuel the boom.

Liar loans (stated income / stated asset (SISA) and no income / no asset (NINA) loans where the applicant's word is accepted without verification), *no-doc loans* (no documentation required), and *adjustable rate mortgages* (ARMs) were born, and anyone who had a pulse could qualify. Everyone in the housing food chain went berserk, from real estate agents to investment bankers, and everyone in between. What a party! But, what a hangover! We still have not recovered from 2008 housing busts, and in 2017 a quarter to a third of American homeowners are still underwater from this housing fiasco!

Such is the legacy of financial deregulation. It seems we never learn, for exactly the same thing happened in the late 1980s when the S & Ls were deregulated. Bankers gone crazy!! Back-to-back housing booms and busts and disasters in the late 1980s and from 2002 2007 in the span of 25 years. In the 1980s, we, the taxpayer, were left with approximately $500 billion in banking losses through the Resolution Trust Corporation (RTC) and in 2008, it was trillions more in taxpayer bailouts under the innocuous, and euphemistically titled Troubled Asset Relief Program (TARP). *Only in America* could bankers get away with such chicanery and malfeasance without doing jail time.

Leave it to bankers and politicians to come up with such benign acronyms for such fraudulent financial activity (TARP & RTC). Not surprisingly, few people did any real jail time for stiffing the taxpayer in either of these fiascos. These asset bubbles and subsequent implosions are all part of the choreographed financial carnage we witness decade after decade in the United States. Bankers blowing asset bubbles to generate increased profits. How many tens of trillions have been lost by the middle class in feeding this voracious beast called the banking sector and Wall Street? How many tens of trillions have been lost by the middle class in feeding this voracious beast called the FED and Wall Street? As noted by DeSoto (1998) of the Mises Institute, without credit expansion by central bankers most economic crises would be isolated events brought on by natural disasters like famine, floods, hurricanes or pandemics.

In other words, without excessive credit (monetary expansion) created by central banks, economic crisis would be the result of naturally occurring events like poor crops, and natural disasters like floods and hurricanes, or earthquakes, and we would see fewer of them (economic disasters). Now we see economic disasters at least once a decade thanks to integrated, and highly coordinated central banking monetary policy worldwide.

DeSoto (1998) also presciently noted that the new money created via the expansionary process of loans (read excessive liquidity created by the FED) is used to finance all sorts of speculative operations, takeover bids, and financial trade wars in which the culture of short-sighted speculation prevails. He noted that easy money and credit ultimately lead to speculation in nearly all asset classes, often generating supernormal returns in a short period of time. This in turn predictably leads to massive malinvestment and speculation, leading in turn to a waning of the entrepreneurial spirit and a general lack of commitment to longer term goals. Ultimately innovation becomes subdued, as planning and working for longer term goals appears stupid when surrounded by friends making record money in record time in the speculative bubble du jour.

As also noted by DeSoto, the entrepreneurial spirit largely evaporated because of these last two crises (2000 Teck Wreck and 2008 housing collapse). It was the middle class, the young, and the poor stuck with the mess for the most part after the housing collapse, as always, and the Millennials, growing up and witnessing such chicanery, predictably have shunned many of the consumption based trappings of their parents and grandparents (cars, houses etc.) after seeing what happened to them in these two recent economic crashes. Why save, invest, or innovate when it can all (and often is) be taken away from you in the next asset bubble collapse?

Gutting Regulation

The second reason for it *all going out the window* was the gutting of financial regulations enacted in the 1930s, particularly the repeal of the Glass Steagall Act of 1934, in 1999 by a Republican House and Senate (106th U.S. Congress). Repeal of this act enabled banks to *commoditize* the housing market, and exponentially compound real estate gains (and losses) through the use of real estate derivatives. The Glass-Steagall Act was depression-era legislation put in place by well-meaning Senators Glass and Steagall in the mid 1930s after the crash of 1929. It created a firewall between investment banks and consumer banks and other financial intermediaries. It was abolished in 1999 under Republican sponsored Graham-Leach-Blyly Act that allows investment banks practically unlimited reign in buying other financial intermediaries like brokers, mortgage companies, and insurance companies (just like the 1920s, and with the same inevitable result). As in the 1920s, this made conflicts of interest in the financial services industry, insurance, and investment banking grow exponentially, leading inevitably to the Crash of 1929.

Why Was Glass-Stegall Passed?

In this current (and past) environment of Republican efforts to deregulate and *privatize* all business, we would do well to remember that there has always been a reason for government regulation of business, to protect consumers from the often rapacious and unbridled greed of corporations and bankers. From the time of the robber barons of the Gilded Age, regulation may have curtailed some of the wealth of the wealthy, but regulation has often been the only thing between the middle class and abject poverty created by the financial chicanery of bankers and crony capitalists.

As politicians always do after such financial disasters like the stock market Crash of 1929, the Senate and U.S. Congress passed the Glass-Stegall Act (similar to the Frank-Dodd or Sarbanes-Oxley Act in recent times). This act squarely took aim at crony capitalism and the rampant conflicts of interest that existed in the roaring 1920s between consumer banks, investment banks, rating agencies, insurance companies, mortgage companies, and brokerage houses. In the 1920s, any of these entities could own the other, leading predictably, to ridiculous and blatant conflicts of interest, crony capitalism, financial fraud, and finally the mother of all crashes, the Crash of 1929 when the stock market lost 90% of its value in less than 18 months.

In the early 1930s, the Securities Acts of 1933 and 1934 were enacted requiring publicly traded companies to issue a prospectus to potential investors and file quarterly and annual financial statements with The Securities and Exchange Commission (SEC), among other things. The SEC was created during the same time. In this somber environment of 30% unemployment and a very disillusioned population, the Glass-Stegall Act was born. This Act prohibited banks from owning brokerage firms and other financial intermediaries like mortgage and insurance companies.

It is hard to realize now just how delicate the state of American capitalism was at this point. The communist party was thriving and the people were fed up with the FED and the shenanigans of the investing elite and moneyed classes. The country was on the verge of anarchy. This was the era of the resurgence of Das Kapital, Carl Marx's treatise on historical dialectic, and the rise of the Communist Party in the United States.Marx's predictions of capitalist economies destroying themselves from within were proving prescient. Legislation that clamped down on the financial services sector, and a leader championing the working class was an absolute necessity to save capitalism from itself. And then who should come along but Franklin Delano Roosevelt (FDR) to save capitalism from itself—and none too soon. Nearly every piece of meaningful social welfare legislation in American history was passed under his first three terms, much to the chagrin of Republicans to this very day. They are still busily trying to gut the last vestiges of the New Deal; to have it replaced or repealed.

Passage of Glass-Stegall in FDR's first term reigned in the Wild, Wild, West atmosphere in the financial services sector and the rampant crony capitalism existing in banking and financial services sector prior to his election in 1933. Many conservatives were, and are to this day, infuriated at its passage. In their myopic arrogance, the wealthy, without realizing that these laws and this man saved capitalism from itself, deemed government intervention an affront to capitalism! What irony!

Bankers worked feverishly, and relentlessly since the passage of Glass-Steagall to have it dismantled. Unfortunately for them, and fortunately for the middle class, the Republicans lost control of government for nearly 50 years after the Crash of 1929, which they were blamed for, and rightfully so in my opinion. In the late 1990s, Republicans had an opportunity at last to scrap Glass Stegall. With a Republican House and Senate, the 106th U.S. Congress, under a Democratic President (President Clinton), and with a massive lobbying effort by the banking sector costing hundreds of millions of dollars over 4 years, they succeeded in overturning the Glass-Stegall Act, and replacing it with the Graham-Leach-Blyly Act (GLBA). This was a puff piece of financial legislation designed by banking lobbyists, giving banks and the financial services sector free reign to use financial leverage not seen since before the Crash of 1929.

The GLBA also allowed for the re-emergence of financial supermarkets whereby consumer banks could now own brokerage firms (Merrill Lynch bought by BankAmerica for example), and investment banks could own or have a controlling interest in, mortgage companies, insurance companies and rating agencies. The result was totally predictable. During the next 8 years, the American people, in particular much of the middle class, suffered the Tech Wreck of 2000 (stock market collapse), and the housing collapse of 2007–2008, wiping out over $10 trillion in savings. Much of the middle class has still not recovered, and sadly, with the continued roll-back of protective legislation designed solely for the further enrichment of the very rich, may never recover.

Trillions were made in the housing bubble by banks and other financial intermediaries, and like every bubble before, and to come, all were happy as long as the bubble kept getting bigger. The U.S. government loves bubbles because of the ability to collect more in taxes. The bankers and real estate elites and players love bubbles because it makes them wealthy beyond their wildest dreams. And the FED loves a bubble because its stockholders and major constituents, i.e., its member banks and billionaires, make trillions lending money to the middle class. (Where did you think the rich got its money? It's nearly always been from the middle class.)

Politicians of every stripe love a bubble because it makes them look great, and of course, they are only too willing and able to take credit for something they seldom have anything to do with, but keep getting re-elected, nonetheless. And many middle class voters unwittingly keep voting against their best economic self-interest by re-electing these very politicians (Republicans) decade after decade, who once in office, back legislation favorable to big business and the wealthy, but seldom working men and women. My Uncle Joe is one of them. He is getting by and feels that someday, somehow, if he works hard and long enough, his ship may come in, just like all those very wealthy Republicans he wants to be like and is told daily via news outlets, like Faux News, can be.

Bubbles and the Pigou Effect (Wealth Effect)

The Pigou Effect, a term coined by Arthur Pigou in 1948 and later adopted by central bankers who called it the *Wealth Effect* , is a moniker created by central bankers describing a process of how the FED, very deliberately, can, and does, decade after decade, create asset bubbles. This bubble creation machine is a miracle, albeit arguably a fraudulent one. Most interestingly, this seemingly innocuous moniker, *the Wealth Effect, regained popular usage by* none other than the vaunted, even legendary head of the FED for over 20 years, Alan Greenspan.

So, why would the FED deliberately create asset bubbles, which when they collapse, have such a destructive impact on the economy, and in particular the middle class and the most vulnerable of all among us, the poor and the aging? What possible rationale could exist for creating such economic carnage, year-after-year, decade-after-decade?

Greenspan and all central bankers know that when asset prices rise for example, (housing which is the preferred collateral of bankers) people would feel, and do feel wealthier. This is not rocket science, but it is diabolically clever in some respects. As people feel wealthier, they consume more. They go out and buy that second home (more loans!), that new car (more loans!), and more collectibles of every stripe (art, cars, match boxes, and old signs), you name it! As asset prices continue to rise, a consumption boom is created through all this newly created debt and GDP expands. Taxes increase to the Treasury, and everyone is happy!

Until the bottom falls out of the bubble! After every collapse, citizens who leveraged up during the boom or used their homes like an ATM machine to maintain a lifestyle that they could not afford, found their balance sheets *upside down*. It rarely dawns on anyone, especially the middle class, that *the expansion* was nothing more than a debt-fueled illusion of prosperity, begun and perpetuated by their own central bank—the FED!

None of the boom bust cycles our economy has grown accustomed to since the founding of the FED could have happened without massive injections of money and credit into the economy by the FED, excess money and credit which in turn encourages malinvestment and speculation. The housing bubble could not have happened without record low interest rates. It could not have happened if the FED had adhered to and enforced its own underwriting guidelines in place for nearly a century. It could not have happened without securitization, the elimination of Glass Steagall, the rise of derivatives, and a complicit and mostly corrupt banking sector willing to loan to anyone with a heartbeat (Hanke, 2017).

What is the economic or social justification for creating one asset bubble after the other? The answer is that in a consumption-based economy where consumer spending is responsible for over 70% of economic activity (GDP) because we don't manufacture much for export anymore (i.e., manufacturing is less than 15% of GDP), it is imperative to keep the investing class consuming, and using services. Making the public feel wealthier encourages the public to consume, in turn driving the economy forward. And surprise, surprise, all that additional consumption always requires additional bank loans in a banking system such as ours. Not coincidentally, that extra lending generates more loans and revenues for the banking sector. In the case of the housing bubble, it resulted in trillions of additional sales and profits.

From a social and public policy standpoint, such bubbles

are a disaster. They create mal-investment, encourage rampant speculation, and make housing for the middle and lower classes much more expensive. They inexorably erode the savings of the middle class and destroy social mobility, two critical components of any democracy.

Not coincidentally, our politicians since President Ronald Reagan (1981—1989) and neo-liberalism's comeback, championed consumption and debt at the expense of manufacturing, savings, and exports, three critical common denominators in the successful democracies of our major competitors. The American people were falsely led to believe that piling on debt and creating asset bubbles to drive the economy was sound public policy! Many in the Republican Party still believe it, espousing the virtues of trickle-down economics at every opportunity. The presidents new *economic advisor* is one such example. But, FED-created asset bubbles are only great for the bankers and Wall Street and generally very bad for middle class Americans like my Uncle Joe, who feels his middle class lifestyle slipping away, but is not sure why.

Why Savings and Investment Over Debt and Consumption?

As any smart businessman and nation understands, an economy or business grows by owners foregoing current consumption and reinvesting profits and savings into more productive capacity (retained earnings in accounting terminology) such as business or infrastructure. It cannot happen by using more debt to create asset bubbles masquerading as growth. Any growth realized through this manner (i.e., more debt) is an illusion, a debt-fueled illusion perpetuated by those who profit from such myopic thinking like the banks and financial intermediaries heavily invested in perpetuating the fraud called fractional reserve banking.

As our major competitors Germany, China, and India all know, one grows an economy by improving and increasing spending on infrastructure and by investing in people. The United States has done neither in 40 years; a time span in which, not coincidentally, wages and living standards for the vast majority of Americans have relentlessly imploded. Coincidence? No, fellow citizens. Misguided and anachronistic economic policies, banking, and trade legislation have had dire economic and social consequences for our nation, as we are learning, very probably too late to reverse course towards a saving, investment, and manufacturing based economy.

We were told under Reagan, Bush 1 & 2, and now Trump and promoted by our central bank the FED, that massive tax cuts, primarily for the wealthy, and taking on more debt, and consuming more, would lead us all to the economic promised land. Instead our politicians, knowing they would be long gone by the time the effects of their blatantly biased legislation for the rich came to fruition, sold us and the nation down the proverbial river. For if these tax policies promulgated by Reagan and the Republicans, and these awful trade deals like NAFTA passed under Clinton and a Republican held Senate and House, were such a boon to our economy, why aren't we all rejoicing in an economic Valhalla? Instead, as noted by 2016 Democratic Party Presidential candidate Bernie Sanders and many concerned citizens from billionaires Bill Gates to Warren Buffet, the tax code has become progressively more regressive and we, as a nation, have gone from the largest creditor nation on earth, to the largest debtor nation on earth in 40 short years, with the gap between rich and poor wider than it has ever been and getting even wider. As Bonner and Wiggin (2006) so eruditely pointed out in *Empire of Debt*, in reality, Reagan's messages of something for nothing, and trickle-down economics was a fraud.

Of course as we all know now, an economy and individuals, must eventually pay the piper. There is no free lunch unless you are the Federal Reserve. These new, and totally untested, ideas of supply side and trickle-down economics infected the country with many now (1980s) believing they could borrow more and spend more and get rich. The idea of a corporate pension went out the window, along with the idea that corporations had any responsibility to their stakeholders, other than maximizing shareholder value for the owners of the firm, shareholders.

Employees were hung out to dry and the era of the leveraged buyout (LBO) championed by Michael Milken, allowed nefarious characters like him to use a company's own assets to borrow against, using these funds in turn to then buy back the company's outstanding stock to take the company private. Once taken private, parts of the company were sold off to the highest bidder. Employees of course lost their jobs and pensions, but those involved in the LBO got very, very rich.

This was the beginning of the end (1980s) for the middle class in the United States, aided and abetted by ridiculous, and often cruel and very esoteric and completely untested economic and academic arguments like trickle-down and supply side economics. As Bonner and Wiggin (2006) concluded in retrospect it was all a cruel hoax, perpetuated by the usual suspects, investing elites and bankers, to strip the American middle class of their pensions and savings.

Michael Milken, the creator and of the leveraged buyout

king (LBO) in the 1980s, received a life sentence in jail for his part in the financial destruction of our economy, but surprise! He was recently pardoned (2019) by President Trump.

This economy created by self-serving bankers and politicians cannot end well for working men and women of America. The situation, as shown in a recent paper by Storm (2017) discussed earlier, is only getting worse. Less than half of the children born after 1980 will enjoy a higher standard of living than their parents.

Who's Next in Line for FED Largesse?

Those second in line for FED largesse are the investing elite, wealthy, and those among us capable of getting a loan so they can take advantage of the bubble du jour. Very simple. Remember, money is only created when a debt (bank loan) is created.

Money = Debt and Debt = Money

Those who can get the loans expand the money supply and through their economic activity, it is theorized, increase consumption, GDP, and employment. This was the entire, specious economic argument behind trickle-down economics (aka Supply Side, aka *VooDoo* economics), which most noted economists will agree, was a total fraud. It was a hoax perpetrated by the few, at the expense of the many, designed and pushed by those at the very top of the income scale, just like the recent tax cut we saw in 2017 (Trump administration). Taxes under Reagan and Bush were cut relentlessly on the wealthy. The spurious argument was that this would provide them with more disposable income with which to consume, in turn propelling the economy on an upward trajectory.

In an economy that is 70% based on consumption, encouraging consumption must lead to greater economic activity, higher GDP, and therefore greater employment. The problem was that the argument that the wealthy would *invest* any portion of that new-found income into productive pursuits and economic infrastructure, predictably, fell flat on its face. The rich consumed, all right, much of it on imports and luxury goods and stock buy backs, but very little of it in real productive economic infrastructure. Most of it went into assets that produce *unearned income*, assets like real estate, bonds, and stocks, with the balance going to spending on luxury imports. Our economy and infrastructure have as a consequence of these policies languished for the last 40 years, with both now in desperate need of repair.

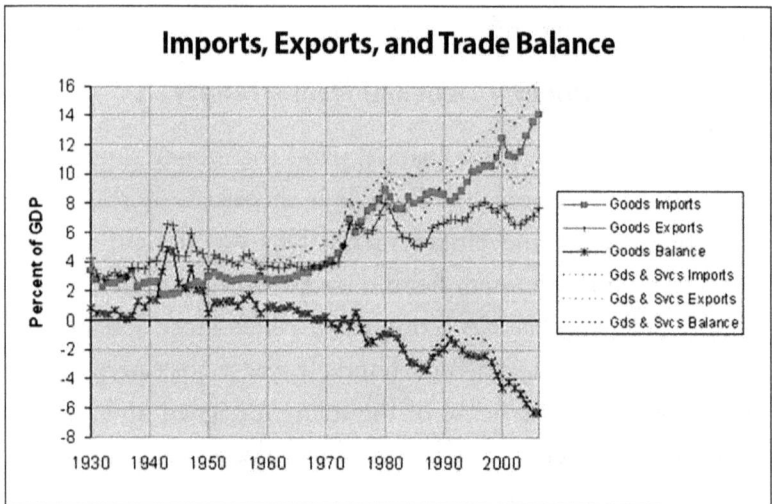

Figure 9: Imports, Exports, and Trade Balance

Note: Reprinted with permission from the Bureau of Economic Analysis: Historical Statistics of the United States. https://www.bea.gov.

As our national debt has expanded so has our trade deficit. Please note the drastic fall in exports (blue line) and the dramatic increase in imports (red line) since 1980 (the Reagan administration and the Tax Reform Act of 1986). As can be clearly seen between 1970 and 1980, our trade balance began to diverge going negative in 1975 (blue line). Imports (red line) rose from 8% of GDP in 1980 to over 14% of GDP in 2000, while our exports (green line) remained flat for the same period. In summary then, right after Reagan's election and the rise of neoliberalist trade policies aka, Reaganomics, imports rose dramatically, and our trade balance began dropping precipitously. This is the OPPOSITE of what Reaganomics, aka trickle-down economics predicted.

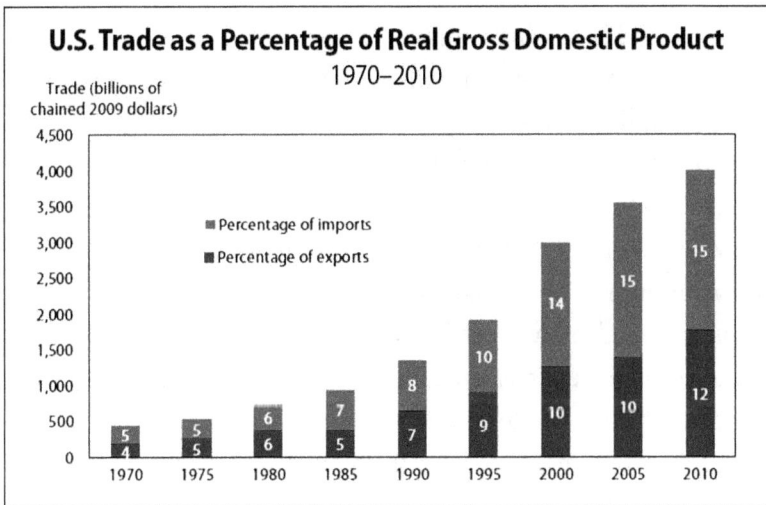

U.S. Trade as a Percentage of Real Gross Domestic Product 1970–2010

Figure 10: Percentage of Imports and Exports in Trillions

Note: Reprinted with permission from the Bureau of Economic Research, Washington, DC. https://www.bea.gov 2019.

In Figure 10, note that as taxes have been cut relentlessly on the wealthy the OPPOSITE of what we were told by Reagan and his acolytes, and subsequent Republican administrations would happen has occurred. Money *trickling down* would put more purchasing power in the hands of the middle class while corporations and the wealthy would invest in productive assets to increase U.S. manufacturing and exports. As can be seen, much of this newfound money from massive tax breaks was used to buy imports and on stock buybacks, providing no net growth in GDP per capita for most Americans, a surge in imports, and very minor gains in exports.

Economists call increased spending based on increases in income the *propensity to consume.* As income rises, so does the propensity to consume. That is, a larger portion of one's disposable income is devoted to discretionary and recreational spending. This helps explain why the FED and the government, and politicians are all too eager to create a bubble. It is an insidious economic model, the belief, perpetuated by plutocrats, and investing elites, and a mostly corrupt financial services and banking sector, that an economy can borrow its way to prosperity, that more debt equals more growth, and creating more debt equals real wealth. It is a chimera, a thing that is hoped or wished for, but in fact is illusory or impossible to achieve. It is a ridiculous argument and one shown through both anecdotal and empirical evidence to be totally false. The U.S. government, in the very short run does collect more real estate and capital gains taxes through such bubbles, but predictably, when the bottom falls out, as it did in 2000 and 2007, the government goes for decades with lower tax revenues.

Qui Bono? To whom is it a benefit?

Answer: The bankers and ancillary services and the very wealthy. Who suffers? The middle class.

Not coincidentally, in the 40 short years since Reagan and neoliberalism (aka *Reaganomics*), the middle class has declined, and our economy has been hollowed out through poor trade deals. We have gone from the largest creditor nation on earth, to the largest debtor nation on earth. Thanks to the reserve status of the dollar and the elimination of the gold standard under Nixon in 1971, we, as a nation, have spent wildly beyond our means with our national debt now approaching $30 trillion dollars. Our debt to GDP ratio is now well over 100% (i.e., debt is more 100% of GDP), a point at which most countries face currency collapses. (cite *collapse* of Chile, Mexico, Argentina, Thailand, Peru, Russia, Zimbabwe, etc.)

The Invisible Hand

The invisible hand, as posited by Adam Smith (1776) in his book *The Wealth of Nations*, basically sought to demonstrate that everyone working in his or her own self-interests allocates the resources of society most efficiently. The *free market*, in other words, in conjunction with the Law of Supply and Demand, is sure to set the correct price.

This quaint, anachronistic economic model, developed nearly 250 years ago is grossly antiquated in that free markets no longer exist in America and have not existed here for decades. We have industries, and an economy dominated by a few very large firms that control over 70% of the market in their respective industries, i.e., oligopoly.

The *invisible hand*, theorized by Adam Smith, has been a

mainstay of dogmatic *conservative* economic doctrine since Reagan. Smith theorized that through the collective purchasing and selling of the population, goods and services would be most efficiently allocated in a free market economy. That is, every individual operating in their own self-interest, making personal buying and selling decisions, allocates goods and services most efficiently, at the lowest prices in the economy. This free market concept has become a mantra for the conservatives. I too believe in free markets that actually exist. As noted earlier, they don't exist in America anymore.

Unfortunately, through the influence of lobbyists, government subsidies, special interests, and the bankers, oligopoly now thrives and small businesses, along with the middle class, die. Or, at least they get sick. The *free market mantra* has been touted far and wide by conservatives and in every business school in the nation as a panacea for everything from higher productivity to longer life! It is of course a lie, one of the greatest lies of all.

Is America Great Again?

If these touted supply side economic policies were correct, then why are we, as a nation, not in economic promised land? With a chicken in every pot? With the best educated children, the healthiest population, and more importantly, the happiest population on earth? As you can see from the indexes below the United States is not even in the Top 10 for happiness and well-being, and not even in the Top 10 of healthiest nations. Because being #1 in anything other than hubris and military spending is pure American fantasy. As the late great George

Carlin (2010) said, "They call it the American Dream because you have to be asleep to believe it" (2013 PBS Newshour).

Today, more Americans than ever are on food stamps and some form of government assistance. We have more people in prison (over 2.2 million in 2017) than any other industrialized nation on earth. According to the World Economic Forum (2019), the United States ranks only 13th in the world's happiest countries, with those countries mostly considered to be *socialist*, that word that Republicans use to vilify any economic model that threatens the status quo, nearly always in the top 10. *Interestingly, these countries are also usually run by women.* According to the World Economic Forum (2018), the United States doesn't even make the top 10 of the world's healthiest countries. Singapore, Italy, Australia, Switzerland, Japan, Israel, Spain, Netherlands, Sweden, and Germany were in the top 10. According to the World Health Organization (WHO) the United States falls between Slovenia and Costa Rica (37th place) in overall health care outcomes (World Health Organization [WHO], 2018).

WHY are we constantly bombarded by political advertising that relentlessly pushes the message that we have the best health care industry in the world? Don't these prescription and medical care costs rising often at double digits annually kill the middle class financially? Of course they do, and are. And, of course, we know why prices rise relentlessly putting more and more pressure on the middle class. Because we are the only G-8 country with a for profit health care system. Prescriptions and medical care are a huge part of our economy (about 25%) and VERY profitable for big pharma and the medical community. How profitable? In 2018, according to Sherman (2018), combined health care costs in the United States were $3.65 trillion dollars, a massive amount of money (about a quarter of U.S. GDP). We spend roughly twice as much as the G-8 on health care and have health care outcomes that rank in overall world ranking by the WHO in 37th place out of 182 countries. Of course, these rising health care and prescription prices are killing the middle class.

We are also reminded continuously how happy we are as a nation but rank behind Denmark, Sweden, Iceland, Norway, Finland, Canada, Netherlands, New Zealand, Australia, Sweden, Israel, and Austria on the World's Happiest Country Index (World Economic Forum, 2012).

According to The World Economic Forum (2018), the United States is not even in the Top 10 of industrialized countries for overall happiness, lagging behind Denmark, Switzerland, Iceland, Norway, Finland, Canada, Netherlands, New Zealand, Australia, Sweden, Israel, and Austria on health care outcomes.

This dog-eared idea (the invisible hand) became the backbone of modern trickle down Reaganomics setting the foundation along with the Reagan tax cuts and the Tax Reform Act of 1986 for financial disaster. It led us ultimately to a nearly $30 trillion dollar national debt and the greatest wealth divide in our nation's history. The price of health care, education, and childcare has exploded disproportionately rising oftentimes at 10% a year, while wages have remained flat, putting a few more nails in the middle class coffin. Education costs for example, have been estimated to be growing 8 times faster than wages (Amadeo, 2019; Maldonado, 2018).

As will be discussed shortly, this major recent tax reduction

(2017 Tax cut) for everyone, but especially for the uber rich and corporations, resulted in effectively no one paying for extant government programs resulting in the U.S. Congress having to borrow more money and the national debt increasing to its highest level in American history to 186% of where it was at the beginning of the Reagan administration in 1981 (186.7% below). As a percentage of increase in debt from the beginning of a President's administration until the end, it is still the highest, including the Obama administration (which was a Republican Congress for 6 years) and the Trump administration (see Figure 11).

President (years in office)	% Total Term Increase of Debt
Eisenhower (8)	10.5
Kennedy (3)	6.8
Johnson (4)	13.6
Nixon (6)	31.8
Ford (3)	35.4
Carter (4)	46.3
Reagan (8)	186.7
H Bush (4)	56.2
Clinton (8)	39.6
W Bush (8)	76.7
Obama (8)	93.4

Figure 11: Percent Increase of the National Debt Under Democratic and Republican Administrations.

*Note: Reprinted with permission from Miles Hamby, PhD, 2019, Arlington, VA, 2019.

Where are the economic miracles and growth promised under Reagan, Bush 1 & 2 (George H. and George W.) and Trump? Where has all that promised prosperity gone to?

I doubt that Adam Smith ever envisioned an era when labor and capital could move virtually (pun intended) unimpeded across borders and trillions of capital could move from one corner of the globe to another in a millisecond. I suspect his thinking would have been very different if confronted with today's economic, technological, and social realities. Clearly, we as a nation, need to look at competing economic models that actually work for their citizens, such as those in Northern Europe, Germany, Canada, Belgium, and France. These countries have societies that actually work for all citizens, unlike the United States, with strong social safety nets, lower illiteracy, lower corruption, retraining for displaced workers, free health care and education, childcare, and not coincidentally, labor forces that are more productive with active union membership. As importantly, our successful trading partners have economies built on manufacturing, not mountains of debt. Their banks and corporations generally do not run their economies, their people do, because they have an active and informed citizenry.

Interestingly, when one takes the time to actually investigate who has the healthiest, happiest, and most productive populations and economies on earth are, these countries mentioned above are nearly always in the Top 10 of the indexes for health, education, and quality of life, according to the WHO (2018), the World Bank, the International Monetary Fund (IMF), and Transparency International. That's right, Germany and France with a 35-hour work week and where every working citizen gets at least 1 month of paid vacation yearly and cradle to grave security, are more productive than Americans with few of those benefits.

Gasp! I can hear the collective groan from every conservative, xenophobic, blue blood, and many blue collar workers in America. Sorry to burst your bubble, but America is not the greatest nation on earth. At least not on any important economic, health, literacy, or social well-being metric. Perhaps in hubris, military spending, student debt, and denial, we rank near the top of all industrialized nations, but we are far, far down the list on those that I find important, such as health, education, happiness, and overall quality of life.

Shared Prosperity—Is it Really?

Real wages in the United States have not risen in 40 years (1980–2020) in inflation adjusted terms, while the cost of everything else from milk to education and health care has risen inexorably (some items like health care and education almost exponentially!) The most vulnerable among us, the young, the poor, and pensioners are the first victims of such a system because they usually have neither the experience (understanding) nor capital to protect themselves against the ravages of inflation created by reckless money and credit creation, or the means to buy inflation hedges like real estate, precious metals, or stocks, to protect their purchasing power. As the price level inexorably rises under such a system, their savings are wiped out and many end their lives in penury. This is unforgivable and an abomination in any nation, but particularly in one of the wealthiest nations on earth.

As noted by Servaas (2017), the American dream of inter-generational progress has now become a chimera, a fairy tale in America, with those born after 1980 halving half the chance their parents did in realizing the dream of a middle class life. What we have now in America, sadly, is a caste system where those privileged children of the investing class and top 20% are doing just fine, thank you very much, because their parents have the money to send them to the *right* school where they can graduate with an *Ivy league* education, which will automatically open the doors of opportunity for them. We now truly have a dual economy as noted by Tmien (2017).

As we saw earlier, the FED founded in 1913, and under very suspicious circumstances, rather than *promoting price stability* has done just the opposite for over a100 years. Policies of easy credit and low interest rates led to the Crash of 1929 and most financial panics and economic disasters since. Prior to the demise of the Second Bank of the United States under Andrew Jackson in 1835, and the founding of our third central bank in 1913 (the FED), the country experienced nearly uninterrupted, zero inflation for 78 years! Can you imagine? Really? No inflation? The country did extraordinarily well, economically speaking, with no central bank. Coincidence? I think not. Please note in the figures below how worker productivity increased steadily from 1979–2013, yet wages in inflation adjusted terms were down to basically flat for middle and low wage earners.

Middle-class wages are stagnant—Middle-wage workers' hourly wage is up 6% since 1979, low-wage workers' wages are down 5%, while those with very high wages saw a 41% increase

Cumulative change in real hourly wages of all workers, by wage percentile,* 1979–2013

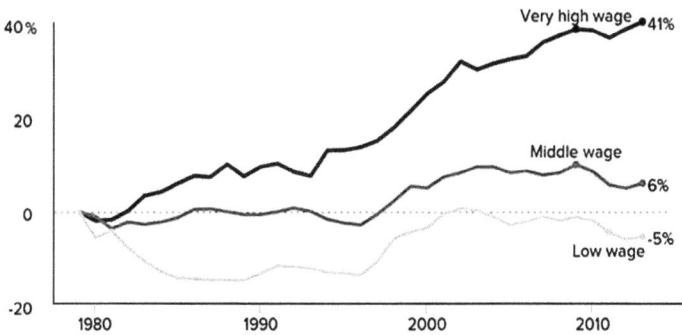

* Low wage is 10th percentile, middle wage is 50th percentile, very high wage is 95th percentile.

Source: EPI analysis of Current Population Survey Outgoing Rotation Group microdata

Reproduced from Figure F in *Why America's Workers Need Faster Wage Growth—And What We Can Do About It*

Figure 12: Cumulative Change in Real Hourly Wages of All Workers, by Wages and Percentile 1979–2013

Note: Reprinted with permission from Economic Policy Institute, Washington, DC, 2019.

Note: Figure F: Cumulative change in real hourly wages of all workers, by wage percentile,*1979–2013, in Elise Gould in, *Why America's Workers Need Faster Wage Growth-and What We Can Do About It*, Economic Policy Institute, 2014. Washington, DC.

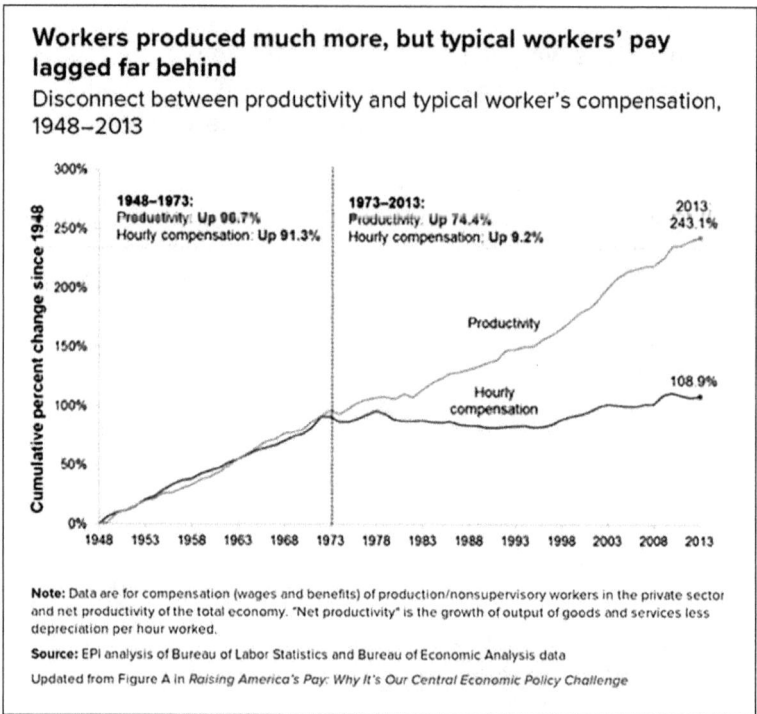

Figure 13: Disconnect Between Productivity and Typical Worker's Compensation

Note: Reprinted with permission from the Economic Policy Institute, Washington, DC, 2019.

*Figure A, "Disconnect Between productivity and typical workers compensation, 194802013," in Josh Bevins, Elise Gould, Lawrence Misheland Heidi Shierholtz, *Raising America's Pay: Why It's Our Central Economic Challenge,* Economic Policy Institute, 2014. Economic Policy Institute, Washington, DC, 2019.*

As is clear from Figure 13, despite rising productivity, real incomes for the majority have been declining steadily since the 1970s, even as productivity increased.

Wealth is basically excess production not needed for immediate consumption. A healthy and prosperous economy turns raw materials into value added products which American labor and industry used to do very efficiently, and profitably. Despite labors rising productivity (more output per hour) their share of national wealth has remained stagnant or gone lower decade after decade, as can be seen from these charts. Please note Figures 12–14. The majority of gains, as noted repeatedly in this book, have gone to the top 5% of the population.

As can be seen from Figure 14, the minimum wage should be $18. Where has the difference between the increased productivity and wages gone? Into the pockets of the wealthiest among us, shareholders of the Fortune 500, and their overpaid executives.

The minimum wage would be over $18 had it risen along with productivity

Real value of the federal minimum wage compared with its value had it grown at the rate of productivity and average hourly wages, 1968–2014

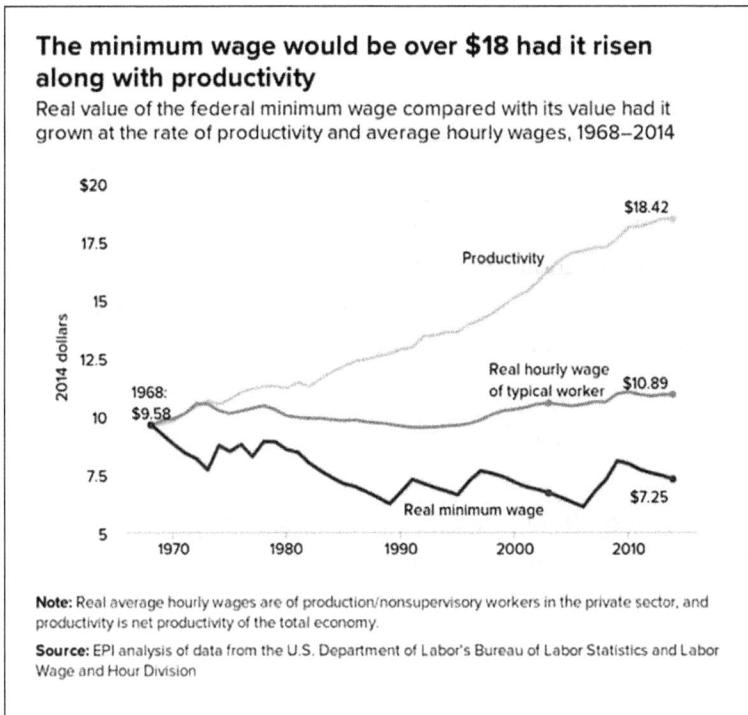

Figure 14. The Minimum Wage Would Be Over $18
Had It Risen Along with Productivity.

Note: Reprinted with permission from the Economic Policy Institute, Washington, DC, 2019.

Once again, the irony of the FED claiming to be inflation fighters is incredibly disingenuous. The FED deliberately creates asset bubbles through low interest rates and easy money policies (where we are now is a typical-stock market bubble in late 2019), discouraging savings, and encouraging speculation and mal-investment (like the housing bubble). More ironically, I find it amusing that the free marketers on the right, fail to grasp that at the very heart of our alleged free market economic system we have a monopoly called the Federal Reserve controlling the nation's money supply and interest rates.

Is this just ignorance, avarice, or pure hypocrisy on conservative's part? Probably, it is a combination of all of these. One thing is for certain—either intuitively, or intellectually, the advocates and defenders of the FED understand that the FED was created by the rich and for the rich, and is comprised of the rich and the super-rich (top 1%) who will defend it to their deaths, raving about the virtues of *free markets*. Indeed, believers in supply side and trickle-down economics have, and will continue to take us to war (among other questionable places) to preserve the *reserve currency* status of the dollar and a fraudulent financial services and banking sector. But that does not surprise those who know and understand financial history. There is much to lose should this current system crumble like all others before it, money, wealth, and power.

Who Benefits?

The primary beneficiaries of the FED's financial largess are (you guessed it!) the money center banks. As demonstrated, the banks are the FED's primary constituents, not you or I, and not the *middle class*. Asset bubbles like the one we recently witnessed between 2002 and 2007 are very deliberately created and choreographed as described earlier. The FED's member banks made trillions of dollars and the FED created a *wealth affect* by providing the investing class with a housing bubble. Those with access to credit did very well in this bubble. Those that had no credit or limited access to credit, such as wage earners and pensioners, did not do so well and saw their buying power drop and the cost of their housing double or triple and their standard of living collapse. We now have a nation truly divided between the haves and the have-nots. The irony is that it is the have-nots (essentially, the middle class) who continue to elect the billionaires to protect their working class interests???

This is truly astonishing to one who expects people to vote in their economic self-interest (the wealthy mostly do). Both Reagan and Trump got elected by making promises to the losers of globalization, free trade and the technology revolution (middle and lower classes), while simultaneously providing huge tax cuts for the wealthy and corporations at the expense of the middle class, the people promised relief from their tortuous economic slide.

These tax cuts will of course, bankrupt our country for good and leave the have nots even further behind. A cynic might argue that it is all part of the plan the rich have in store for us. Destroy the economy, create a panic, and pick up the assets (what's left over) for pennies on the dollar, and get legislation passed ostensibly to ever prevent it (the financial calamity) from ever happening again, while consolidating their choke hold on our economy, and finish gutting any vestiges of the New Deal and any other social welfare legislation. It is a very old trick. Undoubtedly, we will see it again in the near future.

As noted in the *New Normal: Demand, Secular Stagnation and the Vanishing Middle Class* by Servaas (2017), the lack of wage growth has very real and dangerous socio-economic and political consequences. The loss of good jobs and the polarization of the U.S. labor market has put the middle-classes under severe stress. Many other academics noted that the plethora of low wage and alternative work arrangements (a euphemism for sure) resulting from outsourcing, globalization, and union busting since 1980 have resulted predictably, in lower real wages and working conditions for most Americans (Temin 2017; Weil, 2014).

The shift in the U.S. employment structure is one factor behind the major slowdown of average real wages since 1980. The major shift in the American employment structure from high skill manufacturing jobs to service jobs means that around one-fourth of all U.S. workers are in low-paying jobs, earning a poverty wage that is about two-thirds of the median hourly wage (for all occupations) and only half the mean hourly wage. More than 73% of employees in (fast) food preparation and serving earn this poverty-wage (or less), as do 57% of workers in personal care, 54% of workers in cleaning, and 45% of workers in health care support. Poverty-wage jobs are concentrated in just 10 occupational categories. If one chooses to enlarge the definition of *mediocre* jobs (in terms of pay) to include jobs earning up to 200% of the poverty wage, these 10 occupations account for 55% of U.S. workers (in 2010), as reported by Thiess (2012).

It becomes readily apparent, after even cursory research on the subject of wealth inequality, that growth in real wages (or lack thereof) for workers in the stagnant low wage hospitality and service industries have fallen drastically compared to real wages in manufacturing and information technology (IT) for example, in many cases by more than 30% over 60 years in cumulative terms. The primary reason for the increasing wage inequality and the main source of the rise in wage inequality, has been the decline in the relative hourly wages earned in the service vs. information age economy that has drastically altered the U.S. economic landscape in the last 40 years. Fewer hours worked per person ultimately leads to an involuntary reduction of hours worked by an ever increasing percentage of the U.S. labor force (Autor & Dorn, 2013).

The gradual decline of the American middle class since 1980 is a direct result of the fiscal (tax) and monetary policies (interest rate and money supply) put in place by often misguided and disingenuous politicians, lobbyists, and bankers. These economic policies at the heart of Reaganomics are primarily responsible for America's middle class decline (Baumol, Blackman, & Wolff, 1985).

CHAPTER 6.

How Inflation Is Generated By the Banking Sector

Permit me to issue and control the money of the nation and I care not who makes its laws.

—MAYER AMSCHEL ROTHSCHILD, FOUNDER OF THE ROTHSCHILD FAMILY INTERNATIONAL BANKING DYNASTY

Inflation generation is the other big problem with the FED and as pointed out earlier, something central bankers strive for, not fight to avoid. The most pernicious tax of all is inflation, which the FED very deliberately creates, decade-after-decade. Indeed, in a fractional reserve system, inflation is baked into the system. Speculators are rewarded by speculating in the asset bubble du jour, savers, wage earners, the poor, and pensioners are severely penalized because they see the buying power of their dollars go lower and lower, while their savings from investments go down and down in lockstep with declining interest rates. Central banks worldwide, by creating artificially low interest rates, have forced investors seeking a reasonable return on their savings into riskier and risker asset classes like stocks. In finance speak, investors are forced further and further out the risk curve. (from high quality bonds to junk bonds or dividend paying stocks for example).

From a social policy perspective, the deliberate creation and perpetuation of inflation and asset bubbles is anathema to most citizens of this great country of ours, and just exacerbates the already outrageous wealth gap. Many argue like Ron Paul, a Congressman from Texas (retired), that we should end the FED. That the FED tinkering with interest rates and the money supply is always harmful, distorts the free market pricing mechanism for money (interest rates), and always does more social and economic harm than good, leading inevitably to mal-investment, speculation, and financial disasters. Ron Paul and his followers argued we already have a perfect way to set interest rates. It is called the bond market. It is one of the most efficient, deepest, and liquid markets in the world that sets interest rates daily through supply and demand Ron Paul and true free market advocates go on to argue that the money supply and credit can be handled by the Treasury which could grow money and credit at approximately the same rate as growth in the economy, thus obviating the need for a FED. I agree. After all, we went from 1835 to 1913 without a central bank just fine, with virtually zero inflation. Coincidence? I think not. Look at what has happened to inflation since going off the gold standard in 1971.

Please note from Figure 15 (on the following page), the price level went parabolic after Nixon took the United States off the gold standard in 1971. Not coincidentally, gold, the ultimate inflation hedge, has kept pace with rising prices perfectly. From 1665 to 1971, while under the gold standard (dollar was as good as gold) inflation remained flat, but began rising exponentially after the United States went off the gold standard in 1971. Without the restraints posed by the gold standard, government spending accelerated sharply, and has continued unabated to this day (July 2020) with the national debt now approaching $30 trillion dollars.

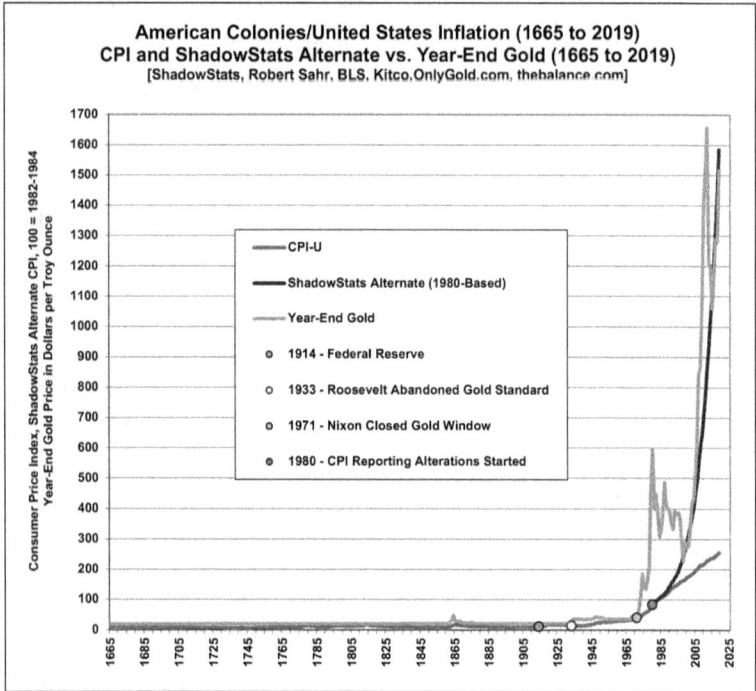

American Colonies/United States Inflation (1665 to 2019)
CPI and ShadowStats Alternate vs. Year-End Gold (1665 to 2019)
[ShadowStats, Robert Sahr, BLS, Kitco,OnlyGold.com, thebalance.com]

Legend:
- CPI-U
- ShadowStats Alternate (1980-Based)
- Year-End Gold
- 1914 - Federal Reserve
- 1933 - Roosevelt Abandoned Gold Standard
- 1971 - Nixon Closed Gold Window
- 1980 - CPI Reporting Alterations Started

Figure 15. U.S. Inflation Since 1665, CPI and Gold Prices.

Note: Reprinted with permission of John Williams of Shadowstats.com: www.shadowstats.com.

Many FED historians and longtime observers like G. Edward Griffin (2010), the author of the definitive history of our current central bank, *The Creature From Jekyll Island*, make a very clear and compelling case for abolishing the FED altogether. He noted numerous times in this book that the FED is an instrument of totalitarianism. As an institution, it is designed to create inflation and create asset bubbles which the *investing class* benefits. Fiat currency created by the FED ultimately leads to more government debt, causing inflation in the process and encouraging malinvestment, ultimately impoverishing much of the population, thus providing an excuse for the government to increase power, inevitably ending in totalitarianism. Simply put, the problem is, and always has been, that asset prices often rise at 10–30% per year per under a fractional reserve banking system, while wages grow at 2–3% a year, if at all.

Others like DeSoto (2006) of the Mises Institute understand the economic danger posed by central banks as well, noting that allowing banks and speculators to accrue enormous profits with relatively little effort ultimately stifles innovation, and kills the entrepreneurial spirit, two essential ingredients for creating and maintaining a healthy, vigorous, and growing economy. Who wants to really work with long-term goals in mind when they can make money more easily by speculating in FED liquidity induced asset bubbles? In other words, the rampant speculation in banking and financial services discourages the traditional entrepreneurial spirit and a job well done, both of which are based on prudent business management and long-term strategic thinking.

Since 2008, we have seen more tinkering than ever by central banks in the form of *quantitative easing*, negative interest rates, and intervention in markets from currencies to commodities, not only in the United States but worldwide. Quantitative easing and record low interest rates have sown the seeds for the next asset bubble here in the United States. Speculation in the stock market is rampant and saving is virtually nonexistent. The economy has been unable to recover from the last asset bubble created by the FED (2007 Housing Collapse), despite injections of massive liquidity, and record low interest rates. Business formation and growth is anemic at best. The FED strayed far afield from its original dual mandates of price stability and full employment, in a seemingly inevitable form of mission creep, trying to correct prior mistakes by compounding them further, throwing more money (debt) at the problem, exacerbating and fueling the next bubble. For example, as I discussed with Uncle Joe, they can and do through proxy investment banks like Goldman, routinely purchase or sell futures, forwards, commodities, mortgages (MBSs), and of course treasuries. Indeed, one could call the FED the world's largest hedge fund. We now have a form of central planning, not by government, but by our own central bank, whose balance sheet ballooned from less than a trillion dollars in 2006 to over $10 trillion today. They have strayed far indeed from their original dual mandates of price stability and full employment.

Uncle Joe asked me somewhat incredulously, where did all the money go?

"Uncle Joe," I said,

It's easy. Remember, they can create and do create, money out of thin air through an electronic book keeping entry. What do they do with much of the money that they create (that we know of?) They often buy *non-performing assets* of their member banks (like mortgage backed securities) for 100 cents on the dollar when they are often worth much less. This re-liquifies their member banks and provides them with fresh reserves allowing their member banks to make new loans, speculate with them, or just leave on loan at the FED itself earning risk free interest. Is this really what we want as a nation? A central bank with more power than our President, Congress, or judiciary? A central bank that controls every aspect of our economy? Free market, and supply and demand be damned?

It's so political!

Our central bank was ostensibly created to provide an arm's length financing mechanism outside of political control of the Executive Branch, or Congress. This was yet another disingenuous argument used by its founders that argued for its creation. The institution by its nature and support of its most ardent adherents, has had a very clear big business, and Republican bias since inception.

Many erroneously blame the Obama (recession chief) administration for our current state of economic disarray. That is like blaming the Hindenburg tragedy on the discovery of hydrogen. He was a convenient target for the right, but he was not the cause of this never ending recession created by a reckless central bank and financial services sector. That dubious distinction (recession chief) belongs to the Federal Reserve.

In an excellent book by DeSoto (2006) *Money, Bank Credit, and Economic Cycles*, he relates that in a fractional reserve banking system every expansion must be followed by a sharp and painful economic contraction. It is mathematically and economically impossible to grow debt exponentially because at some point the amount of interest required to service that debt becomes impossible to raise. Then comes the inevitable crash. This is why capitalism and central banking in particular, requires strict government regulation and oversight.

It is economic contractions and busts after banking created bubbles that lay bare the inadequacies of market economies, proving the necessity for state intervention at all levels of the economy to neutralize the consequences of the recession and to prevent further economic damage. This in turn lays the ground work for market interventions of all kinds (what we have now with the FED propping up, or intervening in nearly all financial markets). These contractions also provide fertile ground for the blossoming of trade protectionism, increasing budget deficits and deficit spending, and increased government regulation of the economy.

The shortcomings of American style capitalism are all too clear to those of us giving it any serious thought. In terms of economic mobility in relation to our major trading partners, the United States is in last place, behind Denmark, Norway, Finland, Canada, Sweden, Germany, and France. I repeat, we are in dead last place for relative economic mobility. This is corroborated by hundreds of empirical studies many of which are noted in these chapters. This is also corroborated by the Gini Index noted earlier and discussed below.

As noted by Chety et al. (2016), recent evidence suggests that the *American dream* of inter-generational progress has begun to fade children's prospects of earning more than their parents, from 95% for children born in 1940 to less than 50% for children born in the early 1980s. America is no longer *great*, as its economic growth falters, but because, as part of the secular stagnation itself, it is becoming a bifurcated, *dual economy*—two countries, each with vastly different resources, expectations, and potentials, as America's middle class vanishes (Temin, 2017). Despite our current presidents wishful thinking, it will take much more than empty rhetoric and mindless cheerleading to make the American economy great again. Restoring crumbling infrastructure, investing in, and supporting new age industries in which we have a competitive advantage, and training our people to fill these newly created jobs of the 21st century will require substantial investments, not more tax cuts for those who do not need them. Add to this free education to all those who need it and secure social safety nets, and you can begin to see the enormity of the task ahead of us. Undoing four decades of tax cutting and the hollowing out of government and our economy by self-serving politicians will not be easy, but all this and more must be done if we are to survive as a democracy.

In economics, the **Gini coefficient** (/ˈdʒiːni/ JEE-nee), sometimes called the **Gini index** or **Gini ratio**, as noted earlier, is a measure of statistical dispersion intended to represent the income or wealth distribution of a nation's residents, and **is the most commonly used measurement of inequality**.

Sadly, social mobility and economic growth have soared for decades in the United States. From 1945–1975, we had one of the wealthiest, most productive economies on earth. Today, we have the highest degree of income inequality on record, and as noted earlier, a dual economy with 20% of the population owning nearly 90% of the country's assets. This puts the United States in an emerging market company along with Argentina, Russia, and Venezuela. Along with declining social mobility and a widening wealth gap has come public antipathy towards our economic and political institutions. Voter apathy is an understatement in the United States.

In line with this discussion, recent studies suggest that the American dream of *intergenerational mobility*, that is, the notion that children will earn more than their parents, has been fading for some time. Chety et al. (2016) performed a rigorous study that demonstrated that since 1940, the proportion of children in the United States earning at least as much as their parents' by age 25 to 35 has been steadily diminishing to only 50% in 1984.

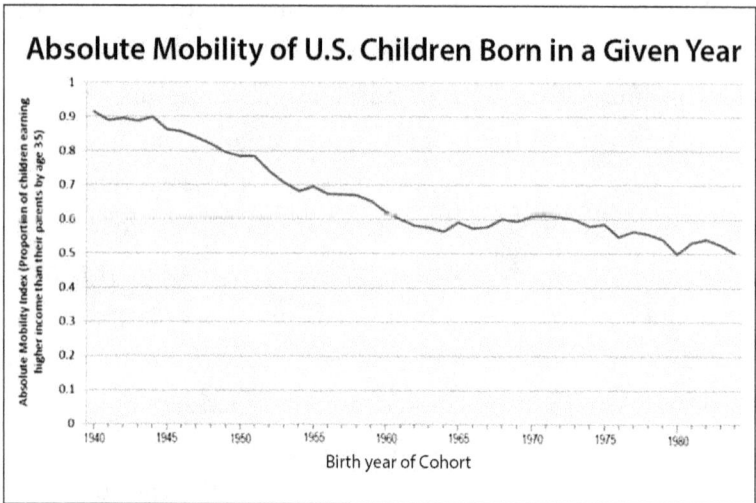

Figure 16. Absolute Mobility of U.S. Children Born in a Given Year

Note: Reprinted and drawn by Miles Hamby, PhD, and reprinted with permission from Miles Hamby, PhD. Alexandria, VA, 2020.

Please note from the chart above that a cohort is a sample of 25 to 35 year-olds born in a given year, whose incomes were obtained at that age (25 to 35) and compared to their respective parents' income in the year they were born. The Absolute Mobility Index is the proportion of children whose income (in constant 2014 dollars adjusted for inflation) equals or exceeds that of their parents' for the year they were born. For example, the Absolute Mobility Index for persons 25 to 35 year-olds born in 1940 is .915 indicating that 91.5% of that cohort had an income equal to or greater than their parent's income in 1940. Notice that the last cohort is 1984 meaning that they were born in 1984 and therefore their income data were from 2009 (25 years-old) and 2015 (31 years-old), the last year of the study with this cohort showing an Absolute Mobility Index of .503, that is, only 50.3% of the 1984 cohort had an income equal to or greater than their parents' income in 1984. *(Data from open source Watson Institute for International & Public Affairs, Brown University, Equality of Opportunity Project databases, Absolute Mobility Estimates and Counterfactuals by Cohort, Parent Income, and State; Retrieved from http://www.equality-of-opportunity.org/data.)*

The Times They Are Changing

In his book *Supercapitalism*, Reich (2007) summarized the United States' rise in power, noting that between 1945 and 1975, the American economy generated the greatest number of middle class jobs in our history, years in which trust in government, business, and democracy itself were at a high water mark. Not coincidentally, this trust in our institutions and democracy has been in rapid decline since 1975.

In short, we had the strongest economy on earth, a growing and prosperous middle class, high union membership (35% of workforce), and much lower income inequality. Unfortunately for us, by the 1980s, things were changing dramatically for the worse. Intensified competition from abroad (globalization), combined with the rise of technology made doing business abroad easier, and oftentimes, cheaper. In addition to this, corporations and notably multinationals, with loyalty to no one except their shareholders began to inexorably take over our political system, through campaign contributions, lobbyists, and an increasingly corrupt political system. Democracy was never designed or equipped to effectively control the amount of money, power, and influence that these capitalist's juggernauts wield in politics and the economy.

American democracy was simply never equipped to deal with

the size and power of industrial capitalism of the enormous scale we have today. The U.S. Constitution germinated in the warmth of an agrarian economy and written by gentlemen land-owners was far removed from the often rapacious, freewheeling, crony capitalism we have in today's America. The founders could not have envisioned (with the exception of a few like Abraham Lincoln) an era where corporations were enshrined in the U.S. Constitution as people (U.S. Supreme Court Citizens United Ruling) and where lobbyist paid by those corporations, often wrote the legislation passed into law on behalf of those corporations. They could not have envisioned corporations with the economic power and profitability of companies like Amazon, Google, or Microsoft.

Along with the rise of the multinational corporation came an increased distrust (and rightly so) of government institutions, corporations, and business in general. The early 2000s were the high water mark for corporate greed and malfeasance, mani-festing itself in the well-publicized financial frauds involving Enron, WorldCom, Parmelat, and many other corporations. These disgraceful scandals merely served to solidify the public's distrust of politicians, business, and *democracy* itself. Capitalism and democracy were both stained and vilified in the public's eye and things have only deteriorated since.

Needless to say, the situation, noted above and throughout this book, has deteriorated further. Since 2007 when Reich wrote his book *Supercapitalism,* the U.S. Supreme Court Rul-ing, Citizens United (January 2010), has since closed the lid on Democracy when the *Supremes* passed this very anti-democratic law (Citizens United) providing corporations the same rights as people and the ability to make unlimited and anonymous campaign contributions to politicians and their political action committees (PACs). This court ruling, in conjunction with the decline in manufacturing and union membership, financialization of the U.S. economy, the gutting of the Glass Stegall Act, the proliferation of derivatives and a *deregulated* and *privatized* economy paved the way for the country we now have. A country where economic inequality is the highest on record and where America lags all major trading partners on every meaningful metric form overall quality of life (World Bank) to health care (World Health Organization (WHO)) to literacy. And of course concomitant with all of the above, we have a rapidly shrinking middle class with severely stunted upward economic and social mobility.

Who Really Benefits from the FED

Now that you know how the FED was created and what fractional reserve banking is and how it works, and why inflation is built into a fractional reserve banking system, let's take a look at who the real beneficiaries are under such a system. Who wins and who loses?

By now this is surely obvious. The winners under such a system are the bankers and other financial intermediaries, the investing class and the top 1%. The losers of course are those without the wherewithal to obtain credit (a loan), those living on a fixed income like wage earners and pensioners, and those without inherited wealth or the necessary capital to build their own wealth or get an education. The wealthy buy influence to perpetuate fiscal legislation that increases their wealth annually and exacerbates the wealth gap between rich and poor with remarkable consistency. (Just like the *tax reform* just passed by Trump and a Republican Congress in 2017). Those with inflation hedges like real estate, stocks, and precious metals thrive under such a system. Those living on wages or a fixed income are financially skewered under such a system, their purchasing power erodes year-after-year, and all the while the U.S. middle class slowly evaporates.

Those who speculate with debt are rewarded because they pay their debts back in cheaper dollars, while those who are savers are penalized as earnings on their savings go lower and lower. Figure 17 (below) summarizes it all pretty well.

Share of adults living in middle-income households is in steady decline, and share in lower- and upper-income households is rising

% of adults in each income tier

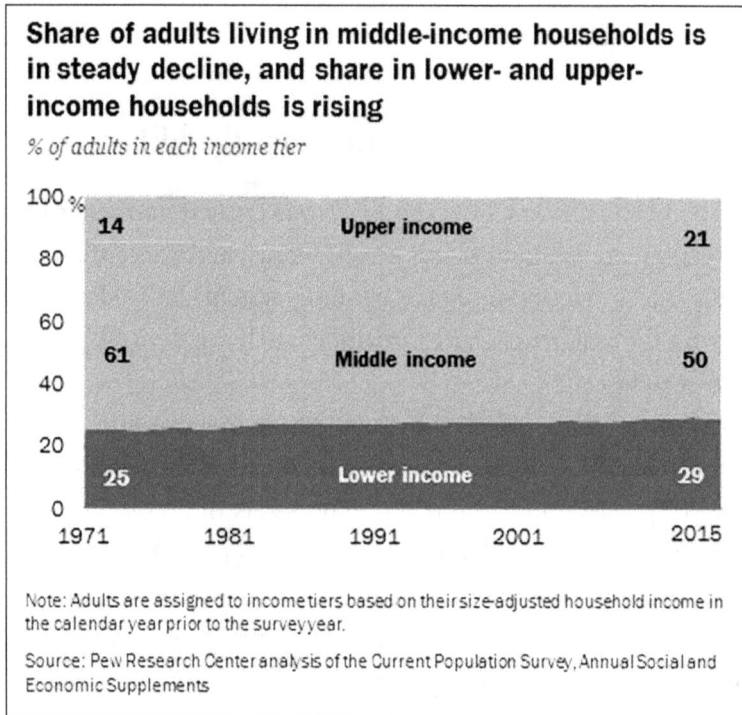

Note: Adults are assigned to income tiers based on their size-adjusted household income in the calendar year prior to the survey year.

Source: Pew Research Center analysis of the Current Population Survey, Annual Social and Economic Supplements

Figure 17. Percentages of Adults Living in Middle Income Households.

Note: Reprinted with permission from the PEW Research Center, Washington, DC, 2019.

One can see graphically what has been happening to wealth in America: a rise in the upper income level of 7%; a fall in middle income of 11%, and a large decrease of those in the middle income of 11%.

As recounted in What's Killing the Middle Class, Richard Eskow (2016) noted a startling and very unsettling statistic. One tenth of one percent of American families, about 160,000 families, have as much wealth as the 90% of Americans, **with 536 people having a combined net worth of $2.6 TRILLION dollars. These are the kind of statistics you'd expect to see in many emerging market economies, but in the United States?**

Corporate profits, although they've taken a hit in recent months, have nevertheless grown at a healthy clip while wages lag far behind as noted above. Those profits have increasingly been used to pay high executive salaries, which has led to an explosion in the gap between CEO salaries and worker pay. (Fortune 500 CEOs earned about 420 times as much on average as the typical worker in 1980. Today, they earn 373 times as much.) Profit-taking in the form of dividends has increasingly taken the place of long-term investment in worker and business growth (Hembree, 2018). **This type of egregious income inequality cannot last for long without severe and disruptive socio-economic consequences.**

So, simply said, **more government debt = more money = more inflation = falling currency = lower standard of living = less social mobility = unhappy citizenry = lower social services and safety nets = Really bad place to live as a wage earner or a pensioner.** And of course, a disappearing middle class.

CHAPTER 7.
Pump and Dump: The Roaring Twenties and the Crash of '29

As Franklin Roosevelt observed over 80 years ago, "our enemies of today are the forces of privilege and greed within our own borders."

—FRANKLIN ROOSEVELT, 1938

As Rothschild so wryly observed over 200 years ago, but what so many Americans fail to grasp today because of the deliberate obfuscation of central bankers and politicians, is that the President, Congress, and the judiciary branches wield very little real power in our *democracy*, especially when the politicians rely on campaign contributions from the wealthy to stay in office.

The real power, as Rothschild understood over 200 years ago, lies with the banks and other monied interests, those able to control a nation's money supply and interest rates. It is those men behind the curtain (think the Wizard in *The Wizard of Oz*), that really control our economy, and thus our economic fate as a nation.

Many of our major competitors including Germany and Canada, understand how dangerous the collusion between bakers and politicians is and thus heavily regulate their financial sectors like we had done from the period after the Crash of '29 (1930s-1999) with Glass-Stegall. Our competitors understand there is a natural and symbiotic relationship between central bankers and the state(s) (Economist, 2017). It is politicians and monarchs who created and allowed the first central banks to thrive in the first place because of their need to spend and borrow beyond their means, thus needing *independent* government financing arms which they could regularly rely on to be their lender of last resort. This is very well documented historically (Chapter 1) and explains in large measure the staying power of our central bank. They are not seriously scrutinized or audited by the U.S. Congress, despite the economic carnage they create. Why? Because central banks are the lenders of last resort to the governments that create them. When the U.S. Congress needs money, they turn to the FED to create it out of thin air. This is euphemistically and ambiguously called open market operations. The U.S. Congress gets its money and what does the FED get? That's right, an IOU called U.S. Treasury bonds. Stacks of them.

Did the FED Create the Crash of '29?

Before establishing the FED in 1913, the 16th Amendment was established (1909) giving the U.S. government the right to raise money through taxes. The money trust, as they became to be known, the Warburgs, Rothschilds, Morgans, and Rockefellers, with their Wall Street agents, championed the idea of course for it would mean more potential for loans to an expanding government, and of course the war machine. As John F. Hylan, the Mayor of New York City in 1922, raged in a famous speech given in August of that year,

The real menace of our Republic is the invisible government, which like an octopus, sprawls its slimy length over our city, state, and nation. *At the head is a small group of banking houses generally known as "international bankers." This little coterie of powerful international bankers virtually run our government for their own selfish ends.* (Hylan, 1922, p. 2)

Clearly, the money trust was firmly in control of the financial sector and much of the government sector at this point (early1900s).

Using their well-worn tricks of creating superfluous liquidity, combined with record low interest rates, they began pumping up the American economy for their greatest, most audacious *pump and dump* since their founding, 16 years earlier.

Charles Lindberg Sr., a distinguished U.S. Congressman and father of the now famous aviator, led the charge against the Federal Reserve Act in 1913 proclaiming on the Senate floor that the act (the Federal Reserve Act, December 23rd, 1913) "established the most gigantic trust on earth" (Lindberg, 1913, p. 1).

As noted by Perloff (2013), in *Trust is The Truth is a Lonely Warrior* noted that when President Wilson signed the Federal Reserve Act into law it created an invisible government of the money powers. Presciently Congressman Lindberg said on the House floor in opposition to the bill.

The new law will create inflation whenever the trust wants inflation. If the trust can get a period of inflation, they figure they can unload the stocks on the people at high prices during the excitement, then bring on a panic, and them buy them back at low prices. The people may not know it immediately, but the day of reckoning is only a few years removed. (Lindberg, 2013: House Floor Speech, December 22nd, 1913)

Brilliant prediction and how very prescient! Sixteen years later, the day of reckoning predicted by Lindberg reared its ugly head in October of 1929, **Black Thursday** as it came to be known, the Crash of '29. This event wiped out millions of small and large investors alike and much of the middle class, bringing on the Great Depression. As James Perloff (2013) said in *The Truth is a Lonely Warrior*, the Crash of '29 was not an accident. It was carefully choreographed by a coterie of international bankers seeking to manage the world economy.

As Perloff (2013) and many other authors and academics have noted, there were numerous strategies used by the international banking cartel and the FED to bring on the Crash of '29. The FED increased the discount rate in that year from 3.5% early in the year to 6% in August. They also began calling margin loans on stock which forced many to liquidate their stock positions. At the time, 90% leverage was allowed. For every dollar invested in stocks, nine dollars could be borrowed. Needless to say, calling in these loans started a panic among stock investors. Huge numbers of these loans were called in simultaneously to bring on the Crash of '29. The rest is history as they say.

There is very little doubt among informed readers of financial history, that this *crash* was carefully planned and choreographed by the FED and the money trust (Warburg's, Rothschild's, Mellon's, and Rockefeller's), destroying most of the middle class in the process (Palms, 2015). It would take 20 years and WWII for them (money trust) and the middle class to recover from this disaster.

The same tactic has been used in various forms by the FED and its minions ever since. More recently, we saw wealth destruction (stock crash of 2000) on a similar scale. The same pump and dump tactics were used by the FED and their minions in the housing bubble, except instead of inflated initial public offerings (IPOs) and stock prices, the FED and its surrogates used the process of securitization, as explained earlier, to pump up housing prices to obviously unsustainable levels, making trillions in the process, until the inevitable crash.

Increased financial activity exacerbates the already enormous wealth inequality in the United States. Peaks in financial activity as represented by new initial public offerings (IPOs) in the stock market and housing starts for example, correspond nearly perfectly to peaks in money supply growth and the housing / stock market bubble tops in 1928 / 29, 1987, 2000, and 2008. Since it is basically the top 10% of the country's population who owns nearly all of its assets, the relentless push by the wealthy towards LESS financial regulation is hardly surprising. Less financial regulation means easier credit, which means more speculation and *easy* money for those at the top of the income and wealth scale.

Financialization of the U.S. Economy and the Danger of Derivatives

As we've seen, the FED was created in 1913 by a group of wealthy industrialists and bankers, ostensibly in response to the Panic of 1907 which they helped deliberately create. As sure as the sun rises and sets fellow citizens, there will be another financial meltdown in the near future, this time caused by something called derivatives. What are derivatives? Warren Buffet (2005) called them weapons of mass financial destruction and incredibly dangerous. Why?

Derivatives *derive* their value from an underlying asset. Like stock options or commodity futures contracts which derive their value from an underlying stock or commodity, these types of derivatives (options and futures) trade on an exchange and are standardized contracts where accounts are marked to market at the end of every day to ensure all account positions in deficit are brought up to the required account balance or sold to raise the funds to pay the counter party to the contract at the end of each trading day. Counter party risk is eliminated by marking trades to market at the end of every trading every day. The exchange is the enforcer, the referee if you will. Trades are transparent, contracts are standardized, and all interest in buying or selling each contract is known and made available to the investing public and speculators daily (open interest figures).

Then there are forward contracts, which are basically customized contracts between two parties (financial intermediaries). These contracts do not trade on an exchange, are not standardized, have little to no enforcement arm or regulatory oversight, and no party to the contract knows with certainty what counter party risk is involved in the trade. It is these contracts that are so dangerous to our financial system and pose the largest risk of a systemic financial meltdown in our financial system. There are now over 1.4 quadrillion (yes, with a Q) of notional value, the value of the underlying assets that the derivatives contracts control. These totally unregulated forward contracts entered into by financial intermediaries (primarily) floating around the world, represent a clear and present danger to our financial system. Why the popularity and parabolic increase in derivatives since the late 1990s, and the insistence by banks and other financial intermediaries that they not be regulated by Dodd-Frank (2010) or any other sensible financial regulations?

Because my friends, this area (derivatives trading) has become one of the most lucrative areas in all of banking. Banks make 5–10% commission per contract, pushing this toxic, unregulated paper out the door. As with mortgages before, who cares about the risk of the parties involved as long as we get our commission (or origination fee)? IF they were to regulate this industry as proposed by Dodd-Frank or as suggested by Elizabeth Warren and many others, trading spreads would shrink dramatically. Commissions would collapse from 5–10% to less than 1% on each trade (as happened with stocks and bonds when they started trading on a regulated, transparent open market) and bank profit margins would suffer substantially as noted in the New York Times story (Story, 2010).

All for the Money. Follow the Money

Unfortunately for us, once one of the major counterparties to these customized contracts cannot pay, it may, and in all probability will, start the dominoes falling, with counterparties to the contracts defaulting on their other existing derivatives contracts, creating a panic in the financial system quite possibly larger and uglier than the housing collapse of 2007–2008 or the Crash of '29.

Impossible you say? I don't think so. Why on earth do you think bankers quake when tiny little countries like Greece or Portugal default on loans? Because my friends, no one knows with certainty what the real counter party risk to those countries having a financial systems melt down would be, because no one knows how many billions or trillions of derivatives the Greek or Portuguese bankers may be on the hook for. That is, no one, even the bankers, often do not understand what the real counter party risk to the contract is.

In this era of globalization and inter-connected markets and financial systems, one little default in Lisbon, could shatter confidence in Shanghai half a world away, setting off a firestorm of fear and panic among banks, governments, and investors. Think good old fashioned cattle stampede, with a 1000 head of cattle trying to get through a gate 20 feet wide at the same time. Many would die in such a stampede and as is customary, it would be the most vulnerable among us, the poor, elderly pensioners, and the young, who will bear the brunt of such an economic disaster. It will happen. It is just a matter of time. It is germinating as I write this in late 2019.

Economists and call such high impact, low probability events, *Black Swan Events* because they are ostensibly as rare as seeing a black swan. In an increasingly inter-connected and *globalized* world with highly interconnected economies and financial markets, such an event as a major derivatives default by say Deutsch Bank, would be catastrophic. Such an event is very likely to occur within the next few years if the financial sectors in the United States and elsewhere are not more regulated, especially the derivatives market. These derivatives need to be put on exchange and regulated just like futures and options.

Unless we as a nation summon up the will to fight the banking lobby, one of the most powerful on earth, and insist on banking reform and legislation, particularly in the area of derivatives, we are doomed to see another Crash of 1929, another 1997 (LTCM), another 2000 (Tech Wreck) or another 2008 (housing bubble).

According to opensecrets.org, The Center for Responsive Politics, the banking lobby alone spent $64 million dollars lobbying the U.S. Congress in 2018 (Open Secrets, 2019). The banking and financial services industry is a formidable lobbying group as well. How formidable?

Not surprisingly, they came in second place, tied with the National Realtors Association at $64 million dollars for total political contributions, behind the U.S. Chamber of Commerce, who spent $103 million dollars. In third place was Blue Cross-Blue Shield at $25 million, followed by the Pharmaceutical Research lobby at $20 million and $19 million respectively.

The lure of derivatives is that these instruments (derivatives) allow players to use enormous leverage on the financial bets they are placing, whether on interest rates, currencies, or commodities. Leverage is what the parties agree to, not what is mandated by an exchange, but . . . the potential risk to our financial system is incalculable. Warren Buffet, the Sage of Omaha, can give us an idea of just how dangerous these instruments are. In Berkshire Hathaway's 2005 annual report, he wrote

> Long ago Mark Twain said, A man who tries to carry a cat home by its tail will learn a lesson that can be learned no other way. If Twain were around now he might try winding up the derivatives business. After a few days, he would opt for cats. (Buffett, 2005, p. 3)

In 2002, the Oracle of Omaha wrote, "The range of derivatives contracts is limited only by the imagination of men (or sometimes it seems, madmen.)" (p. 2). He went on to say,

> Improved transparency, a favorite remedy of politicians, commentators, and financial regulators for averting future

train wrecks—won't cure the problems that derivatives pose. **I know of no reporting mechanism that would come close to describing and measuring the risk in a huge and complex portfolio of derivatives.** (Buffett, 2002, p. 1)

Buffet (2005) continued in a later interview (CNBC) on derivatives,

Auditors can't audit these contracts and regulators cannot regulate them. When I read the pages of some 10k's of companies that are entangled with these instruments, all I end up knowing is that I don't know what's going on in their portfolios (and then I reach for some aspirin. (p. 3)

Numerous experts in the field have similar concerns about derivatives. Timothy Geitner, ex head of the Federal Reserve bank of New York no less, raised concerns in a number of speeches about operational deficiencies that were undermining the rapidly growing credit derivatives market. He also arranged a series of meetings with senior executive at leading financial institutions to address an alarming backlog of unsettled trades.

Panzner (2002) in *Financial Armageddon* noted that The IMF was not uttering bureaucratic happy talk in its 2006 *Global Financial Stability Report* when it discussed the specter of major liquidity issues and potentially massive defaults in the derivatives markets.

Since these writings (early 2000s), unregulated derivatives have only continued to grow, now approaching **$1.5 quadrillion dollars.** To put that in perspective, the entire world's annual GDP is approximately $60 trillion dollars a year. As Stephen Lindman (2015) noted in the book *Global Derivatives: $1.5 Quadrillion Dollar Time Bomb*, the proliferation of credit default swaps (CDSs) and other newly financially engineered financial instruments are now over $1.5 quadrillion, with the number of outstanding derivatives more than anyone can conceive. Designed originally to mitigate financial risk, these derivatives are compounding risk, many times over, with a major default not a matter of If, but when.

The late Bob Chapman (2010) also predicted it (a derivatives financial Armageddon), as does Paul Craig Roberts (2015) who thinks a derivatives bubble meltdown could destroy Western civilization. Financial deregulation has turned Wall Street into a casino with no according to these experts.

Ellen Brown (2016) called the "derivatives casino . . . a last-ditch attempt to prop up a private pyramid scheme—slowly crumbling under its own weight and very likely to crumble in the near future" (p. 3).

As noted earlier, one of the savviest investors of all time, Warren Buffett (2005), called derivatives "financial time bombs . . . for economies and ordinary people" (p. 3).

> Unless collateralized or guaranteed, their worth depends on the creditworthiness of counter-parties. Earnings on derivatives are *wildly overstated*, because they're based on estimates whose inaccuracy may not be exposed for many years. (Buffett, 2005, p. 3)

Suffice it to say here that I'm in good company, when I say unregulated derivatives pose a very real, and systemic threat to our way of life, and the middle class, whose pension funds, insurance contracts, stocks, and bonds, will be wiped out under such a derivatives meltdown scenario. Many financial pundits, myself included, feel that modern civilization's only hope is dismantling them (the banks)—making them much smaller and weaker economic pieces and ultimately putting the money back into the hands of the public where it belongs.

Question: And where were / are the regulators? Those who could curb or mitigate such wild speculation in all these FED created bubbles?

Answer: the same place they were in 1929, 1973, 1987, 1997, 2000, and 2007. Nowhere to be found.

They were muzzled by their financial masters, central bankers, and financial elites. The next financial collapse, rapidly approaching as I write this in 2019, will make all these prior *crashes* look like a picnic in the park thanks to the explosion and proliferation of these financial weapons of mass financial destruction as Warren Buffet calls them.

Big banks are as connected and dangerous as they were before the 2008 crisis. The IMF in 2018 reported that Deutsche Bank (with thousands of derivatives contracts) was "the most important net contributor to worldwide financial systemic risks" (IMF, 2018, p. 4). The threat of banks being so interconnected as globalization continues apace is that once they fail or if they hit market turbulence, it can cause a financial contagion effect globally, with financial markets falling like dominoes (The New Domino Theory). When one bank catches a cold, the next catches pneumonia. Indeed, in *Other People's Money* by John Kay (2015), he noted, as did DeSoto (1998), that financial crises are not natural disasters, they are man-made. Errant and often ill advised economic, fiscal and monetary policies can increase or decrease their severity. Financial crises which used to occur infrequently, are alarmingly frequent now, as the world becomes ever more financially interconnected.

As John Kay (2015) and many others have noted, the increasing globalization of the past several decades, combined with the rise of securitization and derivatives, and the elimination of Glass-Stegall, make an event like the Crash of '29 increasingly likely today. The next financial panic is being wittingly or unwittingly choreographed as I write this in late 2019. Planned by the usual suspects who are well known to us now, the FED, Goldman, etc. they will light the match that starts the financial inferno that burns the country to the ground. A scorched earth policy. They will be short all these derivatives and make trillions as millions of investors and another great swath of the middle class are wiped out. After the dust has settled and enraged populations are pointing their fingers at the politicians they mistakenly believe are responsible for the crash, the *trust* will very quietly start buying up assets at fire sale prices. It's a tried and true formula and will make them trillions again. It will also wipe out what is left of our American middle class.

Pump and dump. These credit bubbles are not uniquely American. When the Group of Seven or G-20 get together in Davos and elsewhere, it's not for cocktails. It is often to *coordinate* monetary policy. Central banks worldwide, then as now, were responsible for the outlandish credit inflations and subsequent inevitable crashes, benefiting enormously financially from the financial train wreck that they themselves choreographed. The only difference between then (2007) and now (2019) of course is that the bubble(s) now are in the bond market and equities, not housing.

CHAPTER 8.
The Quid Pro Quo Between the Military, Bankers, and Politicians

"Patriotism is usually the refuge of the scoundrel.
He is the man who talks the loudest."

—MARK TWAIN, EDUCATION AND CITIZENSHIP SPEECH,
5/14/1908

Politicians love the Federal Reserve and fiat currencies (ours included!) because fiat currencies (currencies backed by no tangible asset) allow them to recklessly spend with abandon, without the constraints that they would have under the gold standard or any currency backed by real assets. As demonstrated in earlier chapters, what we now have in the United States is akin to an unlimited checking account for politicians because there is no brake on their spending. On the gold standard, you could not spend what you did not have. Under the new (post 1971) euphemistically titled *floating rate regime*, a currency's value is simply determined by supply and demand. As long as this floating rate regime exists, which has prevailed since 1971, politicians will recklessly spend beyond their means on superfluous projects at home (bringing home the bacon) or reckless wars abroad.

Indeed, it has almost become cliché for a president to start a war the nation cannot afford to distract the population from domestic troubles at home. Gore Vidal (2002) in his book *Perpetual War for Perpetual Peace: How We Got To Be So Hated*, observed that from V-J Day 1945 (Victory over Japan and the end of WWII), to the turn of the 20th century, we have been engaged in what historian Charles Beard called perpetual war for perpetual peace. He famously compiled a list of our enemy of the month club, noting that every year and decade we seem to be beset by a new horrendous enemy at whom we must strike before the enemy destroys us (Vidal, 2002).

Politicians and bankers love war, for they are hugely profitable, and as noted in Chapter 1, one of the primary reasons central banks were created in the first place. Wars must be funded by bankers, and politicians can't resist having a military base or defense related organization in their state because they too, are profitable, and create employment, and make them look good to their constituents, often ensuring their reelection.

Incredibly, Vidal (2002) commented on this inane propensity for war by U.S. presidents and politicians by saying that we have had SEVERAL HUNDRED wars against Communism, drugs, and often, nothing much at all, between Pearl Harbor and 9-11-2001.

How were all these wars paid for without ever raising taxes you may ask? (Most of them?) Simple. As long as politicians can spend dollars backed by nothing but the *full faith and credit of the taxing authority of the U.S. government* and have a central bank to create unlimited quantities of money, but never dare run a campaign on raising taxes, deficit spending will continue to soar and the national debt will continue to explode. It is approaching $30 trillion dollars as I finish writing this in 2020. In 1970, we were the largest creditor nation on earth. Forty nine years later, we are the largest debtor nation on earth. How much of our accumulated national debt is due to war? For the Afghanistan and Iraqi wars alone, the figure is approaching $7 TRILLION dollars. Indeed, in Washington DC, it has become routine for retired military and retiring Congresspersons to go to work for defense contractors and other *beltway bandits* and *consultancies* and K Street lobbyists in their *new* career. This revolving door between the Pentagon and K Street ensures that there will always be an *enemy* out there to fight and almost as importantly, keep the funding coming for the Pentagon. How else to keep all these people employed and the defense budget growing at 5% a year (minimum)? This incestuous relationship between the Pentagon and Capitol Hill has proliferated unabated, relentlessly marching (or should I say careening?) the nation towards one fruitless and hugely costly foreign misadventure after the next since Korea.

Much of this war spending would have been impossible without the availability of deficit spending. One could argue, that if we eliminated the Pentagon, there would be no deficit (now running at around $1 trillion a year and approximately the same as the defense budget, about $800 billion a year). What made much of this reckless war spending possible and accelerated the nation's race towards profligacy, was the elimination of the gold standard by Nixon in 1971. The elimination of the gold standard paved the way for the exponential increases in deficit spending that we have seen since 1971.

What Was The Gold Standard?

The Gold Standard was pretty simple:

1. Each currency was pegged to the dollar with its value in turn,

determined and backed by a certain amount of gold. Each currency in turn was pegged to the dollar at a fixed rate of gold. Each country's central bank stood ready to convert currencies to gold at these fixed parity's. The British pound sterling for example was defined as 113 grains of pure gold and the U.S. dollar as 23.22 grains. Thus, the exchange rate between currencies were also irrevocably fixed with one pound equal to $4.87 or 113/23.22.

2. These rules meant that changes in the domestic supply of money were inextricably linked to movements in gold reserves. A country with a deficit on its foreign balance of payments would lose gold to its trade partners and consequently experience a reduction in its money supply (less gold=less money in circulation) and a contracting economy. Those countries running a trade surplus would realize a net increase in their gold reserves. These gold flows in turn would trigger corrections in economic imbalances, better known as automatic adjustment mechanisms by economists. If a country were in a deficit position, tighter monetary and credit conditions would result in a combination of rising interest rates and falling domestic prices. This in turn would lead to reduced spending and improved trade competitiveness, restoring equilibrium of trade imbalances, bringing the countries balance of payments (BOP) back into balance.

3. Unlike today's floating rate regime that we have under the gold standard rules, governments had no ability to experiment with monetary policy to alter domestic credit conditions, unlike today, because the domestic money supply was solely determined by gold and capital flows across national borders. Under the gold standard, central bankers were

constrained by the availability of gold, and had little to do besides issuing or retiring domestic currency as the level of gold in their vaults fluctuated.

After World War I, Britain found itself in the unenviable position of having a domestic interest rate which had tripled during the war and they had also run up large debts with the United States which had stockpiled a massive amount of gold. The British government was forced to maintain unusually high interest rates to prevent capital flight and unemployment remained stubbornly high at over 10%. Churchill was urged by his cabinet to maintain the old parity to gold at all cost for the sake of the system (gold standard), but eventually had to go off the gold standard in 1931.

Britain, once the standard bearer of the gold standard, was forced out of the gold standard club because of their inability to service their debt, at which point the gold standard days were numbered. Franklin Roosevelt took the United States off gold in 1933 to enable faster and greater monetary expansion, with most of the so called *gold-block countries* and France following in 1936. De-linking currency from gold allowed governments to create money at will. Politicians, governments, and of course bankers, reveled in this new system.

What Were the Advantages and Disadvantages of the Gold Standard?

Briefly, the gold standard's biggest advantage was to constrain governments and politicians from spending money they did not have. Deficit spending was nearly impossible under such a system. As shown in graphs in Chapters 1–4 if the money supply expands faster than the actual growth in the economy (GDP), so must inflation, if there is not a commensurate rise in the domestic production of goods and services It is painfully clear to even the most untrained eye, that there is a nearly perfect correlation between money supply growth and inflation. After going off the gold standard in 1971, U.S. politicians and the U.S. government, no longer constrained by having a currency backed by a physical asset, went on a spending spree. The national debt went parabolic starting in the mid 1970s shortly after the U.S. went off the gold standard and has been compounding at nearly $1 trillion dollars plus, nearly every year for over a decade now. Interest on the national debt is now the third largest item in the budget behind Social Security and defense (over $400 billion a year $479 billion/ $4.5 trillion=about 10% of the budget). This explosion in debt of course has severely eroded the purchasing power of the dollar. A dollar from 1913 is now worth .03 cents. (see Figure 18).

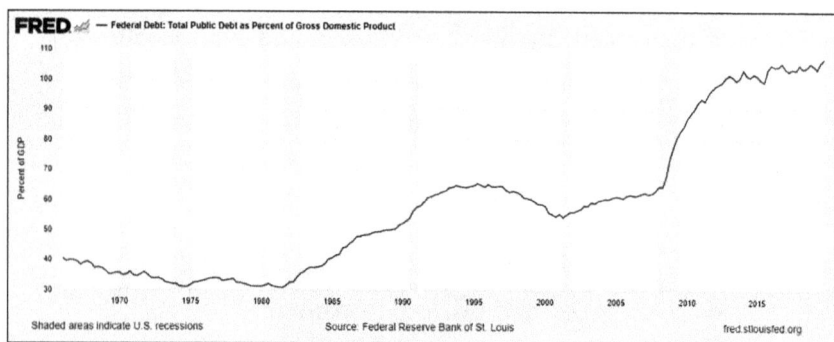

Figure 18. Public Debt as a Percent of GDP

Note: Reprinted from the Federal Reserve Bank of St. Louis.

More disturbingly, these interest payments are forecasted to triple over the next 10 years, devouring a larger and larger piece of the budget as time goes on. By the end of this decade, total debt service on our national debt will be over a $1 trillion dollars a year, greater than military spending (which is really saying something) (Schwartz, 2018).

What Were the Disadvantages of the Gold Standard?

The major disadvantages of a gold standard, seen from the perspective of governments and politicians of course, is the inverse of the advantages mentioned above. Under such a system, governments cannot go to war without raising taxes, and politicians and bankers cannot *expand* the economy by creating excess credit and liquidity. Bankers cannot charge interest on loans created from thin air (they could only loan what they had in actual deposits) and governments would have a much harder time warring with each other if those wars must actually be paid for from tax revenues.

Yes, if we went back to a gold standard or something like it, the economy could only grow as fast as national savings and foreign direct investment (FDI) and gold reserves. And economic growth would therefore slow. BUT, this growth rate would be sustainable because the lending could only come from actual savings (bank deposits) of the country. This would mean the end of much of our banking and financial services sector, but it would end the boom bust cycles that occurs automatically under a fractional reserve banking system. Now we have a financial system where financial excesses build unchecked until the imbalances (malinvestment) must self-correct, which they always do, with a bust. This is a system where banking profits are privatized (bank profits paid out to shareholders) and the losses are socialized. That is, when the inevitable bust comes, the taxpayer foots the bill. This has happened decade after decade since the FEDs founding in 1913.

Bretton Woods and the Fixed Exchange Rate System

In July of 1944 at a New Hampshire resort known as Bretton Woods, John Maynard Keynes, then the head of the English treasury and Harry Dexter White of the U.S. Treasury Department, and delegates from 44 nations met at a conference to set new rules for the international financial system. The system designed and agreed to there, would govern the world's financial system for nearly 30 years. The World Bank, the IMF, and the General Agreement on Tariffs and Trade (GATT) were created during this time, laying the groundwork for freer trade between nations and what is now called *globalization*. As with the founding of the Federal Reserve in 1913, motives for creating a new financial system were hardly egalitarian.

This currency regime envisioned and ultimately crafted by Keynes and White at Bretton Woods, eventually came to be known as a fixed rate currency regime in which the dollar became the reserve currency of the world. Under this system, all other currencies were pegged within a narrow *band* to the dollar, with each dollar convertible at $35 per ounce of gold.

This system had tremendous advantages for the U.S. government. It provided automatic support for the dollar because any country wishing to trade internationally had to acquire dollars to do so. To acquire dollar *reserves* meant providing raw materials or goods and services to the United States, often on very advantageous terms. This system also meant a ready and willing world available to suck up as many dollars as could be created. The dollar became a part of foreign central banks *reserves*. Under this system as noted earlier, international trade between nations grew exponentially. This system ushered in a period now known as *globalization* and not coincidentally, made the American economy and middle class, the envy of the world.

Globalization, however, is a two edged sword. It is not clear that in the longer run, as economists like to say, that it has been a benefit for most Americans. Many would and do argue that the reverse is true. That is, globalization benefited American multinationals and their shareholders enormously, but outsourced and gutted most of our manufacturing base, leaving displaced manufacturing workers with no alternatives for work other than much lower paying jobs in the services, hospitality, and retail sectors. An economy that once was the envy of the world, has now become a *dead man walking*, according to globalization's critics. This is the camp I find myself in.

In the *Globalization Paradox*, Dani Rodrik (2011) noted that Paul Krugman, a highly respected Berkley economist with liberal leanings, was a *free trade* advocate up until the 1970s, but changed his mind when he saw, "the impact of globalization on domestic income distribution" (p. 84). Krugman, a Nobel prize winner in economics in 2008, understood early on the fallacy and dangers to the U.S. economy and working men and women early on, presented by free trade.

So, up to this point, several salient points need to be highlighted. A world under this Bretton Woods system traded goods, services, and commodities internationally in dollars, with all currencies pegged to the dollar, and the dollar convertible by trading partners at $35 per ounce of gold. The United

States controlled three quarters of world GDP after WWII, providing the United States with enormous financial leverage and advantage in international trade, paving the way for globalization. This is why the dollar was considered for many years as good as gold.

The gold standard was abolished by Nixon in 1971 because the United States was bankrupt after nearly 10 years of war in Vietnam (another war we could not afford) and the additional financial burden of social spending, aka *The Great Society* promoted by President Johnson and his contemporaries in the 1960s. The beauty of going off the gold standard was that gold was no longer required to back the currency. Predictably, politicians were quick to grab the new opportunity and spent relentlessly, *bringing home the bacon* and their pet projects (bridge to nowhere??), all without ever having to raise taxes! Do you remember taxes increasing for the dual wars in Afghanistan and Iraq?

It was agreed at this point (1971) that the world would go to a *fiat* monetary system, where no currency was backed by any hard asset (like gold) but whose value would be determined by simple supply and demand. Currencies would *float* relative to one another with their value relative to each other, determined by the supply and demand for that currency. Under such a floating rate currency regime, a currency's value would be determined by how well their economy was deemed to be doing which in turn would affect the demand for the currency, based on foreign confidence in the economy and thus the level of foreign direct investment (FDI) in the economy. There were of course a host of other microeconomic and macroeconomic factors affecting the demand for a currency as well. The relative level of interest rates and inflation were very important in determining demand, as were investor perceptions on the overall state of the economy.

Under this system if a person in the United States bought a BMW from a German dealer, they would have to sell dollars and buy Marks (now Euros) to do so. This puts downward pressure on the dollar (dollar falls) and upward pressure on the Mark (Euro goes up). Multiply this event by $100 million purchases a day of foreign goods and services and you begin to see the problem(s) which free trade, a floating dollar, a spendthrift and unconstrained political and economic system, coupled with an out of control financial services sector, bring about.

As noted by Reich (2006), this bringing on of cheap imports by Americans starting in the 1990s led to massive trade deficits leading to erosion of the dollar's value (more money leaving the country than coming in) and displacement of millions of American workers in industries from furniture making to steel. This hollowing out of America's manufacturing base led to higher unemployment and lower wages throughout much of America, most notably the *rust belt*. Concomitant with this, as noted in prior chapters, there has been an explosion in the national debt, and the costs of health care and education. All of these items in total (anyone would be enough) have led to the predictable financial decline of America's middle class.

Politicians on both sides of the aisle (but usually Republican legislation) contributed to the decline of our middle class since 1980 by deregulating the banking and financial services sector and whole swaths of our services sector and government while agreeing with the Pentagon to get our nation involved in one fruitless, pointless, and yes, very expensive war, after the next. But that is another chapter. War profiteering is as old as war itself. The cozy quid pro quo between politicians and bankers and the FED has existed nearly since the country's inception (1776) and as Jefferson (1786) so presciently warned over 200 years ago, "has brought our nation to the edge of ruin and bankruptcy" (Jefferson, 1786, p. 2).

Politicians are elected by their constituency to *bring home the bacon*. That is, every politician needs government funded social and infrastructure projects that will improve the state's economy, increase jobs, and hopefully, prosperity. This is why politicians are elected. How they stay in office is another matter altogether.

Under our current political system, staying in office requires relying on the special and moneyed interests for campaign contributions from those that often pose the greatest threat to our democracy, and economy, Wall Street, defense, and the Banking Cartel. As noted in prior chapters, they contribute heavily to political campaigns (as shown from lobbying figures noted above). Both major parties feast at this corporate and defense spending trough and both are beholden to plutocrats, corporatists, and monopolies for their political survival. This is why the smart money always places bets on both parties.

What's War Got to Do With It?

Bankers, politicians, and of course the FED, understand that war increases government spending, benefiting them and many of their constituents, particularly those in the metropolitan DC area where *Beltway Bandits* and so called consultancies, often staffed with retired military and Congresspersons, proliferate like a red tide in summer. These *consultants* understand the *system* better than anyone and so are naturals for these positions where securing Department of Defense (DOD) grants is imperative for corporate survival. There are of course *spillover* economic benefits to be had from a $800 billion dollar defense budget, half of which goes to personnel: active and retired military) that benefits many other ancillary industries.

The major point to be made here is that central banks were originally created to fund wars that monarchies could not afford (Chapter 1 and 2). Nothing has changed much in the model since their inception in Switzerland in the 1600s. War is profitable. For governments who gain increased taxes from those employed by war and for suppliers of war material and personnel, and yes, of course, the FED, which is called on to create the money to pay for them because no politician can survive on a *let's raise taxes to pay for more war!* platform. The more things change, the more they stay the same.

The national debt which was nearly zero when Reagan was elected, nearly tripled under his administration and is now approaching $30 trillion dollars as I finish this book in 2020. When the U.S. Congress needs money now to raise the debt ceiling for example, who is the lender of last resort? The FED of course. If we do not have the domestic savings to borrow from (we don't), and foreigners will not lend us the money (they have slowed lending considerably), the U.S. Congress calls the Treasury and says we need a trillion dollars.

The treasury contacts the FED and the FED creates out of thin air, with a keystroke, a trillion dollars, which is deposited in government accounts to fund operating expenses (Chapters 1 and 2). What does the FED get? A stack of I.O.U.'s called Treasury bonds worth $1 trillion dollars. It's a very clever quid pro quo that avoids public scrutiny because of the deliberate obfuscation of the U.S. Congress, the Treasury, and the FED. What does the public get? INFLATION. More money has

WEALTH INEQUITY IN AMERICA

been magically created without a commensurate rise in the production of goods and services, so prices must rise. And they do of course, inexorably, particularly in the two areas critical for a citizen's economic survival, health care and education. Costs for just these two items as noted previously often rise at about 10% per year, while wages during the same period remain flat. This is a recipe for disaster from a public policy perspective. The middle class as noted throughout this and prior chapters, simply cannot keep up.

Not coincidentally, before 1971 we were the largest creditor nation on earth and today, the largest debtor nation on earth. What a legacy for our kids and grandkids! A $30 trillion debt, which doesn't include another $50 trillion in potential unfunded government liabilities. And it will just continue as long as central bankers are running our economy.

But not to worry friends, as "Easy" Ben Bernanke quipped in 2012 to the National Economist's Club in 2002,

> But the U.S. government has a technology, called a printing press (or today, its electronic equivalent), that allows it to produce as many U.S. dollars as it wishes at essentially no cost. By increasing the number of U.S. dollars in circulation or even by credibly threatening to do so, the U.S. government can also reduce the value of a dollar in terms of goods and services, which is equivalent to raising the prices in dollars of those goods and services. **We conclude that, under a paper-money system, a determined government can always generate higher spending and hence positive inflation.** (para. 22)

It's very clear from Bernanke's many remarks and prior monetary policy and actions by FED heads and governors, that the

FED is the purveyor of inflation, not an inflation fighter. As noted in Chapter 1, inflation is baked into a fractional reserve banking system and very intentionally perpetuated because without continuous loan growth, economic growth (GDP), and bank profits will stall, and the economy contract because *consumption* drives 70% of GDP in the United States.

FED monetary policy is never seriously questioned by politicians or the bankers who are tacitly complicit in this nefarious quid pro quo. As explained by William Nordhouse (1975) in *The Political Business Cycle* most politicians (57% when written and higher now) make decisions based on very short-term considerations because of the financial contributions required to assure them victory in the next election. DeSoto (2006) noted that politicians seldom hesitate to inhibit monetary expansion by the FED because these artificially contrived expansions produce a temporary prosperity and optimism, helping them to attain reelection in the short run. Any deviation from this artificial expansion is viewed unfavorably the party in power, often vilified in the press, and used as a weapon against the opposition to suppress unions, non-governmental organizations and business and political entities with different points of view than those prevailing from those currently in power. Seldom is this excessive credit creation questioned by those in power. Of course not. Such a system (fractional reserve banking with the FED at its head) makes developing a ***sustainable economic system*** built on real savings, impossible.

In summary then, what we have in Washington DC now is a revolving door between the Pentagon, K Street, and the U.S. Congress. Some would say, a grossly incestuous set of relationships where retiring military and Congressman peddle their influence garnered from decades in one institution

(Pentagon or Congress) for the benefit of often publicly traded corporations and defense contractors, only too eager to pay them handsomely for their knowledge on how to maneuver the intricacies of the government contracting and procurement process. This situation is rife with conflicts of interest, often reeks of crony capitalism at its worst, and often leads to disastrous legislation, with all in the nefarious Congress-K Street-Pentagon (the DC triangle) food chain benefiting enormously at taxpayer expense.

This uniquely Washington set of seriously questionable relationships also puts pressure on Congress for yet more military spending, resulting in increases in outsized Pentagon spending year-after-year, (10% increase in 2019), and all too often provides the temptation to use a blunt instrument (military) in foreign relations, when a more finely calibrated response (diplomacy) is called for. War is profitable for all involved, except for those who actually have to die in the process. Finally, all this additional spending drains the national treasury and diverts funds from critically needed social programs at home. As noted before, the money for these wars, to add insult to *injury* so to speak, is often borrowed, leaving our children and grandchildren with what now resembles an emerging market economy and infrastructure, and mountains of national debt growing now at well over $1 trillion dollars a year. This burgeoning, and increasingly fascist coordination between the military, U.S. Congress, and K Street lobbyists just increases the tax burden on the middle class, crowding out investments in education and infrastructure , hastening the demise of the middle class.

CHAPTER 9.

The Birth of the Middle Class: Franklin Roosevelt and the New Deal

"If the American people ever allow private banks to control the issue of their money, first by inflation and then by deflation, the banks and corporations that will grow up around them (around the banks), will deprive the people of their property until their children will wake up homeless on the continent their fathers conquered."

—THOMAS JEFFERSON 1816

Many historians credit the FED and its member banks with destroying what middle class existed in the 1920s by using their now well-known tactics of creating a bubble, a selling panic, and then picking up the assets at rock bottom prices after the crash (just like they did in the Tech Wreck of 2000 and the housing crash of 2007–2008. This nefarious bunch of financial opportunists have had over four centuries to perfect this ugly parlor trick.

With the Crash of '29, and the following depression however, they (the banking cartel) nearly killed the goose that laid the golden egg, the American economy, through their avarice. America was on the ropes, falling to the matt, and nearly down for the count. But as often happens throughout history, an unlikely, unassuming hero arose just when we thought America couldn't take another economic punch. Franklin Delano Roosevelt was an unlikely, and unassuming hero. He slowly brought America up on her knees, then her feet, and by the time he and the U.S. Congress were done, America was once again, the envy of the modern world. Not coincidentally, the New Deal (Social Security) and the Civilian Conservation Corp (CCC) were Democratic reforms, with most of the Republican minority voting against them.

As we all now know he initiated public works projects like the CCC to build parks, lodges, and trails across the country. He started the Tennessee Valley Authority (TVA) to put people to work and bring electricity to rural America. More importantly he immediately enacted financial regulation legislation creating the Securities Acts of 33 and 34 and created the Securities and Exchange Commission (SEC). Like his brother Teddy before him, he became a first class trustbuster understanding only too well, what a danger monopoly and oligopoly were to capitalism. Perhaps most importantly, he championed the working man through an eight hour work week, a minimum wage, and the occupational safety and health regulations (OSHA) and many other pieces of legislation designed to improve the lives of working men and women in America.

Perhaps most importantly from a social and public policy perspective, he provided hope. Hope that economic fairness and social justice could prevail in America over the entrenched interest of plutocrats and special interests. Hope, that yes, every man and woman could, if he / she worked hard and played by the rules, could cross class barriers rising from poverty to the upper middle class just like Carnegie!

Yes, this humble, humorous, and unassuming hero saved capitalism from itself, much to the chagrin of his Republican opponents, the wealthy, and of course, the FED and its member banks. Many people give Roosevelt credit for laying the groundwork for a vibrant and prosperous middle class, which as noted numerous times throughout this book is essential for democracy's survival.

This was the golden age of labor in America and a burgeoning middle class. In the 30 years between 1945 and 1975, a unique and remarkable accommodation between capitalism and democracy transpired. The enormously powerful and productive economic engine of the American economy peacefully co-existed with a seemingly well organized and internationally admired American political system (how times have changed). This was an accommodation between capitalism and democracy seldom seen before or since.

America accounted for approximately 75% of global GDP and generated the highest number of high paying jobs in history, with more and more people enjoying the economic benefits of its hugely productive economy. Commensurate with this tremendous economic growth came a heightened sense of economic security, with the majority of Americans expressing a high trust in government and its institutions, a situation that is now ancient history, with most Americans today cynical and disgusted with politics, government, and Washington DC. Those halcyon *Leave it to Beaver* days of the 1940s, 1950s, and 1960s were also accompanied by a truly progressive tax code with the top marginal income tax rate at 90% of income. One of the most economically successful periods in American history was also accompanied by some of the highest marginal taxes in history! Republicans would say this is impossible, but our own history, and the current tax codes of many social democracies prove that high taxes and a powerful economy, accompanied by strong social safety nets in a democracy are possible. Sadly, we as Americans are somewhat brainwashed on this score, with the right routinely excoriating social democracies as moribund, sclerotic economies. This argument, that high taxes destroys economic growth, is of course a complete fabrication when one looks at the facts (more on this later). France for example, is the most productive economies in the G-7, with America coming in at 6th place.

Divided America

In 2020, we have a bitterly divided America, with a hollowed out and anemic industrial base, a tepid *service* economy, and an apathetic population, too disgusted with Washington and the status quo, to vote. Corporations have been enshrined in our U.S. Constitution as individuals (U.S. Supreme Court Ruling Citizens United) and now propagate much of the *public policy* legislation in our country. The corpotocracy has the government well in hand. It is a travesty. American democracy was not designed for or ready for, the size, scale, and reach of today's multinationals that have net incomes larger than many countries' GDP. Think Microsoft or Amazon or Wal Mart. In the face of such capitalist juggernauts, voters feel powerless to initiate meaningful social, political, or economic change that would actually benefit working people (the middle class).

The U.S. Supreme Court ruling, Citizens United, closed the lid on democracy when it provided corporations the same rights as people, and the ability to make unlimited campaign contributions to politicians whose origins did not have to be identified. This court ruling in conjunction with the decline in manufacturing and union membership, financialization of the U.S. economy, the gutting of the Glass Stegall Act in 1999, the proliferation of derivatives, and a *deregulated* and *privatized* economy paved the way for the country we now have a few decades later. A country where economic inequality is the highest on record, where America lags all major trading partners on every meaningful metric form overall quality of life (World Bank) to health care (WHO), to literacy (World Bank). And not surprisingly, concomitant with all of the above, we have a rapidly shrinking middle class with severely stunted upward social and economic mobility.

What Happened?

For approximately 30 years, we had an economy that was the envy of the world. The dollar was the reserve currency of the world and we controlled 75% of the world's GDP, and union membership was at an all-time high at approximately 35% of the labor force (1945–1975). Those halcyon days of the American middle class Renaissance have since faded like a fiery sunset. The creation of our middle class brought with it advances in economic and social mobility as never seen before. Many of these were pointed out by Samuel Huntington (2008) in *The Clash of Civilizations*, where he opined that at the end of WWII, as one of the worlds remaining super powers, along with Britain and France, the United States had the ability to determine the economic fate of most of the world's economy. The United States, along with other Western economies, owned or mostly controlled the international banking system, international capital markets, most hard currencies, the high-tech weapons industry, international sea lanes, and access to space. It exerted tremendous financial and military might worldwide. In addition to this of course, America wielded soft power. That is, it exerted and transmitted cultural and moral leadership through fashion, music, design, and art. In short, the United States was an unrivaled superpower.

This is the flattering and somewhat sanguine viewpoint popularized by U.S. politicians like Trump today, with few of them giving credit to Roosevelt for saving capitalism from itself or paving the way for the extraordinary advances noted above. The more accurate picture of the United States today is painted a few pages later where Huntington (2008) observed that the United States is now a fading power, exhausted from decades of Cold War, with its share of economic, political, and military power in steady decline, with its citizens increasingly focused inward, attempting to, but generally powerless to halt the seemingly intractable problems of stagnating populations and torpid economic growth, rampant deficit spending, low, or nonexistent savings rates, and social upheaval and disintegration. This is the unhappy portrait of America in decline today.

As most Americans know and subconsciously fear intellectually or intuitively, economic power is rapidly shifting to East Asia, and military and political influence are starting to follow. The Indian sub-continent continues to rapidly develop and the entire Middle East, with the exception of Israel, is hostile to the United States.

Many previously *emerging* economies, including China and India (Chindia), are no longer willing to accept the dollar as the reserve currency of the world or accept the often capricious and arbitrary dictates of the West, which they often view with a jaundiced, skeptical eye. Indeed, the United States which has enjoyed the privilege and bounty of an economic system they set up in 1944 at Bretton Woods, making the dollar the reserve currency of the world, is fading rapidly in significance in most parts of the world. The unwillingness of the rest of the world to accept the dollar as a reserve currency, and their desire to seek economic partnerships with each other (Russia and China for example) spells doom for the dollar. As the reliance on the dollar as a reserve currency fades, the support it has enjoyed will evaporate and it will decline. As goes your currency, so goes your standard of living. This inevitably, spells more hardship for the middle class in the years ahead.

In the military realm, the balance of effective capabilities between the United States and a number of growing regional powers (including perhaps Iran, India, and China) will shift from the center toward the periphery. Some of America's structural power will inevitably flow to other nations; while some will find its way into the hands of non-state actors like multinational corporations who many would argue, already own and run most of the world.

Decline in Trust

Along with the rise of the middle class as noted earlier, came a concomitant high water mark in trust for U.S. government institutions, capitalism, and business in general. As the United States struggled with stagflation in the 1970s, an S & L debacle in the 1980s, slow growth in the 1990s, and corporate scandals in the early 2000s such as Enron, WorldCom, and Parmelat, trust in the U.S. government, institutions, and corporate

America slowly disintegrated. Francis Fukuyama (1999) in his historical treatise *The Great Disruption,* explained what happens to a society (and the middle class) when trust in institutions erodes, accelerating the economic and social decline we have witnessed in the United States since the mid-1970s.

As trust in traditional institutions declines and the economic pie begins to shrink, and the population becomes more mobile and secular, the social *ligatures* that used to bind families, communities and societies together begin to disintegrate leading to social behavior that would have been stigmatized, and led to an individual's pariah status in the community 40 years earlier. This tendency of modern societies to move towards *individualism* leads inevitably to a dog eat dog mentality, as exemplified by today's American society, particularly among plutocrats, and businessmen. This is unbridled, rampant, and now totally brazen crony capitalism at its worst that abounds in America today. As Fukuyama (1999) noted, in a secular, mobile society, the societal and familial ligatures that bond individuals to each other, their family, community, and government, often disintegrate, leading to a pervasive distrust of business and government, and a cult like mentality of many whom find solace in identifying with individuals rather than traditional institutions. One need look no further than the current occupant of the White House, J-Lo, or NFL football heroes to see this. Anecdotal evidence abounds that the state has been displaced by the cult, where people in America are no longer bound by bonds of tribe, caste, or religion. In such an environment, the ties of social and economic obligations are greatly loosened.

As a longtime observer of the slow disintegration of the middle class in America, I see trendlines converging, creating an inevitable economic, social, and financial confluence that is hard to ignore, and painful to witness. In short, as the increasing financialization of the economy has occurred since Reagan, and trust in traditional institutions has hit an all-time low, and the societal *ligatures* that bind people to each other, their communities, and their institutions evaporate, society has become highly individualistic and tribal, where a dog eat dog mentality prevails, while our middle class continues to evaporate.

This disintegration of public trust in government and deliberate castigation of government as being incapable of doing anything better than the private sector, was summarized by Reagan's famous speech in the mid 1980s when he said, "I'm from the government and I'm here to help" (Reagan, 1986, p. 2). Reagan prefaced this quote by claiming these were the "nine most terrifying words in the English language" (Reagan, 1986, p. 2). Reagan and Republicans everywhere parroted this notion that government was now the enemy, not the enabler of liberty, health, and the pursuit of happiness. It is this kind of thinking, and the vilification of government in general, that spawned the neoliberalist policies of the 1980s, and the relentless tax cuts for the wealthy and corporations, combined with the continual gutting and defunding of critical government services by Republicans, that has now brought our nation to the edge of bankruptcy and ruin. Today (in 2020), we are witnessing what 40 years of deliberately hollowing out our government and its institutions has wrought. A farsical, incompetent response from the White House towards the greatest public health crisis in a 100 years, a painfully slow response time from major government agencies like the Center for Disease Control (CDC), and the Department of Health and Human Services (HHS), and a total lack of preparedness, even a veneer of preparedness, by the highest government officials in the land, who look to the private sector to fill the void left by underfunded government. The results have been as predictable as they are sad. This sad state of affairs is certainly no cause for the ebullience and the cheerleading emanating from the White House that we are subjected to daily as a nation.

Reagan, much to the glee of conservatives everywhere, played a key role in ridiculing anything government run or regulated by government. This, in conjunction with conservative's deliberate destruction of unions, notably starting with the air traffic controllers strike (1980s), and subsequent dismantling of that union, provided a template for union busting throughout the United States.

When conservatives scoff at government doing anything better than the private sector and ask me, "Name one thing that government does better than the private sector!"

My answer is typically,

"Do you get a Social Security check?"

Their expense ratio is 3% vs. 15–30% for the private sector insurance sector.

This is merely one of the plethora of activities that government does daily better than the private sector. And most importantly, there are many things that are extremely important from a social policy perspective that need to be done, but are not profitable or run counter to the corporate profit motive. Agencies like the Environmental Protection Agency (EPA), the Occupational Safety and Health Act (OSHA), and the Federal Trade Commission (FTC) are such critical government agencies pursuing activities that improve the lives of Americans, and protect us from privately owned or publicly traded interests that would like to see them abolished for greater profit and more power. Indeed, there are many industries such as banking and financial services that need much stricter regulation and oversight by government or they will destroy our society and capitalism with it.

As noted in earlier sections of this book, the dismantling of regulations on financial institutions and ensuing financial calamities wrought by such deregulation (S & L debacle and RTC and Housing bubble and TARP), aided and abetted by an ever expanding financial sector and military industrial complex, has produced extreme income inequality which has grown exponentially, as has public distrust of government and its institutions, with all of these elements combining to create an anything goes atmosphere where the objective of many is to get ahead at all costs, and an ends justifies the means society, with the epiphany of such thinking currently represented by a president who exemplifies the very worst elements in our society, and gloats at creating division, deriding honesty, personal integrity, and lies routinely.

Concomitant with all of this economic and social unrest a mean-spirited division between the have and have nots becomes increasingly apparent. Those with the gold make the golden rules, as the old saying goes. Money and wealth in our current *democracy* provide access to lobbyists, access in turn buys or *influences* Congress people to vote for legislation favorable to the more powerful in society, and inevitably, absolute power corrupts absolutely.

As financial elites and billionaires become inexorably entrenched in business and government, they enact tax legislation favoring income over labor, low taxes on capital gains and *unearned income*, lower or abolish inheritance taxes, and shift taxes from the wealthy and upper class and corporations to the upper middle and middle classes. Thus, not only does the middle class have to keep up with health care and education costs rising at often 10% a year thanks to the inflation created by a fractional reserve banking system and corrupt central bank, crony capitalism and oligopoly, but they must also pay an ever greater share of the taxes in a progressively regressive tax code, built and designed by the wealthy for the wealthy. This is basically what has been happening in the United States since the **Reagan Revolution** and supply side *trickle-down* economics became enshrined in conservative economic dogma in the 1980s. Say goodnight to the middle class.

CHAPTER 10.
The Beginning of the End—
Nixon and the End of
the Gold Standard

*Whenever destroyers appear among men, they start by
destroying money, for money is men's protection and the base of
a moral existence. Destroyers seize gold and leave to its owners
a counterfeit pile of paper. This kills all objective standards
and delivers men into the arbitrary power of an arbitrary setter
of values. Gold was an objective value, an equivalent of wealth
produced. Paper is a mortgage on wealth that does not exist,
backed by a gun aimed at those who are expected to produce
it. Paper is a check drawn by legal looters, upon an account
which is not theirs, upon the virtue of the victims. Watch for
the day when it bounces, marked 'Account Overdrawn.'*

—AYN RAND (1905–1982)

The United States in 1971 was in an untenable and unenviable financial and economic position. Rising competition from export driven economies like Korea and Japan (the Asian Tigers) combined with enormous debts from Johnson's Great Society Program, and of course, the costs of the Vietnam War left the country broke. Literally.

With rioting in the streets, the American flag being burned at protests nationwide, and the Black Panther, Huey Newton, and transformational minister Martin Luther King all demanding social justice and economic fairness for all people, Nixon was hard pressed for a solution to improve America's economic position. And what a simple solution it was! He would simply change the international monetary system! Voila! As the French would say, for it was the French who came knocking on the New York FED's gold window in 1971, demanding gold for their excess dollar *reserves*. Since there was no gold to be had, the solution was simple. Declare bankruptcy, close the gold window, and end the backing of the dollar with gold, making it a *fiat* currency. The dollar was no longer *as good as gold*.

What is a fiat currency you might ask? According to The Merriam-Webster dictionary (2019), a fiat currency is a paper currency issued by a government as legal tender, which is not convertible into coin. As noted in earlier chapters, the dollar was considered *good as gold* up to this point, but with gold no longer backing it, and the conversion ratios of all other international currencies tied to it, how would the international trading system continue to operate? Simple. Each currency's value would be determined by supply and demand, which in turn would be determined by whether the country carried a trade surplus or deficit, relative rates of interest rates and inflation between countries, and a host of other microeconomic and macroeconomic variables. The greater the demand for the currency, the higher it would go relative to its trading partners. If the country ran trade deficits, that is had more money leaving than coming, its currency would fall relative to those of its trading partners.

Under this *floating rate regime* fiat currencies would simply float reaching equilibrium at the point where the demand for, and supply of, each currency was met. It was economics at its simplest and an easy out for America. For now, because the dollar did not have to be backed by any tangible asset, the government, and politicians could spend without restraint. And spend they did of course. A quick review of our national debt and the time at which it went parabolic, the mid-seventies confirms this. What a party ensued, and what a hangover has followed! The numbers from U.S. Government Spending (2019) tell the story. Until 1971, America had virtually zero national debt. Beginning in 1972, the debt begins to rise dramatically and is now compounding nearly exponentially. The expected total for 2019 is $22.7 trillion dollars, and growing bigger every year. By the end of 2020, it will approach $30 trillion dollars.

This was the beginning of the end for the middle class. Not coincidentally, as noted many times in this book, wages and social mobility for the middle class stagnated since the 1970s, but earnings and wealth exploded for the top 1% of our population (Chapters 1 and 2). How did this greatest wealth transfer in U.S. history take place? A combination of factors, many of which have already been discussed.

Our economy being *financialized* by the FED and its member banks creating asset bubbles for the few at the expense of the many (middle class) is perhaps the first and most obvious reason for the demise of the middle class. The resulting inflation in assets like housing, health care, education, and goods and services leave those with earned income (wage earners) far behind economically. This combined with intensified competition with our trading partners starting in the early 1970s, along with the resulting *globalization* and *outsourcing* and destruction of unions put a well-documented *cap* on the earning power of the middle class. But there is more to this tale. Read on.

The Petro Dollar

In Chapter 30 of John Perkin's (2008) *Secret History of the American Empire* titled *King Dollar*, he begins by telling the little known story of the Petro dollar.

Perkins (2008) explained that Nixon's foreign relations team comprised of Kissinger, Shultz, and Cheney worked diligently to work out a deal with King Faisel of Saudi Arabia and head of the oil producing economic community (OPEC) to support the dollar, despite the United States being technically bankrupt. The deal was relatively simple and rapidly consummated. In return for U.S. purchases of OPEC oil, the Saudi's (and all OPEC members) agreed to recycle most of those U.S. dollars back into U.S. assets, primarily Treasury bonds, stocks, and real estate. This provided numerous advantages. First and foremost, it underpinned the dollar, preventing further currency depreciation. This in turn had the salutary effect of keeping interest rates on treasuries lower than would otherwise have been the case, and providing a prop for U.S. financial markets.

What did the Saudi's receive in return for this financial largesse? Unconditional U.S. military aid and protection in the form of military hardware and logistical support in perpetuity. The House of Saud was, and is, in continual conflict with the Wahibe's in their own country and Sunni's in Iran and elsewhere in the Mideast. The *Petro dollar* was a small price to pay to ensure the continuance of a monarchy (House of Saud) that is generally reviled in the region, with enemies on both flanks and nipping at their heels. The *House of Saud officially* took over from Britain in 1932, and was hardly legitimate. They had been installed as leaders of Saudi Arabia by the British when they departed the Middle East in the 1930s.

As noted above, the entire Middle East (OPEC members) were a key Nixon ally from the Petro dollar formation on. OPEC, in response to being beaten and humiliated by Israel in the Six Day War of 1967 deployed the oil weapon, a euphemistic moniker provided by Sadat for the 70% increase in oil prices in the early 1970s. It was OPEC's belief that America needed to be punished for their overt support of Israel. The rest is history as they say. A history most American's ignore, but integral to an understanding of why the United States remains constantly at war in the Middle East.

Effects of the Petro Dollar

The economic impact on America was catastrophic. Oil more than quadrupled between 1971 and 1974, creating oil shortages, and long lines at gas stations throughout the United States. The economy was on the verge of a 1929 style collapse.

In hindsight, we now know that the corporatocracy played an active role in the driving up of oil prices to these record highs in the 1970s. Although business and political leaders, including oil executives, feigned outrage, they were the ones responsible for helping create the economic carnage. They knew that by supporting Israel, OPEC would spend billions of dollars in joint ventures with U.S. companies in the Middle East, and that formation of the Petro dollar would help replace the gold standard, with an oil standard (the Petro dollar), and the corporatocracy knew as well, that Saudi Arabia, as *swing producer* was the lynchpin for such a standard.

In summary then, in return for U.S. military aid and support in perpetuity, the House of Saud agreed to three conditions. (a) they would invest a large portion of their Petro dollars in U.S.

government securities; (b) allow the U.S. Treasury Department to use the trillions of dollars in interest from these securities to hire U.S corporations to Westernize Saudi Arabia, and (c) maintain the price of oil within limits acceptable to the American corporations. In return, the U.S. government promised to keep the Saud family in power.

Many people scoff at the notion that the U.S. government would be involved in such nefarious activities to enrich a few shareholders and keep the Pentagon busy in the Middle East (Really???). They are simply naïve. Maintaining such a world view despite the now mountains of anecdotal, and empirical evidence that the United States is constantly conducting *covert ops* and war worldwide, is living with your head in the sand. If you simply Google P*etro dollar,* a synopsis and timeline of the Petro dollars existence is all there for anyone to read.

In short then, in exchange for American military protection and technological know-how the Saudi s, along with OPEC, would recycle dollars earned from oil sales to the United States, back into U.S. government securities and other U.S. assets. In a floating rate currency system, this demand for dollars would provide support for the dollar, and provide America with cheap oil in perpetuity. This, some would say, artificial demand for the dollar also kept U.S. interest rates lower than they would have otherwise been without OPEC's demand for U.S. government securities.

So, I hear many of you asking, what is the problem? It's a win / win as Tony Robins likes to say. What does any of this have to do with the demise of the middle class? Ponder the facts for a few moments if you will. A greater demand for dollars artificially supports the dollar and keeps U.S. domestic interest rates lower. This is good, but at what cost?

THE BEGINNING OF THE END

The U.S. taxpayer has footed the bill for one military incursion after the next in the Middle East starting with Libya, then Afghanistan, Iraq, Syria, and now Iran. What do all of these countries have in common? Their leaders all wanted to move away from the Petro dollar regime set up by Nixon and King Faisal in the early 1970s. They wanted to be paid for their oil in gold or in other currencies like the Euro, Yen, or Yuan. In short, they were tired of Western bankers, notably U.S. banks, forcing them to invest in a nation's currency and government bonds that now is the largest debtor nation in the world, the United States.

To protect dollar hegemony worldwide, we invaded and removed all of the leaders of these countries. The cost of the war in Afghanistan and Iraq alone, according to recent estimates is between $6–7 trillion dollars alone. Think of the U.S. infrastructure improvements, health care and education, and domestic programs that could have been made with all this money. Instead much of this vast amount of war profiteering went into the coffers of Blackwater and Haliburton, eventually being funneled to shareholders and overpaid executives of multinationals involved in military operations in Iraq and elsewhere like Enduring Freedom (a euphemism if ever there was) and hundreds of other overt and covert operations throughout the Middle East.

Who Pays?

The U.S. middle class ultimately pays for these military incursions in the Middle East, even though they are not taxed directly. The needed money, was created (much of it) out of thin air by the Federal Reserve. Trillions of it. Or borrowed from investors abroad (trillions more). This deficit spending ultimately creates inflation, which devalues the dollar over time, making everything from bread to bombers more expensive.

Why is it so important to bankers and politicians that the dollar be artificially inflated at all costs? Simply because it provides some United States citizens a lifestyle they could not otherwise afford, and more importantly, if the dollar were to lose its reserve status worldwide, all those profits and power realized through a strong dollar would flow to other countries. Our central bank and all of the monied interests beholding to it would realize a sharp and painful decline in their wealth and standard of living.

War Profiteering and the End Game

So, there it is. Here we go again, using American tax dollars to support a corrupt regime, the House of Saud. This is hardly anything new, that is, the CIA or its proxies using American influence and taxpayer money to oust unfriendly governments, and destroying often Democratically elected governments. All of this ostensibly to serve U.S. strategic, economic, and military objectives, with the tacit inference in the media that it's all being done for us, the American taxpayer, to preserve our envied and privileged lifestyle and cherished way of life.

That is naïve thinking. Who really benefits from toppling governments from Nicaragua to Iraq? Decade after decade? Might it be Dole Pineapple in Nicaragua and Haliburton in Iraq and their shareholders? Indeed. Who are the major beneficiaries of such political, military, social, and economic reengineering you might ask? Would it be the American taxpayer? Or the shareholders of those corporations making trillions in those faraway lands?

170

Corporations and their shareholders of course are the primary beneficiaries of such costly global misadventures. Who else benefits? That's right, the Pentagon, the military, and the myriad of companies providing *ancillary* support to the war effort too, of course. The Pentagon with its $800 billion dollar a year budget must continuously justify its existence or God forbid, shrink. The two (corporations and military) must work hand in glove. That is, corporations need *protection* (think protection racket) to set up shop, and operate, often in counties and communities openly hostile to their presence. Hence the need for the most powerful military on earth to *calm the natives*. Dick Cheney, CEO of Haliburton during the Iraq war, for example, saw the stock price of Haliburton quintuple under the Bush administration. This is typical of U.S. war profiteering, and fascism. Between 2003–2006, it's estimated Haliburton made approximately $17 billion dollars. This situation where the U.S. government works hand in glove with corporations, and the military to remain in power and wield international influence is often called fascism.

And of course, we cannot forget the bankers, especially our own central bank, and its acolytes, for *financial services* and related industries are big business. How big? Very big. About 20% of U.S. GDP, according to the Washington Post article from March 2016. That would be about $4 TRILLION dollars today. (20% * 18 trillion U.S. GDP = $3.6 trillion in 2016) (Monkey Cage, 2016).

Fascism is:

**fascism : noun. fas·cism | \ ˈfa-ˌshi-zəm also ˈfa-ˌsi- **
(The Merriam-Webster Dictionary, 2019).

Definition of Fascism

1: often capitalized: a political philosophy, movement, or regime (such as that of the Fascisti) that exalts nation and often race above the individual and that stands for a centralized autocratic government headed by a dictatorial leader, severe economic and social regimentation, and forcible suppression of opposition

2: a tendency toward or actual exercise of strong autocratic or dictatorial control early instances of army fascism and brutality. (The Merriam-Webster Dictionary, 2019)

Remember, much of the recent militarism in the Middle East and elsewhere occurs when countries express concerns about using the dollar as their reserve currency, or openly expressing the notion that they will begin trading oil internationally in currencies other than the dollar. Why would our central bank be so concerned with propping up the dollar at all costs, as the world's reserve currency? It's not complicated. If the dollar loses its reserve currency status, it will fall relative to competing currencies, the FED, its member banks, and all the other entities that gain status, power, social, and political position, and WEALTH, from an active and ongoing association with the FED, banking, and associated industries, stand to lose much, if not all of it. Remember, as Voltaire said in 1729, all paper currencies eventually return to their intrinsic value . . . zero. The FED knows this as well as anyone. Who is going to buy the dollar as a store of value when the United States is approaching $30 trillion dollars in debt as of this writing in 2020? And the debt is compounding at nearly a trillion dollars a year! (U.S. Debt Clock, 2019).

Nobody in their right mind is going to buy the currency and government securities of such a profligate nation unless they are forced to. As I write this, many countries are actively seeking alternative reserve currencies, and or buying gold and precious metals as their preferred *reserves*. Once the dollar loses its reserve currency status, and it will, the economy will begin a downward spiral, our purchasing power will evaporate, and America will go the way of Great Britain, rapidly losing its *superpower* status.

An Extraction Economy

What does all of this have to do with the well documented demise of the American middle class? The American economy has been called by many pundits and academics an. What does this mean? It means that our economy can now be looked at as a milk cow. A milk cow? Yes, a milk cow. Each teat on the cow's udder could be considered an industry or entity trying to *extract* as much from the cow as possible, without killing it. The military industrial complex, the financial services sector and banking, multinational corporations and their shareholders, and plutocrats and conservatives all, who derive a living from ensuring its continued existence, and maintaining the status quo. An extraction economy is, according to David Atkadjian (2017) in an article titled *The US is Becoming an Extraction Economy,* sums up the concept succinctly by noting that an extraction economy, is an economy that works for a few people, leaving the majority behind. An inclusion economy on the other hand, is one that works for the majority of its citizens. Extraction economies are typified by authoritarian regimes, whereas inclusion economies benefit more in the society (Atkadian, 2017).

The political system of the country is highly correlated with the degree to which the economy is an extraction economy or an inclusion economy. A study by Acemoglu and Robinson (2012), along with many other empirical findings, demonstrate that to create an inclusion economy requires an open and transparent political system and press, and largely determines whether the economy will be one of inclusion or exclusion. An autocratic political system as noted earlier, encourages exclusion, while an open, socially Democratic one encourages inclusion. These findings are consistent across cultures, religions, and countries.

When power is concentrated (in the Executive Branch for example) an extraction economy is likely the norm, while the opposite is true for an inclusion economy. Concentrated power typically leads to extraction economies where the free flow of ideas and people are rigorously discouraged, as are those economies where in the words of Geert Hofsteed, noted expert on cultures, *uncertainty avoidance* is high. That is, the culture does not readily embrace change and is controlled by an autocrat or monarchy. North Korea and much of South America exemplify this type of economy.

In other words, if the distribution of power is narrow and unconstrained, then the political institutions tend to be absolutist, as exemplified by the absolutist monarchies reigning throughout the world during much of history. Broadly distributed power on the other hand (democracy being the best example) leads to inclusion economies. What we don't tend to hear from corporate media is (a) how important democracy is to an inclusion economy and (b) how inclusion economies require reinvestment in education and most notably, people.

The middle-class taxpayer is being *milked* by a military industrial complex which saps the nations vitality while providing little in the way of value added goods or services. Our massive military is a tremendous drain on our economy, diverting public funds to foreign military misadventures, using money that might, and should go into domestic programs and infrastructure, health care, and education. Instead those monies (taxpayer dollars) are squandered in foreign lands benefiting no U.S. citizens other than those who own stocks or bonds of the multinational corporations whose bottom lines are expanded at the expense of the U.S. taxpayer. Our vaunted military is just another wealth transfer mechanism / ploy used by politicians and the wealthy to create more wealth for themselves at taxpayer expense.

The FED and the financial services sector as well, provide little in the way of value added goods and services to the real economy, unless you consider rampant speculation and pushing piles of paper from one end of the globe to another, value added. As noted throughout this book, central banking is perhaps one of the most diabolically clever wealth transfer mechanism ever created by man. By creating money out of thin air and excess liquidity to the economic system, central banks create asset bubbles, whether in real estate, stocks, or bonds, which enrich the investing class and upper 1% enormously, but just increase the cost of everything from housing to health care for the average American. This is how the rich have grown much richer, and the poor much poorer since the FEDs founding in 1913.

Thus, the rich get richer, the poor get poorer, and the middle class shrinks.

CHAPTER 11.

The Backlash Against Neoliberalism: The Rise of Neoliberalism as Economic Dogma Under Reagan and Thatcher

"I see in the near future a crisis approaching that unnerves me and causes me to tremble for the safety of my country . . . corporations have been enthroned and an era of corruption in high places will follow . . . until all wealth is aggregated in a few hands and the Republic is destroyed."

—ABRAHAM LINCOLN

Why was neoliberalism such a destructive economic model and what exactly is it you might ask? Neoliberalism, which has its roots in neoclassical economics, is defined generally as an economic and social policy model that seeks to limit protectionism (encourage free trade), open foreign markets, actively encourages privatization of state owned assts, and promotes deregulation of business, and the free unimpeded flow of capital worldwide.

During the *Reagan Revolution* in the 1980s, neoliberalism was touted as a panacea for economic revival. The nation was recovering from the gas shocks and stagflation of the 1970s and hyperinflation. Neoliberalism it was argued, would cure everything from a struggling and stagnant economy, to declining incomes and a yes, shrinking middle class. Reagan and a key economic advisor, Arthur Laffer (of the Laffer Curve or Laughter Curve) touted this economic dogma from the bully pulpit of the White House to a tired and gullible public, yearning for a change. Neoliberalism as touted by Reagan and his apostles focused on (a) deregulation of business, (b) privatization of government controlled or regulated businesses, and (c) the free, unimpeded flow of capital, goods, and services (free trade) worldwide with no constraints or capital controls between countries.

On its face, neoliberalism appeared relatively benign and innocuous. It even had some *face validity* as the statisticians say. On the margins, it had some intuitive appeal, and of course big business, multinationals, and banks were cavorting in the streets, gleeful at the prospect of a business environment with no regulations. Businessmen loved the idea of allowing them to buy and profit enormously from heretofore regulated assets in communications, airlines, savings, and loans, etc. The banking and financial services sector reveled at the thought of being able to move capital at the speed of light into and out of emerging market and G-20 economies at the touch of a button. Freeing up the business and banking sectors it was theorized by Laffer and others, would put more money into the corporate sphere, prompting the wealthy and corporations to invest their increased wealth into productive assets, increasing production, spurring employment, and thereby increasing consumption. This virtuous cycle, it was theorized, would gather momentum propelling the economy and driving GDP per capita higher. Increased earnings for corporations and the wealthy would *trickle down* like manna from heaven to the masses. It would be a win / win. The rich would get much richer, and spend more, thereby putting more people to work. So it was theorized and sold to the American public by a grade B actor from Hollywood.

In economics, there is something called the Law of Unintended Consequences, which states:

> The **law of unintended consequences**, often cited but rarely defined, is that actions of people—and especially of government—always have effects that are unanticipated or **unintended**. (The Merriam-Webster Dictionary, 2019)

Likewise, the first law of thermodynamics states that for every action there is an equal and OPPOSITE reaction. These two laws are germane to the discussion of neoliberalism because although possibly well intentioned (emphasis on *possibly*), the economic and societal ramifications of actually putting these policies into legislation and law would have very negative and unforeseen consequences, and result eventually in creating a society that was the opposite of what trickle-down and supply side economics believers originally predicted, prosperity and equal opportunity for all. (If you can believe that it was what they actually wanted!)

Did Money Ever Trickle Down?

Trickle-down economics under Reagan in the United States and Thatcher in the United Kingdom (UK), laid the groundwork for the undoing of the middle class, and provided the economic impetus for the glaring wealth divide discussed in prior chapters. It was a false paradigm, created by the wealthy, for the wealthy. Supply side economics was developed along with *trickle-down* economics to provide a patina of academic legitimacy to a collection of economic policies designed purely for the benefit of big business and the banking industry. As Bonner and Wiggin (2006) said in *Empire of Debt* regarding the state of our financialized economy then (early 1980s), that with Reagan came a message of hope and optimism to a tired and gullible public worn down by the gas crunch and stagflation of the 1970s, a public that would soon learn that the entire thing (Trickle down / Reaganomics / Supply Side) was a giant hoax, perpetrated by the well-known usual suspects, bankers, politicians, and the investing class.

Think about it. If you owned a big business or a multinational bank, what would be on your wish list? Probably (a) deregulation, (b) privatization, (c) free unimpeded flow of capital directed anywhere you wanted to invest / disinvest in the world with no regulatory oversight, and (d) the destruction of collective bargaining via union membership. Reaganomics was a dream come true for big business and the banking and Wall street cartels.

Yes indeed, it is very clear in retrospect who really benefited from *supply side* economics. It wasn't working men and women of America, that much is certain. Reagan wasted no time in privatizing and selling off state run businesses (like Russian Oligarchs after the fall of the wall), drastically reducing regulations on an often rapacious corporate sector, deregulating the savings and loan industry (S & L) leading to the savings and loan fiasco and bailout of the S & Ls via the Resolution Trust Corporation (RTC) in the late 1980s, and union busting starting with the air traffic controllers union in the early 1980s. Union members were *locked out* and scabs brought in to replace them at airports nationwide. This was the beginning of the end for unions, and not coincidentally, the middle class.

As noted in earlier chapters, collective bargaining is a prerequisite to a strong middle class, and good paying jobs. Union membership peaked between 1945 and 1975, from about 35% of the work force in 1945 to 12% today. Not coincidentally, this coincides with the dramatic and deeply troubling decline of the middle class.

Globalization and Technology-Pressure on the Middle Class

In fairness to conservative economic dogma (trickle down) and corporate myopia, the 1980s in America was a very economically turbulent time with globalization and technology exerting inexorable downward pressure on wages and prices. Competition from abroad intensified while cheap imports flooded the U.S. market. This in conjunction with the economic policies promulgated under Reagan and supply side economics, many would, and have argued, just accelerated the economic decline of the United States and the demise of the American middle class.

What is often not discussed in economic circles is the powerful political influence brought to bear since Reagan, and continuing with Bush 1 and 2, and now Trump. Remember, the Republicans were out of power basically from 1930–1980, 50 years, and for good reason with many pundits and academics blaming them for the Crash of 1929 and Great Depression. Fifty years of wandering in the wilderness like the lost tribe of Israel (it was actually only 40 years for Israelites), taught them a few lessons about economics and power, and how to keep it, at any cost. When their hero Ronald Reagan was swept into power they wasted no time in enacting their wealth friendly, antilabor agenda. And it continues to this day, nearly 40 years later. It appears to me that the right simply will not be happy until every pro-labor piece of legislation enacted since the 1930s under FDR is dismantled or destroyed completely, including but not limited to, Social Security.

In *Take This Job and Ship It* by Senator Byron Dorgan (2006), he cautions that all the social and economic gains from FDRs New Deal and an active labor movement can disappear as quickly as frost on an April morning. First written in 2006, his words are prophetic. Think of the destructive outsourcing, labor displacement, and the massive tax cuts for corporations and wealthy under Trump and his Republican predecessors..

Presciently, Senator Dorgan (2006) noted further that under FDR working men and women were empowered, and social welfare legislation passed into law like the Fair Labor Standards Act (FLSA) in 1938, which set a minimum wage—twenty five cents—and overtime requirements, both of which are under assault these days by the same conservatives who embrace out-sourcing. Under FSLA, the work week was shortened to 44 hours. It required employers to keep time and payroll records and did away with child labor. It was of course, denounced as socialism and a tremendous burden on free enterprise and an example of big government at its worst.

Republican attempts to dismantle any semblance of a social safety net is painfully obvious to this day. Conservatives, nota-bly the Republican party, attempted, and partially succeeded, in dismantling every piece of social welfare legislation enacted under the New Deal. Bush and his recent attempt at *privatizing* social security is just one of many recent examples of their avarice. President Trumps stacking of the U. S. Supreme Court with obviously conservative and partisan judges, and his massive tax breaks for the wealthy and corporations are several more recent examples of the *flowering* of neoliberalist policies, firmly planted and cultivated with care by conservatives, big business, and the religious right, starting with Reagan.

Predictably, the deregulation and privatization of business along with very loose FED monetary policies, neoliberalist economic policies, and lack of financial regulation in the 80s led to the Crash of 1987 (a 25% drop in the Dow Jones in one day), the S & L fiasco leading to the taxpayer bailout of the S & Ls (late 1980s), oligopoly (now) in most industries where only the very largest corporations can survive, the Asian Contagion and collapse of the Thai Baht (1990s) (free flow of capital UNIMPEDED across borders), the Russian Ruble, and the Mexican Peso, the rise of hedge funds like Long Term Capital Management (LTCM, 1997), the Tech Wreck of 2000, and the housing bubble of 2002–2007. More on this later.

The banking cartels (primarily United States), after *deregulation* moved into *emerging markets* like Thailand to exploit growth opportunities in economies without the economic infrastructure or government regulations required to accommodate such massive influxes of capital. Loans were made in local currency by these banking cartels with repayment due in dollars. When the local currency (Baht) depreciated relative to the dollar because of persistent trade imbalances, it became more and more expensive for the local businesses to pay these loans back in dollars, and much of the foreign direct investment (FDI-Western banks) fled the country, exacerbating and accelerating the decline of the Baht. Banks pulled up stakes and fled, leaving the Thai companies bankrupted and much of the population impoverished. This same scenario was played out in Russia after the *Wall* came down, in Mexico during Clinton's presidency, and many other countries. The collapse of these currencies was primarily the result of the rapid and unimpeded inflow of capital and easy borrowing terms from *deregulated* American banks that had moved into the country. Such is part of the legacy of Neoliberalism.

Free Trade?

With the advent of the Internet and globalization the U.S. populace was persuaded by Reagan and his *acolytes* that deregulation, privatization, and the free flow of capital was absolutely necessary for the United States to survive economically. We had to throw open our doors to *free trade*. Oligopoly (4–5 firms dominating each industry) had to be encouraged to compete globally it was argued, and *free trade* was required to compete with the G-8. This specious argument (the need for a few dominant firms in each industry) became the conservative mantra, and touted by the conservative right, and even President Clinton (passing NAFTA as an economic cure all. Corporations, now rule the world, not governments. *Free trade* was in the interest of multinational corporations, not working Americans. This was plain long before passage of NAFTA, and now has become glaringly obvious, even to the most myopic among us. Ross Perot warned us on national TV BEFORE passage of NAFTA exactly what would happen. It was not difficult for anyone with any business sense to see. As Ross Perot said, we'd hear a "giant sucking sound" emanating from Mexico, which would swallow America's manufacturing base, after 's NAFTA passage, and very shortly thereafter, Mexico did indeed, swallow a vast portion of America's manufacturing base.

As Cornelius Vanderbilt (1882) one of the plutocrats of the Gilded Age, once snorted, "The public be damned. I am working for my shareholders." Vanderbilt's sentiment is alive and well, and corporations have only gotten larger and more powerful. This snippet summarizes, in my opinion, the opinion of the right in our country today. The more things change, the more they stay the same.

The situation in American capitalism (oligopoly actually) is now incredibly lopsided with corporations and billionaires wielding far more power and wealth, relatively speaking, than Vanderbilt ever did. Some recent facts on multinational to ponder: Amazingly, of the world's largest 100 economies, 51 are global corporations while 49 are countries (Anonimo, 2008).

Fact: With $258 billion in sales in 2005, Wal Mart is economically more powerful than 161 countries (Out of 182). That is an enormous amount of power and it is wielded every day by shipping jobs overseas.

Senator Dorgan (2006) summarized his take on *deregulation* and free trade emphatically by concluding that trade is hardly free when our workers and small businesses are expected to compete with often exploited labor, and corrupt businesses in third world countries that could care less about environmental and human degradation, that often runs rampant in those countries.

The virtues of free trade, a mainstay of neoliberalist theory, is usually touted by those with the most to gain from so called free trade, as we all know now. The argument, for free trade based on David Ricardo's (1817) theory of comparative advantage and Adam Smith's (1776) *Wealth of Nations* are clear, if not often disingenuous. Free trade makes all countries and people better off it is argued. These arguments have intuitive appeal, but again are not really thought through or closely scrutinized in our modern world. Trade is often a zero sum game. That is, for every winner, there is often a loser (like the stock market) There is not an equal distribution of benefits to all parties as is so often argued. The rise of a middle class in China coincides with the decline of one in America.

As Dan Rodrik (2011) pointed out in *The Globalization Paradox*, there are winners and clear losers from free trade. Those economic sectors that are most viable and have a competitive advantage against trading partners are likely to benefit from free trade while those employed in shrinking sectors of the economy will take an economic hit and are generally forced into a lower lifestyle. When a manufacturing job is outsourced for example, those employed in manufacturing generally suffer a permanent fall in income.

Trade, as noted by Rodrik (2011), by its nature, has often subjective socio-economic advantages and disadvantages, causing some business activities to contract and others to expand which is essential if the full benefits from trade are to be realized. If gains from trade are to be realized those groups whose economic fortunes are tied to shrinking sectors will necessarily take a hit (think steel, textiles, and manufacturing here in the United States). Wage and job losses from trade are not transitory for those affected, but usually permanent, with the losers to globalization having to often settle for lower paying jobs. These socio-economic losses by labor to free trade are usually permanent.

Free trade, a centerpiece of conservative, neoliberalist, trickle down dogma, is not free, and it has been an obvious and significant factor in the decline of the middle class for decades. Ricardo and Smith did not live in the era of high speed Internet, electronic funds transfer, and worldwide labor mobility. Their theories are quaint, but destructive, anachronisms. Destructive, because they are often used by the right to provide a patina of academic legitimacy to ridiculous economic arguments. One empirical study after another demonstrates that *free trade* is often not free, and seldom benefits all parties or countries at the same rate, or in the same economic manner.

The conservative arguments for unfettered trade swirling around the *free trade* debate are at best suspect, at worst totally disingenuous. It cannot ever be made entirely clear who the primary beneficiaries of trade are. Yes, Americans enjoy cheap goods made in China but are prices falling faster than the wages of the displaced manufacturing worker? What is clear, very clear, is that the American middle class is foundering since the advent of neoliberal economic policies and passage of NAFTA. The statistics tell the story, and are there for anyone to see. Generally speaking **The reality is, no pain, no gain.**

As can be seen from the points made above, and mountains of empirical evidence, in reality, *free trade* may well be a zero sum game. That is, for every winner in free trade, there is a loser. This is certainly what we have witnessed in the United States since the *Reagan Revolution*. As I've noted many times in previous chapters, it is more often than not that those with the most to gain financially push a free trade agenda. The anecdotal, and much empirical evidence suggests that *gains* from trade are ephemeral and short lived for the majority of Americans. The economic *adjustments* required, a euphemism for job disintegration in many sectors of the economy, destroys lives and communities, lowers real incomes, and hollows out huge swaths of the productive capacity (manufacturing) of our economy.

Who would those organizations and individuals be that benefit the most from trade, that push the free trade agenda claiming its good for us all? After all exports are less than 15% of U.S. GDP, so how many average Americans actually benefit? Multinational corporations and their shareholders primarily. This ugly truth is seldom discussed in economics classes or society in general. In fact, there is seldom any national debate on the issue of free trade, period. Legislation favorable to those that gain the most from free trade is quietly passed by the U.S. Congress (Republican sponsored legislation), and nursed through the legislative process to final enshrinement in law, by the usual suspects, big business, the wealthy, and lobbyists that often write the legislation themselves. And, of course, corrupted politicians, often aided and abetted by a suspect U.S. Supreme Court and corrupted financial services sector.

In the final analysis, it is these neoliberalist economic, fiscal, monetary, and trade policies promulgated and shepherded through the U.S. Congress, starting with Reagan, that have, very intentionally, I would argue, gutted the middle class.

CHAPTER 12.
The Military Industrial Complex

"This conjunction of an immense military establishment and a large arms industry is new in the American experience. The total influence — economic, political, even spiritual — is felt in every city, every statehouse, every office of the federal government. We recognize the imperative need for this development. Yet we must not fail to comprehend its grave implications. Our toil, resources and livelihood are all involved; so is the very structure of our society."

—DWIGHT EISENHOWER (1961)

So dear reader, I suspect you ask why I might have a chapter in a book devoted to understanding the destruction of the middle class discussing the military industrial complex? What is the connection between the growth in defense spending, and the destruction of the middle class? In its simplest the formula for the linkages between the inexorable rise of the Pentagon since the beginning of the Cold War (1950s) and current veneration of the military and all who *serve* would look something like this.

Increased military footprint abroad (70 countries that we

know of) and too many wars to count in my lifetime = increased taxes or money printing by the FED to enable **deficit spending = crowding out of domestic programs and higher inflation = lower real and discretionary incomes for the middle class = lower standard of living.**

Let me first discuss the often reckless, and always expensive rise of military adventurism and its impact on government spending and the private sector, and finally the negative impact such a militarized economy has on the middle class.

One of the characteristics of empire is veneration, and elevation of the military caste. This is a common denominator in all empires and military and fascist states from ancient Rome to Hitler's Germany, to yes, Trump's America. One does not need to look any further than an NFL football game to see the nationalistic fervor and xenophobia that now grips much of America. Military men and women on the field before the game and often at halftime as well. When did this start?

Answer: recently. The national anthem is one thing, but military on the field?

Ill-advised military adventurism, it seems, is built into America's genetic code now. The military industrial complex that Eisenhower warned us about in his farewell address is pervasive, influential, and VERY expensive. At last count, the Pentagon's budget for 2019 was somewhere between $800 and $900 BILLION dollars, that we know of. The IRS collected $3.5 trillion dollars in taxes in 2018. (SOI Tax Facts, 2020). That means our military budget is about a quarter to a third of all tax revenues.(Even the Pentagon doesn't know how much they spend).

As noted in *Empire of Debt*, Bonner and Wiggin (2006) misplaced patriotism, nationalism, and xenophobia are some of the things that makes empires so attractive to politicians, bankers, and the military. Once underway, illegally or not, wars assume a life of their own, with little domestic resistance. The nation sacrifices everything to the Joint Chiefs of Staff, including the domestic liberties for which these wars are allegedly fought.

There has been no shortage of war in my lifetime. It seems every president must have his war. In the 1950s, it was Korea, the 1960s and 1970s, Vietnam, the 1980s, various *mini* wars in South America, Central America, and Europe, and lately of course, the Middle East.

Then came September 11th, 2001 and we were at war again, and how. Better still, this time against an illusory enemy called terrorism, with President Bush then announcing a War on Terror. No one bothered to inform President Bush that a nation cannot wage a war against a TACTIC. Wars are supposedly ideological. There is a good guy, think capitalism and bad guy, think communism. The IDEOLOGICAL lines are clearly drawn. But a War on Terror is truly a Pentagon dream come true, and a politician's party! A party that never ends. Terror, an amorphous and subjective enemy if ever there was, can be used in nearly any situation to justify military incursions, covert ops, or outright war. How convenient. Let's not forget that every military on earth, including the United States, uses terror (think Guantanamo Bay) at one time or another, with the popular adage being that one man's terrorist is another man's freedom fighter. The war on terror is very convenient for governments, military, and politicians in general, for terror can be defined almost any way that is expedient for the moment, and ensures active and ongoing military actions all over the world, with of course, increased military spending in perpetuity.

Bonner and Wiggin (2006) wryly observed in *Empire of*

Debt, how and why the United States is kept on a perpetual war footing, and why there is a seemingly endless, misguided, and disingenuous public policy crafted decade-after-decade by those that benefit from increased military spending of imminent threat to our national security through the application of external force is pure nonsense.

War profiteering is big business obviously to keep the business going (Pentagon), fear of the enemy and terrorism must be continuously stoked by the nation's propaganda machine. Senator Flanders elaborated in 1951, that spreading and stoking fear in the American populace is deliberate and unending. Keeping America in a perpetual state of fear of course ensures the State Department, the Pentagon, and military's continued existence. Another center from which fear is spread, according to Senator Flanders is the State Department. This leaves diplomacy playing second fiddle behind the massive war machine called the American military. A hammer is now used (military), a very blunt force, when a scalpel (diplomacy) would work better, and more cheaply. But of course, when the only tool you have is a hammer, every potential looks like a nail.

This scenario of fear mongering and war profiteering, from countless and endless wars, has been well documented in prior chapters and in many other places. It is sad to me as a citizen that my fellow countrymen seem to fall for this tired ruse decade-after-decade, so that the Pentagon may continue increasing their budget year-after-year, while our domestic infrastructure crumbles and faith in our democracy and the political process inexorably wane. The *ligatures* that bind us as Fukyama (2000) observed in *The Great Disruption*, tear at the social fabric as more and more resources are consumed by the military. Domestic priorities, like improving infrastructure are left unattended, and faith in our institutions and those that run them deteriorate.

As eruditely said in *Empire of Debt*, empires, from Rome to Turkey to America, must, and do, put their faith in arms, while collective fear of the enemy becomes a patriotic obsession. This collective fear is stronger than any political party.

Ultimately, when the country is increasingly and persistently on a war footing (such as the United States), there is still Congressional debate regarding the allocation of our tax dollars (borrowed dollars), for war material and munitions, but debate becomes acrimonious and bitter. Even though many can see the clear drift of the country towards war and fascism, we feel powerless to stop it. Congress becomes increasingly dysfunctional and marginalized, and executive power becomes increasingly concentrated. Ultimately, the Executive Branch does what it likes because it controls the enforcement end of the state, the military.

Does this not remind of our current situation on Capitol Hill and in the country at large? Eerily accurate in describing the current day state of affairs in our politics, military, and government institutions. Slowly but surely, we creep towards fascism as the economic pie shrinks and the middle class fades into obscurity.

Fascism?

Does economic hardship, corporatocracy, and rampant militarism all equal rising fascism in the United States? A fascinating cross cultural study on fascism was done by Britt (2003) in which common denominators of fascist states were cataloged. He did an excellent and scholarly work in dissecting and categorizing common threads that linked all of them (fascist regimes) in patterns of national behavior and abuses of power. Some of these common denominators found in fascist and quasi-fascist regimes are listed below and often cited in the extant literature as being early warning signs of fascism. I am not alone in my concern for the relatively recent fascist drift of the country. Madeleine Albright (2018), Secretary of State under President Clinton, recently wrote a book titled *Fascism: A Warning*, in which she warns us all about the fascist drift of the country in politics, social norms, increasing militaristic and nationalistic fervor, and fraudulent elections and rampant sexism, all early warning signs of fascism.

Early Warning Signs of Fascism

I like to discuss with my friends and students what are called the 14 points of fascism. Some of these include (a) powerful and continuing nationalism, (b) obsession with national security (Homeland Security), (c) identifying of enemies / scapegoats as a unifying cause (War on Terror), (d) Supremacy of the military, (e) rampant cronyism and corruption, (f) intertwined religion and government, and (g) fraudulent elections and sexism.

Does powerful nationalism and militarism seem familiar to you? How about disdain for human rights? Rampant sexism and fraudulent elections? Remind you of anything?

And so on . . . we have seen every one of the items on this list accelerate over the last two decades from crony capitalism to fraudulent elections, with the master accelerator of these trends being the current occupant of the White House. Need I say more?

Most disturbingly, war and empire are expensive, and are often the excuse to take away the very liberties for which we have fought so hard since the country's inception, and for which so many have died. As Vidal (2002) noted in *Perpetual War for Perpetual Peace*, Osama Bin Laden, though dead, was entirely successful in his strategy to entangle us seemingly forever in the Middle East, bankrupt us as a nation, and severely curtail our civil liberties here at home. We now have an Orwellian sounding Homeland Security, a huge and very expensive bureaucracy annually sucking down massive amounts of tax dollars, coupled with the Anti-Terrorism Act of 1996, giving the FBI and CIA heretofore unheard of powers as they relate to wiretapping, illegal search and seizure, and surveillance.

As noted earlier, politicians love to use war as a pretense for curtailing liberties at home, and expanding military adventurism abroad. This tactic of creating a war to obfuscate unlawful domestic intrusions, wiretapping, and deportations is straight out of a very old playbook. Presidents have been using war since the founding of this Republic to exercise influence, obfuscate unpleasant domestic realities and eviscerate our civil liberties.

Defense spending in 2015, according to the National Priorities Project, was $598 billion dollars (now, 2020- $800 billion) or 54% of all government discretionary spending. Discretionary spending that year was $1.1 trillion dollars (National Priorities Project, 2015). This is outrageous and unsustainable. Our annual budget deficits are close to $1 trillion dollars a year. Where does the money come from? Out of thin air? Oftentimes yes.

Clearly, we built our economic might and worldwide dominance after World War II by making ourselves the world's reserve currency and largest military on earth. As noted earlier, at that point the United States controlled nearly 75% of world GDP.

Vidal (2002) when explaining the reason for perpetuating the big scare of the *red menace* during the Cold War was obvious. To benefit the few (military industrial complex) at the expense of the many. How, you might ask? By making the U.S. the world's policeman after WWII and to maintain the newfound prosperity after the war, they (the usual suspects) would create an arms races with John Foster Dulles the high priest of the movement. As Dulles (1953) noted at the time, it would be ENORMOUSLY profitable AND we would win, because the Russians would go broke first. A win / win. The ending of the race, even from the beginning (early 1950s) as Dulles understood, was never in doubt. We could and would, being the world's reserve currency, simply outspend them, for as you now know, we can create as much of it (money) as we want with a little help from the FED and a touch of a button. It was not Reagan who brought down the Wall, it was unbridled government spending with money created by the FED that ended the Cold War.

One does not have to be a rocket scientist or an Albert Einstein to figure out how this massive defense spending drains our economy, and bleeds the nation, while claiming to protect it, and slowly, but very surely, kills the middle class. As Vidal (2004) noted, Einstein understood the nature of the military rip off, who said at the time that the men with the real power in the country never had any intention of ending the Cold War (Vidal, 2004). War, was then and is now, much too profitable to all involved in its creation and perpetuation.

Nearly 70 years later after Dulles said this, we are still at it. *Defense* spending eats an enormous amount of the budget and puts the country deeper and deeper into debt, year-after-year, decade-after-decade.

Crowding Out

Economists use a term *crowding out* which is a euphemism for government borrowing taking virtually all available domestic savings for their overt and covert operating accounts. Domestic savings and foreign borrowings are limited in supply, and at some point the availability of funds to run the government, empire and associated covert operations is simply not enough. Thus, the need to sell drugs to buy guns for the *contras* in Nicaragua (for example), a U.S. backed fighting force attempting to depose a duly elected government (History, 2019).

What gets *crowded out* by government borrowing for wars abroad? Domestic programs from food stamps to Planned Parenthood, childhood education programs like Head Start, and food banks for the poor, are just a few of the myriad of programs whose funding is cut relentlessly by Republicans (generally), so that we can spend more on the military. Why just last year President Trump increased military spending by 10%. Who paid for it? Cuts in badly needed public programs, health care, and education paid for it, and money created out of thin air by the FED.

These endless wars against communism, terrorism, drugs, and the enemy or ideology du jour, is simply, fought and paid for on borrowed dollars, are extraordinarily expensive. According to the Congressional Budget Office (CBO), government outlays exceeded 2018 receipts by over $700 billion dollars (CBO, 2018), giving us a nearly $800 billion dollar deficit in that year.

Defense

All areas of defense spending were up in 2018. This is not much different than prior years and decades. The defense budget is sacrosanct apparently, an unregulated, unbridled entity that now eats up nearly a third of every tax dollar the U.S. government collects (over 50% of discretionary spending). Citizens objecting to such obscene, often profligate spending on the part of our military, are immediately marginalized, or ridiculed by conservatives as unpatriotic. Not surprisingly, the majority of military contractors, beltway bandits, and those providing ancillary services to the military, as well as much of the military itself are and of course vote, Republican (Newport, 2009). Remember Samuel Johnson (1774) remarked, "Patriotism is the last bastion of the scoundrel" (p. 56).

Hard working, tax paying citizens who have paid into social security for 40–50 years meanwhile are labeled leeches by Fox and Friends, and the monies they have saved all their lives for retirement (Social Security), are disdainfully labeled *entitlements* by those same conservatives, and their minions, who have profited from this bloated government entity (Pentagon) since the Cold War.

Desperately needed money for the nation's infrastructure, health care, childcare, literacy, education, and a myriad of other domestic programs are all put on hold while the spending in and for the questionable military actions throughout the Middle East continues unabated. The costs of just the wars in Iraq and Afghanistan is estimated at between $7 and $8 trillion dollars (Brown, 2017).

As Vidal (2002) so eloquently, if not a bit derisively noted in the last chapter of *Perpetual War for Perpetual Peace*, it is time to curb the Pentagon warlords and spend the money for war on our own domestic infrastructure. The relentless, usually compulsive interference in the affairs of often democratic governments to sustain military spending, and the position power of the Joint Chiefs of Staff, and the military, has become obviously unsustainable. Endless wars make much of the world our bitter enemies and have proven to be, and are generally, pointless, a mindless waste of money. Nearly always.

How does all this military spending harm the middle class? Notably, while indeed providing America's *best and brightest* an avenue towards financial stability, and thus increasing employment, all this spending must be paid for out of the public purse.

Increasing debt = increased money = increased inflation

erodes the purchasing power of the dollar and lowers the standard of living for all of us, while driving prices for health care, education, and goods and services, ever and inexorably higher. As seen in in prior chapters, this military spending is done, much of it, on borrowed money. This compounds our already enormous national debt ($30 trillion) the interest of which is now the third largest item in the U.S. budget, behind Social Security and *defense.*

Clearly, the system as currently configured, is not sustainable. Something must give and will, and it will not be the investing class or the top 1%. It will be the middle class shouldering the increased military spending to come.

CHAPTER 13.
Speculation and Debt vs. Real Economic Growth

The first panacea for a mismanaged nation is inflation of the currency; the second is war. Both bring a temporary prosperity; both bring a permanent ruin. Both are the refuge of political and economic opportunists.

—ERNEST HEMINGWAY

A big part of the problem(s) facing the middle class stems from the misguided notions, promulgated by politicians like Reagan, Bush (father and son), and Trump, and central bankers including but hardly limited to, Greenspan and Bernanke, and Madison Avenue and K street, is the specious idea that a consumption based economy built on debt and consumption, is preferable to an economy built on savings and investment and manufacturing. Although consumption is a lot more fun than saving, which is delayed gratification, there are numerous reasons why such an economy, that is, one based mostly on consumption, cannot work for its citizens in the longer run.

But before delving into the somewhat esoteric social, economic and political ramifications of a debt and consumption society vs. a savings and investment economy, let's pause and simply ask, why would bankers, politicians, businesspeople, and Madison Avenue be interested in the former over the latter? If you follow this line of questioning, it becomes readily apparent why politicians, bankers, and businesspeople generally favor a debt and consumption economic model over a savings and investment economic model. **Follow the money!** Why following and perpetuating this consumption and debt based economic model is so dangerous to the country generally, and the middle class in particular, I'll talk about this in the following pages.

As demonstrated in Chapters 1 and 2, in the United States we have a fractional reserve banking system. In such a system, money is created when a loan (your debt) is created by a bank, and when a debt is created that new debt can compound nine times in the banking system. The initial debt becomes reserves for subsequent banks that can now make loans from what was basically a bookkeeping entry on the original banker's general ledger. In other words, for each new dollar of debt created, the money supply can magically grow nine fold with a 10% reserve requirement. Bankers love this system! Of course! They can make loans without having 90% of what they are lending as *reserves*. That is, create money out of thin air. And of course, they *earn* (what a misnomer for the *money* was never theirs in the first place) interest on the difference between what the money costs them, and what they charge the borrower. This is called the net interest margin. The higher the net interest margin, the more money the bank earns from money that was seldom theirs in the first place.

It is obviously in the banker's interest to push debt, and push debt they do. U.S. total household debt has grown from $17 billion in 1929 when the debt to GDP ratio was 16% to $22.7 trillion dollars and 108% debt to GDP ratio in 2019. That is, our national debt has gone from $29 billion dollars in 1929 to nearly $23 TRILLION today (Amadeo, 2020).

This is a staggering amount of money so one must ask *why*. That is, why the propensity in the United States to consume rather than save? Could it be that most Americans understand intuitively or intellectually, that taking on debt makes tremendous sense when you can pay it back years later in deflated dollars? Inflation remember, is an automatic by product of a fractional reserve system, and inflation is a debtors best friend, and a savers worst enemy. Since inflation is built into such a system consumers, businesses, and government are actually acting rationally by taking out as much long term debt at low locked in low interest rates, as they can. Yes, of course they do. It can be paid back in *cheaper* dollars.

Most advanced economies like the United States are consumption based economies. What makes the United States different is the rapidity with which this *consumption* has grown. As noted in an article, *Don't Expect Consumer Spending to Be the Engine of Economic Growth It Once Was*, the author notes that consumer spending (PCE) has grown at approximately 3.5% in the quarter century prior to 2007 while net exports, investment, and government spending grew at only 1.7%.

Notably, personal consumption (PCE / consumption) contributed 81.3% to the overall economy, while the other major components that measure economic activity, investment, government spending, and net exports contributed only 18.7% to GDP. The takeaway? Consumer spending is the dominant driver of the U.S. economy, and MUST be stoked, by any and all means possible. Thus, the relentless onslaught by banks,

Madison Avenue, politicians, and financial services to encourage Americans to consume, consume, consume rather than save, save, save.

Debt and Consumption and the Middle Class

As noted in prior chapters, the *wealth effect* was, and is created deliberately by Western central bankers in their misguided attempts to make consumers *feel* wealthier, and therefore, spend (consume) more, for without ever expanding debt creation and *consumption,* the economy will stall, as will corporate and banking profits. This is why a cadre of economists from the *Chicago School,* along with politicians like Dick Cheney (Deficits don't matter Cheney), and central bankers like *Easy* Alan Greenspan, encourage debt and consumption. It's patriotic to consume! Remember George Bush urging Americans to go out and "spend after 9/11?" A central banker's worst fear is deflation (lack of loan growth). Why? Because without a continuous expansion of *consumption* corporate and bank profits stall, and prices for goods and services might actually fall, creating a deflation that is usually very difficult to reverse. Secondly, the government does not know how to, and cannot tax deflation. That is, if prices fall by 10%, they simply do not have the tools to measure how it can be taxed. Rising incomes and prices are no problem of course. They just tax you more!

Why are such consumption and debt arguments specious, and detrimental to the working poor, the middle class, and American society in general? Because

debt = slavery

and indentured servitude. Real wealth, as most economist

are taught in school, is created through savings being reinvested in the productive capacity of the economy. In business and accounting this amount of money left after paying all expenses and dividends, is called retained earnings, earnings available to be retained by the business for investments in property, plant, and equipment, inventory etc., to grow the business.

It is no different for a country. For a country to truly grow wealthy, there must be savings, reinvested into the country's infrastructure, people, and businesses that have a comparative advantage, for the country to maintain a competitive advantage against its trading partners. A country cannot borrow its way to prosperity. Investments in long-term assets, and notably, people, is required. Our major trading partners know this. Most of them have national health care systems, free education, and cradle to grave security, and social safety nets which not only make them more productive economies, but much better places to live and work. Governments invest in their people because most governments know people are their biggest asset (except the United States apparently) and to prosper and compete, they must have health, education, and a secure home life and retirement.

The culture of consumption and debt perpetuated by the banking sector, politicians, and businesses in the United States, spawns speculation and asset bubbles, encourages debt, and ultimately increases poverty because there are no *savings* being generated by the middle and lower classes to invest in the assets that can move them into the middle class (stocks, bonds, housing etc.) Infrastructure degrades, money moves offshore, and the divisions between the haves and have nots increase. Not coincidentally, Americans have one of the lowest savings rates of all advanced economies, about 2.4% in 2017 vs. 8% in 1960

(Szmigiera, 2019). In addition, this economic model is not fair, or more importantly, sustainable, without one bust after the next. Simply put, the FED can do nothing else other than expand the money supply/banking reserves, which if not loaned out by banks for productive, value added economic activities, find their way into asset classes like real estate, stocks, and bonds, creating asset bubbles which are economic catastrophes when they collapse, as they do, and must. These bubbles cannot grow exponentially for debt service cannot keep up with the growing debt burden forever.

Our top five major competitors save at much higher rates, According to *Something 20 Finance*, the United States came in 16th out of 28 countries in savings rates of disposable income. The five countries with the highest savings rates? France (15.4%) (also the most productive of the G-7-coincidence?); Australia (11.1%), Germany (9.9%), Spain (9.1%), and the UK (5.8%) (Miller, 2019).

These are depressing statistics and a big reason for our falling further and further behind our major trading partners, socially, economically, and financially. We have virtually no domestic savings to invest back into our own country, mainly because most of our tax dollars and savings go into nonproductive, non-value-added pursuits like financial speculation and war. And most Americans, simply have no money to save at the end of the day. Many, 78%, live paycheck to paycheck (*Forbes*, 2019).

The middle class falls further and further behind, deeper and deeper in debt, trying to maintain a middle class lifestyle, which of course, becomes increasingly difficult under these circum-stances. As demonstrated earlier in this book, the theory that popularized and gave a patina of academic legitimacy to cutting taxes on big corporations and the wealthy was *trickle-down* aka, supply side economics, which, as we all know now, was a false argument born in mendacity and steeped in greed. It was then, and is now, nothing more than a flimsy sham of a reason to give money to those who don't need it, corporations, and billionaires. Who paid for the most recent giveaway by Trump et al. ? The middle class, of course. Even the billionaires in their right minds, those with any sense of social responsibility at all, have admitted as much publicly. Bill Gates said of the Trump tax cuts, "wealthy individuals such as himself should be made to pay substantially higher taxes" (LA Times, 2020, p. 2).

Deliberately encouraging consumption and debt while simultaneously cutting social spending, and economically hammering the most vulnerable among us, to provide tax cuts to corporations and the wealthy, in the long run has been, and is, disastrous social and economic policy. It simply accelerates social disintegration, stifles upward social mobility, and financially destroys entire swaths of the American public, notably, the middle class.

Social mobility, income inequality, and intergenerational earnings are highly correlated. As noted many times prior in this book, upward social and economic mobility in the United States. have become much harder in just the last 20 years. Can you hear the social fabric ripping? The top 10%, as in Argentina and Brazil, are just fine and will remain so. It's the rest of us, the bottom 90% who will suffer as the economic pie continues to shrink.

CHAPTER 14.

Towards a Brighter Future: Is a Return to Sustainable Growth Possible?

The trouble with the world is that the stupid are cocksure, and the intelligent are full of doubt.

—BERTRAND RUSSELL

What struck me most about the recent presidential elections in 2016 was the obvious and profound polarization of the American electorate. Running as an independent candidate, you had Bernie Sanders, an avowed Democratic Socialist who won 22 states in the primaries, and on the Democratic ticket you had Hillary Clinton, a lightning rod for the right touting universal health care coverage since the 1990s. On the Republican side was the astonishing Donald Trump, a businessman of mediocre achievements and very questionable moral fiber, who had beaten 16 rivals running on an essentially isolationist "make America Great Again" platform. Mr. Trump has the extraordinarily dubious talent of galvanizing those left behind by outsourcing and globalization by appealing to their visceral, often subconscious social and economic fears, and weaponizing them. In this regard, he is much like all great transformational leaders like Kennedy, Gandhi, King, and Obama. Disturbingly, these charismatic qualities are also the hallmarks of many fascists, neo fascists, and dictators like Stalin, Hitler, Franco, and Mussolini. In this latter case, the ability to distill and weaponize collective fear of change, economic demise, or social instability is one of President Trump's finest talents.

The irony of a billionaire businessman purportedly seeking to lift the working men and women of America up and out of their downward economic spiral leaves me incredulous. I find it incredibly ironic. What irony you ask?

Think about it. The untenable economic situation the United States finds itself in today has its roots in neoliberalist and monetary and fiscal policies designed and put into law (or the tax code) by those very elites in the 1980s who benefited the most from those policies, like Donald Trump and The Fortune 500. The tax cuts for the wealthy and multinational corporations, in the 1980s, part of the economic dogma of *Reaganomics* aka, *trickle-down economics*, along with the gutting of financial regulations and *privatization* and *deregulation* all combined in a toxic mix to benefit the extraordinarily wealthy few, at the expense of the many left behind by globalization and outsourcing, as demonstrated in this book in earlier chapters.

And yet, it is this constituency, the middle lower and lower class, that was a big reason for President Trump's rise to power (kind of like Hitler's Germany). This curious, and to me, astonishing event seems to occur decade-after-decade. That is, those most harmed by globalization and outsourcing voting the very people into office, and keeping them there, that were, and are responsible for the economic and social downward spiral that many of them find themselves in. It is a conundrum, within an enigma, on the horns of a dilemma that never ceases to amaze me. These individuals vote against their own economic self-interest decade-after-decade. Will these displaced manufacturing and middle- income workers never learn?

What we have been witnessing lately in our politics (2016–2020) in my opinion is a backlash against neoliberalism, globalization, and free trade. These economically, and socially damaging fiscal, monetary, and trade policies promulgated since the 1980s provided impetus for movements on the right and left, attempting to restore social fairness and economic justice for all back into our democracy. This was the appeal of Donald Trump who ran on an isolationist (build the Wall!) and pro worker (supposedly) platform. The recent retaking of the U.S. Congress by Democrats who now have a majority, and is the most diverse Congress ever with many women and minorities, is a cause for hope and optimism in my opinion.

What are some things we can do as a country to curb the militarism, crony capitalism, and xenophobia that the country is currently afflicted with? And stop the destruction of the middle class?

1. Repeal Citizens United

One of the first items on the agenda must be the repeal of the U.S. Supreme Court ruling, *Citizens United,* a euphemistic title if ever there was, for legislation that is perhaps the most dangerous threat to our would be *democracy*. This legislation granting corporations the same rights as individuals and allowing for unlimited and anonymous campaign contributions by corporations and political action committees (PACs) is a pox on our house, a cancer that must be excised if we hope to survive as a democracy.

Our democracy has been steadily undermined, unduly influenced, and pervasively corrupted by the increasing, and ever present corporate interests on K. Street, and the U.S. Congress, growing from a trickle in the 1970s to a torrent of corporate campaign contributions today, with the passage of the euphemistically titled Citizens United ruling from the U.S. Supreme Court.

As Reich (2006) noted in *Supercapitalism*, political contributions to those seeking political office increased significantly after the 1970s (beginning with Reagan) and have mushroomed after the U.S. Supreme Court Ruling Citizens United passed in 2010. It has been and is increasingly obvious that Big Business is running the show on Capitol Hill. Trump's recent tax giveaway of hundreds of billions to big business and the uber wealthy and military is testimony to the venality of our current political system and the mendacity of our politicians. The solution? Publicly funded elections with a spending cap and total transparency of campaign funding, along with term limits.

2. Fair Trade Not Free Trade

Another pressing issue is that of fair trade, not *free trade* which is paramount to reversing the economic decline of the United States where the propaganda machines of big business and our paid for politicians have relentlessly sold the untruth to the public that free trade benefits all of us. This must end. For better or ill, globalization is with us to stay. Economies have become increasingly integrated, and the world has become a much smaller place, thanks to technology and FedEx. To believe that we can bring back jobs in industries that we no longer have a comparative or competitive advantage in is naïve, in my opinion. What we can do as Senator Dorgan (2006) pointed out in his book, *Take This Job and Ship It*, is to negotiate trade terms more favorable to the United States. He noted that we need to stop accepting the happy talk and propaganda touted by economic elites that free trade is good for us (as in United States). For the most part, free trade works against our economy, not for it.

Senator Dorgan and a plethora of other well-known businessmen, Congressmen, and political and economic pundits, have discussed for decades the demise of the American middle class and what poor fiscal, monetary, and trade policies have to do with our nation's steady decline into third world status. As Senator Dorgan (2006) noted however, because of the partisanship and acrimony between political parties, stoked by the usual suspects, and the major news organizations, has made compromise impossible, and any thoughtful, meaningful debate between the parties, impossible.

Much of what we hear about the touted benefits of free trade is of course pure propaganda, pushed resolutely and relentlessly by the editorial pages of the Wall Street Journal, The Washington Post, and New York Times along with think conservative think tanks like the Heritage Foundation, all of whom seldom, if ever, offer a contrary viewpoint. Those pushing a free trade agenda, corporate America, and multinationals, stand to gain the most from free trade, not the American middle class. Senator Dorgan merely confirms what anyone taking an honest look at American trade policy since 1980 must conclude, U.S. multinationals and banks create the trade strategy to outsource American manufacturing to low wage countries so they and their shareholders can earn still larger profits. One needs to ask, why the relentless push for free trade and more importantly who is selling it? Who are the lobbyists? The usual suspects of course.

Things have just continued to worsen, unabated since the writing of his book in 2006. Those with the most to gain from *free trade* push it relentlessly through conservative think tanks like the Heritage Foundation, the media (CNBC and Fox News, for example), The Wall Street Journal, and nearly every business school in America and elsewhere. It has become the siren's song for conservatives, luring an unsuspecting population onto the rocks that will sink the ship of state. Conservatives and Republicans tout free trade as the panacea for all that ails us economically, with its virtues shouted from every rooftop, even as the country burns, its manufacturing base is gutted and outsourced, and external debt compounds year-after-year. This debt will eventually destroy the dollar, and along with it, most, if not all of what remains of the middle class, unless we reverse the tide.

3. End or Highly Regulate the Federal Reserve

Most of my conservative friends and *economists* that I know consider the idea of ending the Federal Reserve heresy. Of course, they consider it heretical. Why would those with the most to gain from perpetuating the status quo, a basically corrupt financial services sector including brokerage, banking, real estate, and insurance, elect to do away with the very system from which they garner financial and social succor and support? A paycheck in perpetuity, as long as you don't ask too many questions or rock the boat?

As discussed in earlier chapters and proven by financial calamity after financial calamity brought on by excess liquidity created by central banks, an unchecked central bank with basically no Federal oversight and whose constituents are its member banks (80% of bank in the United States), often operating at the behest of rapacious corporations, an often venal military industrial complex, and often corrupt or misguided politicians, is a recipe for one financial disaster after the next which is what we have had since the founding of our third central bank (The FED) in 1913.

Money printing (now electronic credits) and expansion of the money supply at a rate greater than the growth of GDP will always lead to inflation, either in the form of asset bubbles or in an increase in the prices of goods and services or in greater purchases of imports or all of these things, simultaneously, all of which are generally harmful to our economy, society, and the nation.

Asset bubbles are the preferred method for perpetuating and increasing the wealth of the *investing class* as I've demonstrated in earlier chapters. Growing money supply faster than GDP, will raise the prices of goods and services, if there is not a commensurate rise in the production of those goods and services, creating inflation, the ugliest tax of all. A propensity to purchase more imports must ultimately result in a falling dollar (more money leaving the country than coming into it) and with it, a falling standard of living for most of the population because of the loss of purchasing power. Those on fixed incomes and wage earners, are economically skewered under such a system because their wages will seldom, if ever, rise as fast as inflation. As all Americans know intuitively, two of the most important items required to live a dignified and productive life in an information age economy in America, are education and health care, which have been rising for decades at approximately 10% a year, which puts them both out of reach for many in the middle and lower class (Martin, 2017).

Ironically and sadly, the nemesis of our current central bank and banking system is wage growth! God forbid that wages should rise as fast as the inflation banks create, so that wage earners, those with EARNED income, could stay even in inflation adjusted economic terms. In the FED's *beige book* reports, it is always rising wages that they are concerned about (targeting), not the inflation that they themselves create or the destructive asset bubbles they perpetuate for the benefit of the few at the expense of the many. It is an outrageously unfair economic system.

As Edward Griffin (1994) noted in *The Creature From Jekyll Island*, there is no happy economic ending now for the United States. The FED has gone too far and will soon take our economy into the land of negative interest rates, from which there is no return, economically speaking. Corporate power and the banking and related lobbies are much too strong. Financial disaster looms.

As things stand now, for the country to reverse course, we must restore fiscal prudence, and heavily invest in the American people, plant, and infrastructure. Unfortunately for us (as in United States), the entrenched elites in corporate America, the financial services sector, and the military industrial complex, will never relinquish power voluntarily. The American people must demand fiscal prudence and investment in infrastructure and people, not more corporate giveaways and war. Is this possible? Recent elections give me reason for hope.

Why is ending the Federal Reserve imperative? Griffin (1994) summed it up nicely by simply saying that under a fiat money based system, what exists currently: more money

= more inflation = economic destruction = destitute population = an excuse for more authoritarian and concentrated government=totalitarianism.

Griffin does not mince words and goes on to provide 16 other reasons why the FED should be eliminated, and opportunities to improve the current system. He recommends freezing, among other things, the present supply of Federal Reserve notes, going to a gold backed currency system, paying off the national debt with Federal Reserve notes, converting all contracts based on Federal reserve notes to dollars, and abolishing the Federal Reserve system among other things. I must agree, for as long as the money trust are allowed to flourish, our economy is doomed (Griffin, 1994).

As discussed throughout this book, the idea of a monopoly controlling interest rates and the money supply, the very heart of a *free market* capitalist system, should strike most who give it any thought at all, as total hypocrisy at the least, and extremely poor public policy at worst. Such a system encourages speculation, malinvestment, and creates inflation, and provides many opportunities for obvious financial and economic conflicts of interest.

John Kay (2015) in *Other People's Money* summarized the major problem with central banks by saying the primary consequence of central banking has been to keep asset prices high, while compounding their liabilities which ultimately the taxpayer is responsible for. This state of affairs is outrageous. The FED is a privately held corporation, and now it appears, the largest hedge fund on earth. Despite this, the American taxpayer must and will foot the bill for their bank and corporate bailouts. If the FED were treated like any other corporation, there would be quarterly and annual reports required, along with annual audits, which are now impossible to obtain. But not to worry, the FED can simply print (electronically credit) its way out of any financial problems it may incur. With liabilities on their balance sheet now over $7 trillion dollars, creating the credits required to pay them off, will of course, create massive inflation, again.

So you see, it is a totally reasonable question to ask to anybody that has given it any thought at all, that is, why? Why should an elite cadre of unelected officials exercise such outsized and undue influence on an economy that would function fine and sustainably without them? Sustainable because without fractional reserve lending, banks could lend only what they earned from deposits. Yes, we'd have slower growth, but not the boom-bust cycle we've seen under central banking. And bankers would act with a degree of investing prudence heretofore unknown if they actually risked losing their business (bank) from reckless and feckless lending.

As John Kay (2015) noted, it is a perfectly reasonable question to ask, whether nations need central banks and their accompanying, often destructive monetary policy at all. Importantly, he emphasized the contradictions in an alleged free market economy relying on unelected and often unproven, banking elites to control the supply and price of money and interest rates, respectively. ***THIS (monopoly) should strike true capitalists and free marketers as heretical.***

Yes, of course. Any believer in *free markets* or the invisible hand, which would include most classically trained economists, conservatives of every stripe (supposedly), and most of those working in sectors reliant on easy credit and asset growth to ensure their job, i.e., those in real estate, banking, financial services, insurance, and many other sectors, would readily agree that supply and demand is the appropriate, and best model for setting prices and allocating goods and services. This is what I believe, and why I cannot understand those that still insist on having a cabal of unelected army of businessmen and bankers set the price of money (rate of interest) and determine how much money and credit should be available in the economy (money supply). The concept of monopoly control of money and credit flies in the face of everything these people and I believe that the free market is the best way to set prices and allocate goods and services.

So why all the squawking and cries of heresy for anyone questioning the current banking system and the need for the existence of the FED or any central bank? Either because they are ignorant of their own banking system OR they understand that their often privileged positions in the economy and society are a direct result of such a system.

Kay (2015) in an erudite summary concluded that the low cost funding to the banking system simply compounds liquidity thereby pushing up asset prices leading to significant and persistent income inequality between those with access to capital and education, and those without, often creating generational wealth inequalities which are very difficult to reverse.

This is another way of saying that easy money and credit disproportionally favor those with access to credit and those with inherited wealth (the majority of millionaires are not self-made). This system thus excludes about 80% of the American public. Kay (2015) noted that the enormous growth in financial services in the last two decades has come from the packaging and repackaging of financial assets, and that the sector (financial services) performs many redundant, and often unneeded activities. As I have said before, much of the financial services sector provides no economic value added to the economy.

Here Mr. Kay touches on one of my other major points about the inherent inequity in the American economy. With deregulation of savings and loans in the 1980s and the consumer banking sector in the late 1990s (repeal of the Glass-Steagall Act) the American economy became increasingly financialized. A plethora of financial products and services mushroomed overnight, but there was little in the way of value added to the real economy. Concomitant with financial deregulation of course, there was an ever widening ripple of corporate malfeasance and financial fraud culminating in the Enron fiasco in the early 2000s. Culminating however is a misnomer for the financial fraud and consumer abuse by financial intermediaries continues unabated to this day. Just think of Wells Fargo and the hundreds of thousands of fake bank accounts opened a few years ago. The banking and financial services sector is indeed deregulated. Just the way the bankers like it. As Kay (2015) noted, there has been and will be a culture of criminality in much of the financial services industry where everything from LIBOR to commodities markets are manipulated for profit. Financial services merely takes its cues from the FED, whose actions often border on fraud.

The FED, by proxy, is responsible for the actions of its agents (member banks) and has often abrogated even the veneer of social and economic responsibility it has in regulating the actions of its member banks. This was aptly demonstrated in the housing bubble in which underwriting guidelines were thrown out the window in favor of rampant and rapacious profiteering by the FED and its member banks, and the more recent criminal activity of Wells Fargo in opening false customer accounts. Clearly, this is a financial system, out of control, *managed* by a complicit and morally and ethically questionable central bank.

The crony capitalism must end. Tighter regulation of banks, a return to a non-fractional reserve banking system (gold standard). and a change in incentive systems from a transaction and commission based system to performance, fee based system throughout banking, and financial services is needed badly.

4. Reform Wall Street and Our Government

What is the binder for the military industrial complex, Capitol Hill power, and K Street lobbyists, Corporatists and the FED?

Answer: the binder is greed, and lust for profit and power (the same old suspects). Our economy and privileged way of life, relies on the supremacy of the dollar as the world's reserve currency. The supremacy of the dollar in turn relies on the military, to force those that would challenge the dollar as a reserve currency, or use other currencies to trade internationally, to submit to American dominance (think Russia, China, Libya, Iraq, and Afghanistan), Countries that challenged the dollar's supremacy have been taught a quick, and ugly lesson from the largest military on earth. Think Libya, Iraq, and Afghanistan, and all other countries that challenge dollar hegemony (such as Iran-crippling sanctions) and Syria (U.S. troops and special ops).

If the dollar loses the artificial support provided by being the world's reserve currency, it will fall precipitously, the fall exacerbated by a tremendous and rapidly growing national debt and trade deficits. As goes the currency, so goes our standard of living. A falling standard of living and collapsing economy of course means an end to corporate, and especially bank profits. The international money center banks understand this all too well. As Panzner (2007) recounted in *Financial Armageddon,* the looming demise of the dollar and a national debt growing exponentially, means foreigners are more likely to question the viability of the dollar as a reserve currency and international unit of account. I have noted repeatedly that the United States is rapidly losing its reserve currency status, and has continually intervened in the politics of other counties, often on Trumped up charges, to prevent these countries (generally OPEC countries) from going to alternate currencies or gold as their central banks preferred reserves.

The dollar has continued under pressure since Panzner's writing in 2006. In 2020 as I write this, China, Russia, and many other nations central banks have continued to diversify out of the dollar as a reserve currency. This trend will only accelerate as our debt burden continues to rise, putting downward pressure on the dollar and increasing inflation, and interest rates, exacerbating the already horrific wealth gap in America, and of course, decimating the middle class in the process.

The United States is approximately 4% of the world's population but consumes approximately 25% of the world's resources. This lopsided consumption is driven in large measure by incessant corporate propaganda encouraging debt and consumption, rather than savings and investment, as a way of life. Corrupt politicians, and plutocrats and bankers of every stripe, as well, encourage the relentless consumption driven economy, for it is loans from such consumption that a large portion of their profits come from. Without consumption, GDP growth ceases, along with interest payments and dividends. Remember, under a fractional reserve banking system money is debt, and as debt increases (loans), so does consumption.

Who else benefits from such corporate propaganda and profit? Wall Street, of course, shareholders (the investing class), and let's not forget, politicians who under our current political system, are now tenured bureaucrats for life.

In *The Secret History of the American Empire,* John Perkins (2007) discussed changing the existing paradigms of Wall Street, corporate America, and our political system through such political activists organizations like MoveOn.Org. Many of the points Perkins makes, like improving voter records, publicly funded elections, and ensuring the viability of Social Security, are all essential to keeping our somewhat shredded democracy and what is left of the middle class, intact.

Putting pressure on corporations and their shareholders to act in a socially responsible fashion, through the *Green Movement* and activist shareholders and pension funds, and encouraging corporate social responsibility (CSR) are all ways to emphasize to Wall Street, bankers, and plutocrats, that corporations have an obligation to give back to the society from which they derive their profits. This idea, CSR, is given lip service by much of the Fortune 500, but needs to be pushed, and insisted on, by an increasingly informed consumer. Those companies not giving back to the communities from which they derive their profits need to be ostracized, and stigmatized. It cannot be *business as usual* in America. Our country cannot wait. The usurping of our U.S. Supreme Court, political system, banking system and military are a citizens call to arms. It is past time for the slumbering, somnambulant middle class, to rise, and rise with a fury that we have not seen since the Minutemen and Bunker Hill. This is not a time for complacency, it is a time for action!

Writers like Friedman (2005) in his book *Flat World* exclaimed that globalization is a competition, with technology providing all of us with heretofore undreamed of opportunities and of course, threats we have never faced before. Many like Senator Byron Dorgan (and I) note that the world is not flat as Friedman asserts in his best seller, *Flat World*, but rather, grossly tilted in favor of mega-multinationals and economic elites (Dorgan, 2006). I strongly agree. Reforming Wall Street requires a dramatic shift in business, and our way of thinking about business' responsibility to America and all her citizens. Not just the privileged few.

5. Prevent Social Unrest and Disintegration

If we do not change the tilt of this very unfair economic and political system currently in place, our very way of life in America and our political system will cease to exist. In an incredibly prescient book, *Financial Armageddon* by Panzner (2007), he discussed the social ramifications from an increasingly marginalized and angry middle class by noting that the continued displacement of American manufacturing workers and their continued downhill socio-economic slide will create a pattern of political intransigence which will become more pronounced as the economic pie continues to shrink (what we have today) where Democrats and Republicans, rather than working together, will be increasingly at each other's throats. Remember, he wrote this 13 years ago! Prescient. Does this sound familiar? Is it not what we have across the nation and on Capitol Hill now?

Panzner (2007) continued by noting that eventually a climate of total intolerance, and obstructionist behavior will follow with politicians appealing to the *wounded spirits* of those left behind by globalization and technology. This in turn will of course lead the rise of potentially despotic and increasingly tribalistic populists looking for an opportunity to use the collective angst for their often dangerous and anti-democratic ends (Pazner, 2007). Remind you of anything?

Does this not describe to a tee the current and continuing political landscape in Washington and our nation? Does President Trump's appeal to *wounded spirits*, the *collective angst* or the *disenfranchised* ring a bell? Incredibly, this was written over a decade ago. There is no longer such a person as a conservative Democrat or a moderate Republican in Washington, and this has severely curtailed the ability of our government to function. The partisanship and vitriol now displayed on Capitol Hill is more akin to the generational acrimony between the Irish Republican Army and the Protestants of Northern Ireland. The acrimony, patronage, and tribalism on display makes anything resembling a democracy that works for the people, utterly impossible under such circumstances. A house divided cannot stand. We must, and can, find common ground to move our nation forward.

6. Put an End to the FED, Trading Culture, and Reform Banking and Financial Services

It should be painfully obvious to all Americans that our financial, economic and political systems are all in desperate need of reform and greater public scrutiny, and that a paradigm shift in the financial services and banking sectors is required, or we will see yet more financial disasters, and as pointed out numerous times in this book, we are unlikely to survive the next one as a democracy.

The first step to take is to alter personal and financial incentives. A system oriented on commissions and bonuses which in turn are based on the number of financial transactions done per day is inherently flawed. People and institutions operating in such a system most often operate in their own self-interest, not their clients, regardless of the platitudes you hear from Wall Street brokers to the contrary. As Kay (2015) noted so eloquently in *Other People's Money*, a new regulatory framework is needed for the banking and financial services sector, with the guiding principle being that those handling other people's money have a fiduciary responsibility.

As I have argued for many decades, finance and financial services need to be incentivized within an entirely new framework where incentives are congruent with the *customer first* orientation that the banking and the financial services industry publicly espouse, but privately reject, because *management* feels that such a system based on customer needs, could never be as profitable as the transaction driven, commission only pay scales currently in place in the financial services sector. There needs to be a paradigm shift in finance with an emphasis on putting clients first.

Some other reforms Kay (2015) recommends that should underpin economic reforms are, notably, creating and instilling a sense of fiduciary responsibility in all people handling other people's money and decreasing the length and complexity of the financial supply chain between those that have the capital to invest, and those managed to help them invest. There also obviously needs to be SERIOUS enforcement and punishment of those breaching their fiduciary responsibility. This must take place so that a clear and ever present signal is sent to all those in financial services, banking, brokerage, real estate, and insurance that they should not do the crime, unless they are willing to face considerable jail time. White collar crime, simply, has proliferated because it pays. Financial fraud and chicanery are seldom severely punished in our society. Remember from prior chapters, the real estate and banking industry are two of the largest contributors to lobbyists and political campaigns. Stricter regulation of these sectors is desperately needed, and until that happens, the financial fraud will continue, as sure as the sun rises and sets.

These are all relatively obvious and essential elements needed for anything resembling *reform* in the banking and financial services sector. Another very simple step would be to re-enact the Glass-Stegall Act, the depression era bill that was designed to restrict, and mitigate the rampant conflicts of interests and crony capitalism that existed in the financial services sector in the 1920s, leading ultimately to the Crash of 29.

This legislation, along with the Securities Acts of 1933 and 1934, provided the regulatory framework which separated investment banks (the casinos) from consumer banks (lenders and trustees of PUBLIC funds). The rationale then, as now is simple. Allowing unfettered merger activity between financial intermediaries and the growth of *super financials* encompassing everything from mortgage brokerage to insurance, ultimately must lead to obvious, and economically damaging, conflicts of interests. Banks would of course be less profitable under such a system, but the temptation to abuse the consumer, and most importantly, curtail financial speculation, would be greatly reduced (Burnett, 2019).

As Joseph Stiglitz (2009), a well-known economist and winner of the Nobel Prize in economics at Columbia University noted in 2009, commercial banks were never meant to be risk takers, they were, and are supposed to be conservators of the nation's savings, with the tacit understanding between the banking sector and government being that the government would foot the bill if they failed. This agreement between the banking sector and government has been, and continues to be abused by both consumer and investment banks. This often uneasy alliance between banks and government has been sullied, and abrogated, at every opportunity by the banking and financial services sector.

As noted in earlier chapters, with the elimination of Glass-Steagall, there was no longer a firewall between investment banks (the casinos) and consumer banking (stodgy lenders). The financial sector mushroomed into one stop financial centers with banks devouring mortgage companies, insurance companies, brokerage firms etc. Just like the Roaring '20s! And with the same conflicts of interest, crony capitalism, and the same inevitable, sad result. Massive wealth destruction, much of it middle class savings and pensions.

The banking lobby spent hundreds of millions (about $300 million) in the late 1990s to end this depression era regulation (Glass-Stegall) claiming that it restricted competition (and of course profits). After a lot of lobbying, and a lot of money being spent to *influence* the *right* people on Capitol Hill, Glass-Stegall was unceremoniously consigned to the dustbin of history, under a Republican Senate and House. It was replaced by the Graham-Leach Blily Act (GLBA) a puff piece of legislation cultivated in a warm and receptive Republican senate and Congressional hothouse (106th Congress; 1999–2001) replacing Glass-Stegall, and to the delight of banking and financial services everywhere, removed the barriers between banking, insurance, and securities companies, thus allowing once again, the proliferation of financial supermarkets.

Most importantly, *it failed to give the SEC or any other financial regulatory agency the authority to regulate large investment bank holding companies.* The results were as ugly, as they were utterly predicable. Shortly after passage in a Wild Wild West atmosphere prevailing on Wall Street came the Crash of 2000 (March-May) wiping out trillions of dollars and much of the savings of the middle class (The Tech Wreck, 2000). This of course (pump and reflate by the FED) was followed up with the housing crash of 2007–2008, leading us to today (2020), where we currently have a stock market being levitated on piles of newly created money from *quantitative easing* and negative interest rates in many parts of the world.

Once again, we find ourselves crossing the Rubicon, into financial disaster, and social calamity. The free market pricing mechanism for the true cost of money (interest rates) is destroyed by central bankers worldwide, and money creation and central bank meddling in futures, stock, and bond markets is at a crescendo worldwide, with negative interest rates prevailing in many economies, and quantitative easing now an acceptable method for floating economies on a sea of artificial liquidity. It cannot, and will not end well my friends.

The clamor on the right and Wall Street for elimination of Glass Stegall, was, and still is, obvious. The odious new act that replaced it, the Graham, Leech, Blyly Act (GLBA), allowed for basically unfettered merger and acquisitions of financial intermediaries, and the *too big to fail* institutions we now have today. This could not have happened if Glass-Stegall had been left in place. The passage of this bill (GBLA) increased the profitability of the entire banking and financial services sector overnight.

The big money center banks wasted no time in taking full advantage of their new found freedom, frenetically merging real estate and stock brokerages with investment banks, consumer banks, rating agencies and insurance companies. This frantic, and often fraudulent merger activity led inevitably and so predictably, to the Tech Wreck of 2000 (stock bubble), the housing crisis of 2006–2009 (The Housing Bubble), which many in the middle class are still trying to recover from, and now as I write this in 2019 a bond and stock bubble (again). Using a centuries old, tired old ploy of explained in earlier chapters, central banks worldwide have *coordinated* monetary policy providing excess liquidity to the marketplace, resulting in the same old asset bubbles, and inflation, which ironically, they created, but pretend to fight on behalf of *society*. Financial markets are integrated as never before so the next collapse will be as bad as never before. The world will have seen nothing like it.

As noted earlier, stricter regulation of the banking and financial services sector with *fail safes* put into place to protect consumers, NOT TOO BIG TO FAIL INSTITUTIONS, need to be put into place immediately. Proponents of "self-regulation," an oxymoron if ever there was, that argue that the sector can self-regulate, are on hallucinogens, and have obviously never read any financial history. Self-policing will not ever work for obvious reasons. There is simply too much money involved. Think of the Medien Drug Cartel or OPEC. Like any cartel, the banking cartel must be kept on a short leash if we are to save our society, and the middle class. Ideally they should be broken up. But where is the FTC?

Sadly and ironically, those on the right, in conservative think tanks funded by the Koch brothers et al., never seem to get it. Regulation, especially financial regulation, is imperative if we are to save capitalism from itself. Imagine a snake eating its own tail. This is unregulated capitalism. It will consume itself, and most of the middle class, and society with it. Of this we can be certain. The 1% is not concerned with the current state of our political, economic, military, educational and financial systems, which now resemble those of an emerging market economy. No, they will be safely ensconced in their *safe rooms* far, far from the fray that will finish off the middle class for good. Unless we act decisively, and quickly.

7. Make the Tax Code Progressive

Warren Buffet, the shrewdest investor of all time, and a multi-billionaire, when being interviewed in 2017 said the following on CNBC regarding taxes and the Trump tax giveaway,

> "Everybody that wants a cut in taxes can hire some academics and they look for dynamic scoring and they say the country will really be better off if I pay less tax," Buffett said. "I don't blame them—it's very understandable, so be very, very, very suspicious of dynamic scoring." (Business Insider, 2017, p. 2)

Buffet is notoriously skeptical at using tax cuts to boost GDP. What often happens is the major tax breaks are used by corporations for stock buybacks to increase share prices, benefiting primarily shareholders, and the investing class (top 20%).

Buffett was also dismissive of the suggestion by the Trump administration that increased economic growth would help pay for the tax cuts and make up the loss in government revenue, a justification that comes from a method called dynamic scoring.

Bill Gates in the same interview said any tax cut was unlikely to benefit businesses in the tech sector but would most likely help shareholders.

I don't think that the success of the technology sector will be improved by some tax change, Gates said. The tech companies are not starving right now, and this only comes up when you have profits, and these companies have very high profits. It's not like we're going to be stronger in the tech sector by making owners of those stocks richer. (CNBC, 2017)

Many market pundits and academics, myself included, observed that this tax giveaway to the corporations and uber wealthy was, from an economic standpoint, dangerous fiscal policy, and more importantly, **not needed**, as Gates, and Buffet and many other billionaires have already agreed. Indeed over a year after this *tax reform* was enacted, it is clear that most of this money has not been reinvested in our economy. There was some increased initial corporate spending but mainly these "cuts" were used for *stock buybacks* as a way to increase stock value and shareholder wealth, more mergers and acquisitions, and a boom in the stock market, thanks to these *buybacks* and a more optimistic outlook by businesspeople about the future.

Predictably, there was a stock market rally, which as of this writing in late 2019, is peaking, as have autos, housing and many other *leading indicators* of the economy. The sugar high from the tax cuts is predictably wearing off, and our infrastructure, literacy rates, health care, education, etc. lag far behind our major competitors in the meantime, as the rich get richer. The only areas the United States seems to maintain a competitive advantage is in military spending and hubris.

What many, including myself predicted, has indeed come to pass. A boon for Wall Street and stock buybacks, another tax giveaway to the wealthiest people in the country who did not need it, and a U.S. Congress more divided than ever on how to spend what tax dollars still trickle into the treasury. And of course, our national debt and deficit spending are worse than ever, with the national debt now approaching 30 trillion dollars or approximately 150% of GDP, and growing at nearly a trillion dollars a year. As we all know, this debt is not sustainable.

Interestingly, and somewhat ironically, in the Keynesian economic model government needs to *cut taxes and increase spending* in a **recession** to stimulate end (consumer) aggregate demand. These fiscal and monetary tools are counter-cyclical and traditionally have been used by the U.S. Congress and our central bank in times of economic distress. Ironically, the Keynesian economic model is often ridiculed by conservatives and the corporatocracy, as *wasteful* government spending but it was, and is, these corporate entities, that receive the lion's share of *tax breaks* decade-after-decade from Reagan, Bush, and Trump tax giveaways.. As noted above, there has been no significant gain to the economy, but the deficit has predictably soared, and will continue to do so, for who is going to pay the taxes to support government? More and more of the burden will be shifted to the middle class, until there is no middle class. What will the plutocrats do then?

8. Rebuild our Manufacturing Base

It has become almost a proverb that Western economies, as they go from agrarian to industrial economies, and then to information age *service* economies, that heavy manufacturing should be outsourced to countries with cheaper labor. This is what has happened in the United States, steadily since the 1980s, with the process being greatly accelerated with passage of the North American Free Trade Agreement (NAFTA) in 1999. As noted in earlier chapters, this is not a panacea for economic growth. Frankly, it is just the opposite. For an economy to truly prosper it must produce things (goods and services) that the rest of the world needs, at a cheaper price, and of higher quality, than its competitors.

The United States has a plethora of all that is needed in economic terms, i.e., land, labor, capital, innovation and knowledge, to excel in many industries from biotechnology to nanotechnology. Unfortunately for us, the United States is no longer a free market economy. It is now basically an oligopolistic economy. That is, one where a few firms (5 or less) dominate the majority of the market share in their respective industries. Just think of insurance, banking, communications, health care etc. The list is endless. The point is, such an economy stifles innovation, and reduces competition, both hallmarks of a *free market* economy. Without innovation, productivity stalls, and without true competition, prices for all major services, controlled by a few firms, rise inexorably, especially for products where demand is inelastic, that is where demand is not affected by price. Think gasoline, communications, transport, and health care. These are all items essential to surviving in our economy. Because of the nature of this *new age economy* those left behind economically by globalization are at the mercy of these oligopolies. This would be true of most of the middle and lower class in America and yet another reason for the demise of the middle class.

When one ponders how to reverse this outsourcing trend and bring back better paying manufacturing and service jobs to reinvigorate the middle class there are some obvious solutions that could be put in place. Manufacturing does matter, regardless of what economists from the *Chicago School* and other conservative pundits opine. Nearly all of our major trading partners have higher standards of living, better education, superior health care, and lower corruption, and not coincidentally, more manufacturing as a percentage of GDP than the United States.

To give you an idea of just how bad the United States is doing in manufacturing and everything else, I've taken the time below to compile some statistics to clarify just how badly and why we need manufacturing.

Incredibly, but not surprisingly, the United States is in 59th place between Uganda and Haiti, **on the GINI index** (scale = 158–25 with 25 (Ukraine) being the lowest income and South Africa (63) being the highest in inequality. Iceland, Sweden, Denmark, Germany, and the Netherlands are between 26 and 33 on the scale.

According to the WHO (2019), the United States is in 37th place when it comes to overall health care outcomes, between Slovenia and Costa Rica. The top 15 are France, Italy, San Marino, Andorra, Malta, Singapore, Spain, Oman, Austria, Japan, Norway, Portugal, Monaco, Greece, and Iceland.

France? Italy? Singapore, Norway? What countries keep appearing at the top of these indexes? Again and again? Not the United States (WHO, 2018).

Now look at the Transparency Internationals Corruptions Index top 15 least corrupt countries for 2017. They are New Zealand, Denmark, Finland, Norway, Switzerland, Singapore, Sweden, Canada, Luxembourg, Netherlands, UK, Germany, Australia, Hong Kong, and Iceland.

Note that many of the same countries appear in this index as well. Note the United States did not even make the top 15 of least corrupt countries (Transparency International, 2017).

Not to put too fine a point on it, look at the most productive economies on earth as measured by the World Bank. They are Luxembourg, Norway, Switzerland, Denmark, Iceland, the United States, Australia, Ireland, Netherlands, Sweden, Germany, Finland, Canada, France, and Japan. Finally, the United States did make the list but not even in the Top 5 (World Bank, 2018).

The Brookings Institution puts out a report called The Global Manufacturing Scorecard: How did U.S. companies compare to 18 other nations? In this report, they rank manufactured exports as a total of GDP. Counties included in the top 10 are China 27%, United States 12%, Japan 19%, Italy 16%, Germany 23%, South Korea 29%, India 16%, France 11%, Spain 14%, and Switzerland 18%.

Please note that China, Japan. Italy, Germany, South Korea, India, Spain, and Switzerland all have higher output of exported manufactured goods than the United States (Brookings Institution, 2018).

Finally, to make my final point, The World Bank's Index of Economic Freedom shows just that, economic freedom, included in the top 15 are Hong Kong, Singapore, New Zealand, Switzerland, Australia, Ireland, Estonia, UK, Canada, United Arab Emirates, Iceland, Denmark, Taiwan, Luxembourg, and Sweden. Once again, the United States did not even make the top 15 (The World Bank Index of Economic Freedom, 2018).

HOW are all these related you might ask? The countries that keep showing up in the top 10 for quality of life, productivity, etc.? The top 10 are New Zealand, Denmark, Sweden, Canada, Luxembourg, Netherlands, Germany, Hong Kong, and Iceland. Are there some common denominators between these countries? Yes. Many are social democracies with strong manufacturing, union membership, national health care, basically free education, and solid cradle to grave social safety nets. Some like Sweden, Canada, Germany, and Hong Kong have very strong export manufacturing sectors, as well as social safety nets, and better health care than the United States.

What don't they have?

Answer: A nearly $1 trillion dollar (as of 2020) annual defense budget, larger than the next seven countries' defense budgets combined, with troops and bases in 70 countries (that they admit to) according to Politico's David Vine, August 2015 (Vine, 2018).

As discussed in an earlier chapter this kind of military footprint is unnecessary and costly. Much of the fear mongering, xenophobia, and cries for constant wars come from a bloated Pentagon and military industrial complex clamoring to justify their existence, by creating often fictitious, or relatively harmless enemies, one after another. Military spending saps our domestic economy for the sake of the few, at the expense of the many, and of course, is another reason for the demise of the middle class in the United States.

Could we learn something from these social democracies that perform so much better than we do, on nearly every meaningful social, economic, and quality of life scale or metric? Once again, being a realist, I am not optimistic. To repeat, there are two areas where America truly excels however, military spending and hubris. No one can touch us.

We need to learn that an economy cannot grow through the proliferation of speculation and crony capitalism. We need to learn and be told by those in power that saving, and manufacturing items the rest of the world needs is critical to economic survival. The economy cannot grow on hedge fund speculation (the FED being the biggest hedge fund of all), nail salons, and real estate agents (sorry Mom).

Manufacturing matters, and is critically important to increasing the standard of living in America. As Senator Dorgan (2006) noted throughout his book, our manufacturing base has been systematically dismembered and shipped overseas, with the tired old refrain from free traders being it's good for the economy! It's a win!! Really? In retrospect we all now know who wins, the investing class, multinationals, and top 1%. Who loses? The middle and lower class.

Some critical items that Senator Dorgan favors include developing an American free trade plan, repealing the tax breaks for exporting jobs, prohibiting imports from companies that abuse overseas workers, encourage stronger labor unions, and lower health care costs and insist on education excellence (Dorgan, 2006).

These are all excellent ideas for improving American infrastructure, health care, education, and manufacturing, many of which have already been suggested in prior pages. Add to these, government incentives should be provided to encourage American multinationals to bring as much manufacturing home as possible. Repatriate production and investment as much as possible.

9. Stigmatize Neoliberalism and the Washington Consensus as Economic Dogma

In general, many of the notions embedded in the myopic and often dogmatic theology of neoliberalism need to be shown for what they are, false economic idols, with bases built on quicksand. The idea that *trickle-down* economics ever worked for a majority of Americans must be refuted everywhere, including Fox news, and its major tenets, shown to be what they are, tools for an often tainted plutocracy and corporatocracy, used to further their own worldwide hegemony and fatten their bottom lines at any cost.

In *The Globalization Paradox*, Dani Rodrik (2011), discussed an extension of neoliberalism which came to be known as the *Washington Consensus*, a term coined by John Williamson in 1989. This view was promulgated primarily by graduates of the Chicago School of Economics, who began promoting the theory that government was not a promoter of economic growth, but rather, an obstacle blocking business and economic growth. This point of view was lent academic legitimacy by the so called Washington Consensus, and became a central tenet of neoliberalism and conservative economic dogma. No matter how misguided, and now discredited, this dogma was popularized by Reagan (neoliberalism), and fueled with ugly rhetoric from Reagan, Bush 1 and 2, Cheney, Wolfowitz, and nearly all conservatives at the time (starting under Reagan). Yes, the same group that brought you the Crash of 1987, the recession of 2001–2002, and the Afghanistan and Iraq wars, the longest and most costly in our nation's history, were quick to latch onto this new scapegoat, government itself, as source of all our problems. Desperate for better times and gullible about the disastrous economic and social consequences that result from such neoliberalist policies, much of America bit the hook, and conservatives wasted no time in perpetrating this theory through every avenue available (think Fox News and the Heritage Foundation)

In a post industrialist, capitalist society such as ours, it is easy to see how eventually, if one extrapolates the current trajectory of social and economic inequalities existing in America, how the entire, obscene economic and social edifice as currently configured, could come crashing down on itself, capitalism collapsing in on itself like a mushroom cloud, to be replaced by anarchy, social disintegration and mayhem. Every plutocrats nightmare. Their heads on spikes lining Constitution Avenue in a dystopian, Mad Max post-apocalyptic nightmare.

One has to wonder why? Why do financial and economic elites, acting out of enlightened self-interest not see the seeds of capitalism's demise germinating in front of their very eyes and try to spread the wealth more evenly to avoid anarchy? Destroying those that created capitalism itself and the *wealth* of the country, working men and women, and vital to all true democracies, the middle class to which they once belonged? Carl Marx in his theory of historical dialectic argued that capitalism would indeed destroy itself and as noted throughout this book, there is ample historical evidence to lead a reasonable person to this sad conclusion.

Francis Fukuyama (2000), in his celebrated treatise on society, capitalism, and morality noted in his book, *The Great Disruption,* the inherent and curious historical dichotomy between the very rich and the rest the of society in which they live, by discussing this dichotomy. That is, one would think the rich would want to spread the wealth to avoid class conflict and keep their heads. Instead, the opposite seems to occur decade-after-decade, century-after-century. In the *Cultural Contradictions of Capitalism*, Schumpeter (1950) noted that capitalist development ultimately undermines itself by producing norms at odds with those necessary for the operation of markets. In other words, not surprisingly, as the wealthy accrue more money and position power, they begin favoring monopoly over free market capitalism and become increasingly hostile to those who made their wealth possible in the first place (the middle class).

Profound as it is prescient! Why would elites consciously or subconsciously, seek to destroy that from which they grew their wealth? It seems totally counter intuitive but we as a nation have seen it happening in our own society for decades, with the denouement being President Trump's recent election. Pluto-crats running the country and seemingly hell bent on destroying every vestige of the New Deal, and all the social progress made since FDR, and ruining those responsible for his (Trump's) election (the middle class).

In brief, Fukuyama (2000) explained that economic abun-dance has a symbiotic relationship with the cultural elite that finds itself systematically at odds with established rules, con-formity, the status quo, and authority. Remind you of Donald Trump?

As further explained, successive generations of elites find it more and more difficult to shock people out of their con-formism, because there is very little of it left. This explains the current president's tiring and daily outrageous flaunting of his misogyny to our Constitutional processes. Eventually what arises from such elites is an entire class opposed to middle class values and norms, ultimately destroying the society that makes their existence possible. Remind you of anyone?

Ominously, Fukuyama (2000) also observed that market economies routinely elevate as cultural heroes those adept at making money, nearly always at the expense of those who have far greater, but non-monetizable skills.

Incredible!! Keep in mind, this was written two decades before the current occupant of the White House was elected president. This propensity for market, capitalist societies to slip into personality cults, and for elites in those societies to destroy the very base of people responsible for their privileged position in that society, is well documented, here, and throughout history. We as a nation can and must, reverse these trends through collective action, and the vote.

But first, we need to understand the causes of our current situation. Hint: It is not Gay marriage. It is not Roe vs. Wade, and it is not unions. These are cultural wedge issues deliberately used by those in the media, banking, politics, the corporatocracy, and the military, to divide us as a nation. Unfortunately, they have become all too adept at doing so. Hopefully, this trend is reversing with the recent midterm elections ushering in a Democratic majority with the will and votes to fight for the middle class. Anything other than a true return to social justice and economic fairness for *all* American's will not do. Power never concedes willingly as Frederick Douglas noted so eloquently and certainly it will not here. We, the middle class, must fight for it, and VOTE!

References

Acemoglu, D., & Robinson, J. (2014). *Why nations fail: The origins of power, prosperity, and poverty.* New York, NY: Crown Publishing. Retrieved from https://rampages.us/wpnecon491/inclusive-and-extractive-institutions/

Aldridge, J. (2017). *On fascism.* Retrieved from http://www.woodville.org/documentos/140801political

Albright, M. (2018). *Fascism, a warning.* New York, NY: Harper Collins.

Alinsky, S. (1971). *Rules for radicals.* New York, NY: Random House.

Amadeo, K. (2018). The rising cost of healthcare by year and its causes. *The Balance.* Retrieved from https://www.thebalance.com/causes-of-rising-healthcare-costs-4064878

Amadeo, K. (2019a) Equity in education and its impact. Why equity is better than equality for the economy. *The Balance.* Retrieved from https://www.thebalance.com/equity-in-education-4164737

Amadeo, K. (2019b).National debt by year compared to GDP and major events. *The Balance.* Retrieved from https://www.thebalance.com/national-debt-by-year-compared-to-gdp-and-major-events-3306287

Amadeo, K. (2020). *Interest on the national debt and how it affects you.* Retrieved from https://www.thebalance.com/interest-on-the-national-debt-4119024

Anonimo, K. (2006). *Cultural globalization and language education.* New Haven, CT: Yale University Press.

Atkadijian, D. (2017). *A working economy. The United States is becoming an extraction economy like Puerto Rico.* Retrieved from https://www.thebalance.com/interest-on-the-national-debt-4119024

Autor, D., & Dorn, D. (2013). The growth of low skill service jobs and the polarization of the U.S. labor market. *American Economic Review, 103,* 1553–1597. doi:10.1257/aer.103–5.1553

Banton, C. (2019). What is securitization?: Who bears the risk of bad debts in securitization. *Investopedia*. Retrieved from https://www.investopedia. com/ask/answer/07/securitizationrisks.asp

Barry, C. (2018). Wealth Redistribution *Stanford Encyclopedia of Philosophy*, 1. Retrieved from https://plato.stanford.edu.entries/redistribution

Baumol, W., Blackman S., & Wolff, E. (1989). *Productivity and American leadership: The long view*. Cambridge, MA: MIT Press.

Bell, D. (1996). *The cultural contradictions of capitalism* . New York, NY Basic Books.

Bellamy, J., & Mafdoff, F. (2014). *The great financial crisis: Causes and consequences*. New York, NY: New York University Press.

Bernanke, B. (2002). *Deflation: Making sure it doesn't happen here*. Washington, DC: National Economist Club (speech). Retrieved from https://www. federalreserve.gov/boarddocs/speeches/2002/20021121

Bernanke, B. (2012). Bernanke by 2012 (in his fourth lecture at George Washington University on March 29, 2012). Washington, DC: CNN Money. Retrieved from https://money.com/2012/03/29/news/economy/ Bernanke-lecture-economy/index.htm

Bernays, E. (1928). *Propaganda*. New York, NY: Ig Publishing.

Blinder, A. (2004). Quote PBS Newshour. https://doi.org/10.1016/j. jweia.2014.10.009

Bonner, B., & Wiggin, A. (2006). *Empire of debt*. New York, NY: Wiley & Sons.

Britt, L. (2003). The 14 characteristics of Fascism. *Free Inquiry Magazine*. Retrieved from https://ratical.org/ratville/CAH/fasci14chars.html

Brookings Institution. (2919). *Country Rankings*. Retrieved from https:// www.heritage.org

Brown, E. (2016). Brexit and the derivatives time bomb. Retrieved from https://dandelionsalad.wordpress.com/2016/07/01/ brexit-and-the-derivatives-time-bomb-by-ellen-brown/

Brown University. (2017). *U.S. spending on Post 9–11 wars to reach $5.6 trillion by 2018*. Retrieved from https://www.brown.edu/news/2017–11–07/ costssummary

Buffett, W. (2002). Berkshire Hathaway Annual Report. Chairman's Report To Shareholders. https://www.berkshirehathaway.com/letters/2002.pdf

Buffet, W. (2005). Berkshire Hathaway Annual Report. Chairman's Report to Shareholders. https://www.berkshirehathaway.com/2005ar.pdf

Buffett, W. (2017). Warren Buffet: CNBC's Becky Quick Interview (Television interview). Retrieved from https://www.cnbc.com/video/2019/03/28/watch-warren-buffetts-full-interview-with-cnbcs-becky-quick.html

Burnette, M. (2019). The Glass-Stegall Act and why it matters. *Banking News.* Retrieved from https://www.nerdwallet.com/blog/banking/glass-steagall-act-explained/

Camilo, M. (2018). The cost of college is rising eight times faster than wages. *Forbes.* Retrieved from https://www.forbes.com/sites/camilomaldonado/2018/07/24/price-of-college-increasing-almost-8-times-faster-than-wages/#3e3d670366c1

Carlin, G. (2011). *Quotes.* Retrieved from https://www.commondreams.org/views/2011/03/19/george-carlin-knew-why-they-call-it-american-dream

Carr, W. (2013). *Pawns in the game.* Las Vegas, NV: Dauphin Publications.

Chapman, B. (2010). International forecast for the world. *The International Forecaster.* Retrieved from http://www.theinternationalforecaster.com/topic/international forecaster weekly/liquidity Forecast for the world economies

Chety et al. (2016). The fading American dream: Trends in absolute income mobility since 1940. Working paper 22910. *National Bureau of Economic Research*, 356, 398–406. doi:10.1126/science.aal4617

Cohan, W. D. (2011). *Money and power: How Goldman Sachs came to rule the world.* New York, NY: Doubleday.

Comfort, C. (2016). Deutsche Bank say the top contributor to systemic risk recording of the International Monetary Fund. *Bloomberg News.* Retrieved from https://www.bloomberg.com/news/articles/2016–06–30/deutche-bank-may-be-top-contributor-to-systemic-risk-imf-says

Congressional Budget Office (CBO). Non Partisan Analysis for the U.S. Congress. (2019). *The long term budget outlook.* Washington DC: Government Printing Office. Retrieved from https://cbo.gov/publication/55331

Conzemius, J. (1969). Lord Acton and the first Vatican Council. *The Journal of Ecclesiastical History, 20*(2), 267–294. Cambridge, England: Cambridge University Press. https://doi.org/10.1017/S0022046900054695

Corak, M. (2013). The Gini Coefficient: Income inequality, equality of opportunity, and generational mobility. *Journal of Economic Per-*

spectives, *27*(3), 79–102. Retrieved from https://pubs.aeaweb.org/doi/pdfplus/10.1257/jep.27.3.79

Cowen, T. (1998). *Praise of commercial culture*. Cambridge, MA: Harvard University Press.

Dahendorf, R. (1979). *Life chances: Approaches to social and political theory*. Chicago, IL: Chicago University Press.

Daniels, M. (2012). Mitch Daniels gives Republican Response to Obama's State of the Union Speech. speech of Indiana delivered to Barak Obama's 2012 State of the Union Address. *CNN Politics*. Retrieved from https://www.cnn.com/2012/01/24/politics/sotu-gop-response-transcript/index.html

DeSilver, D. (2017). Who pays the taxes? *Pew Research Center* (charts & graphs). Retrieved from https://www.pewresearch.org/fact-tank/2017/10/06/a-closer-look-at-who-and-doesn'tpay-u-s-income tax/

DeSoto, J. (2006). *Money, bank credit, and economic cycles*. Auburn, AL: Ludwig Van Mises Institute.

Dimmitt, M. (2015). 15 of the world's most productive countries: Who's getting it done. *The Collective*. Retrieved from https://collectivehub.com/2018/15-of-the-worlds-most-productive-countries

Dirksen, E. (1965). *U.S. Senate (quote on Senate floor). A billion here and a billion there, pretty soon you're talking real money*. Retrieved from https://www.barrypopik.com/index.php/new_york_city/entry/a_billion_here_a_billion_there_pretty_soon_youre_talking_real_money/

Dorgan, B. (2006). *Take this job and ship it*. New York, NY: Thomas Dunn Books / St. Martin Press.

Douglas, F. (1857). West India Emancipation Speech. Canandaigua, New York 1857. *Black Past*. Retrieved from https://www.blackpast.org/African-american-history/1857-federick-douglas-if-there-is-no-struggle-there-no-progress

Eberstadt, N. (2017). An economist in the miserable 21st century. *NPR Business Interview*. February 25 Weekend Edition. Radio Interview.

Eisenhower, D. (1961). Farewell speech. Retrieved from https://ourdocuments.gov/doc.php?flash=true&doc=90&page=transcript

Emmanuel, R. (2020). As Rham Emmanuel quipped not so long ago never let a serious crisis go to waste. *Wikeyquote*. Retrieved from https://en.wikeyquote.org/wiki/Rahm_Emmanuel

Eskow, R. (2016). What's killing the middle class? *People's Access Blog*. Retrieved from https://www.commondreams.org/views/2016/what's-killing-the-middle-class

European University Institute. (2019). *Eurostat: Official EU Statistical Data*. Retrieved from www.eui..eu/Research/Library/ResearchGuides/economis/Statistics/DataPortal?HUS

European University Institute. (1975). *Historical statistics of the United States 1775–2000*. Retrieved from https://www.census.gov/library/publicationas/1975/compendia/hist_statscolonial-1970.html

Fernald, J., Byrne, D., & Reinsdorf, M. (2016). Does the United States have a productivity slowdown or a measurement problem? *Brookings Papers on Economic Activity*. Retrieved from file://C:/Users/17034/AppData/Local/Microsoft/Windows/NetCache/IE/C4JW4KJR/byrnetextspring16bpea.pdf

Fernald, J., Hall, R., Stock, J., & Watson, M. (2009). The disappointing recovery of output after 2009. *Brookings Papers On Economic Activity*. BPEA Conference Drafts, March 23–24, 2017. Retrieved from https://www.brookings.edu/wp-content/uploads/2017/03/1 fernaldetal.pdf

Foster, J., & Magdoff, F. (2009). *The great financial crisis: Causes and consequences*. New York, NY: NYU Press.

Fukuyama, F. (2000). *The great disruption: Human nature and reconstitution of social order*. New York, NY: Simon & Schuster.

Garrett, G. (1992a). *The peoples pottage*. San Diego, CA. Truth Seeker.

Garrett, G. (1992b). *The peoples pottage: The revolution was Ex America, the rise of empire*. New York, NY: Truth Seeker Press.

Geitner, T. (2006, February 28). Risk management challenges in the U.S. Financial System. Global Association of Risk Professionals (GARP) 7th Annual Risk Management Convention and Exhibition, New York. Retrieved from https://www.bis.org/review/r060303a.pdf

Ghilaraducci, T. (2018). Who benefits from the tax cuts 10 months later? *Forbes*. Retrieved from https://www.forbes.com/sites/teresaghilarducci/2018/09/28/who-benefits-from-the-tax-cuts-10-months-later/#7509ab0026bb

Gini Coefficient—chart. (2018). Retrieved from https://en.wikipedia.org/wiki/Gini_coefficient

Goldwater, B. (1953). *With no apologies*. New York, NY: William Morrow Company.

Griffin, E. (2010). *The creature from Jekyll Island: A second look at the federal reserve* (5th ed.). Westlake Village, CA: The Reality Zone.

Hammermesh, D. (2002). *Economics is everywhere*. New York NY: McGraw Hill.

Hanke, S. (2017). *Does the FED create asset bubbles?* Retrieved from: https://www.forbes.com/sites/stevehanke/2017/10/31/how-the-greenspan-and-bernanke-fed-blew-and-deflated-bubbles/#1038658e4bbHartcher

Hartman, T. (2015). *How Federal Reserve policies led to the Crash of '29*. Retrieved from https://www.thomhartmann.com/users/de-peterpalms/blog/2015/10/how-federal-reserve-policies-led-crash-1929

Hembree, D. (2018). CEO pay skyrockets to 361 times that of the average worker. *Forbes*. Retrieved from https:www.forbes.com/sites/dianahembree/2018/05/22/ceo-pay-skyrockets-to-361-times-that-of-average-worker/#7f06373776dd

History of public debt. (2019). *Wikipedia*. Retrieved from https://en.wikipedia.org/wiki/history-of-US-public-debt

Huntington, S. (1996). *The clash of civilizations: Remaking of the world order*. New York, NY: Simon & Schuster.

Hylan, G. (1922, December 10). Hylan adds Pinchot to presidency list: Berates wealth lords. *The New York Times*. Retrieved from https://timemachine.nytimes.com/timesmachine/1922/12/10/109339923.pdf

Internal Revenue Service (IRS). (2006, September). Tax Statistics. Retrieved from http://www.irs.gov/taxstatsindtaxstats/article/o.id=129406.00.html

Jackson, A. (1832). Our republic-Andrew Jackson. Retrieved from https://www.ourrepubliconline.com/author/110

Jakaria, F. (2018). Interview with Washington Post Columnist Fareed Jakaria.

Jha, J. (2011). A Pareto Optimal multi-objective optimization for a horizontal axis wind turbine blade airfoil sections utilizing exergy analysis and neural networks. *The Journal of Wind Engineering and Industrial Aerodynamics. 136,* 62–72. https://doi.org10.1016./jweia.2014.10.009

Jefferson. T. (1791, December 3). Jefferson quotes and family letters. Retrieved from https://tjrs.monticello.org/letter/1541

Johnson, S. (1775). Patriotism is the last bastion of the scoundrel. Retrieved from https://en.wikipedia.org/wiki/Political_views_of_Samuel_Johnson.

Kay, J. (2015). *Other people's money: Masters of the universe or servants of the people*. London, England: Profile Books Ltd.

Kelton, S. (2012). Where did the Federal Reserve get all that money? *New Economic Perspectives*. Retrieved from https://neweconomicperspectives. org/2012/03/w/where-did-the-federal-reserve-get-all-that-money.html

Kertscher, T. (2019). Bernie Sanders on target saying 3 richest families have as much as the bottom half of all American. *PolitiFact*. Retrieved from https://www.politifact.com/factchecks/2019/jul/03/ bernie-sanders-target-saying-3-richest-have-much-w/

Keister, L. et al. (2015). Rising wealth inequality: Causes, consequences, and potential solutions. *Poverty Solutions*. University of Michigan. Retrieved from https://poverty.umich.edu/research-projects/policy-briefs/ rising-wealth-inequality-causes-consequences-and-potential-responses/

Klobuchar, A. (2014). Wealth inequality in the United States. *Joint Economic Committee-Democrats, United States Congress*. Retrieved from https:// www.jec.senate.gov/public/ cache/files/d72ff522-e470–496d-90ff-b8f7ac-9c4c2c/income-inequality-in-america.pdf

Krugman, P., & Wells, S (2006). *Economics*. New York, NY: Worth Publishers.

Lindman, S. (2015). Notes in global derivatives: $1.5 quadrillion dollar time bomb. *Lindman Deytch Group. Global Research*. Retrieved from https://www. globalresearch.ca/global-derivatives-1.5-quadrillion-time-bomb/5464666

Magdoff, F. (2009). The treat financial crisis three ears on. doi:10.14452/ MR06205

Massey, D. (2007). *Categorically unequal: The American stratification system*. New York, NY: Russell Sage Foundation.

Meldanado, M. (2018). Inequality matters. *LIS Cross National Data Center: Luxembourg,5*. Retrieved from https://www.lisdatacenter.org/wp-content/ uploads/files/nl-2018–5.pdf

Merriam-Webster. (n.d.). *Fascism*. Retrieved from https://merriam-webster. com/dictionary/fascism

Merriam-Webster. (n.d.). *Neoliberalism*. Retrieved from https://www.merri-am-webster.com/dictionary/neoliberal

Merriam-Webster. (n.d.). *Fourteen points of Fascism*. Retrieved from https:// www.merriam-webster.com/dictionary/fascism https://www.merriam-web-ster.com/dictionary/fascism

Miller, J., & O'Hanlon, M. (2020). *Focusing on quality over quantity in military spending. Brookings 2020.* Northampton, MA: The National Priorities Project. Institute for Policy Studies. Retrieved from https://www.brookings.edu/wp-content/uploads/2019/11/Big-Ideas OHanlon Defense.pdf

Mishkin, F. (2016). *Economics of money, banking, and financial markets.* London, UK: Pearson Publishing.

Mohamed, T. (2020, December 31). The rich should pay more: Bill Gates for higher taxes on the wealthy. *Markets Insider.* Retrieved from https://markets.businessinsider.com/news/stocks/bill-gates-calls-tax-hike-wealthy-new-years-eve-blog-2020-1-1028791394

Molms, F. (2018). Take a peek at what the top 1% have in savings. *Forbes.* Retrieved from https://www.forbes.com/sites/greatspeculations/2018/10/18/take-a-peek-at-what-the-top-1-percent-have-in-savings/#739b8be06dff

Money Facts. Questions and answers on money. U.S. Congress House Banking and Currency Committee. (1964). *Money facts: 169 questions and answers on money-a supplement to a primer on money, with index, Subcommittee on domestic finance.* Washington, DC: Publisher?

Newport, F. (2019). *Military voters of all ages tend to vote Republican.* Princeton, NJ: Gallup. Retrieved from https://news.gallup.com/poll/118684/military-veterans-of-all-ages-tend-republicam.aspx

Newton, L., Englehardt, E., & Pritchard, M. (2013). *Taking sides: Clashing views in business, ethics, and society.* New York, NY: McGraw Hill.

Nordhouse, W. (1975). The political business cycle. *Review of Economic Studies, 42*(130), 169–190, 457–466. doi:10.230712

Office of Management and Budget (OMB). (2018). *Monthly budget review: Summary for fiscal year 2018.* Retrieved from https://www.cbo.gov/publications/54647

Open Secrets Center for Responsive Politics. (2019). *Industry profile: Annual lobbying of commercial banks.* Retrieved from https://www.opensecrets.org/federal-lobbying/industries/summary?cycle=2019&id=F03

Oppenheim, G. (2012). Bill Gates says he and other rich people should pay significantly higher taxes. *Independent.* Retrieved from http://www.independent.co.uk/news/americas/bill-gates-tax-rich-people-pay-higher-cnn-trump-reform-a821/431.html

Orman, S. (2018). *Do prices really double every 20 years?* Retrieved from https://www.quora.com/Do-prices-really-double-every-20-years-as-claimed-by-Suze-Orman-due-to-inflation

Palley T. (2012). From financial crisis to stagnation: The destruction of shared prosperity and the role of economics. *Research Gate.* doi:10.1017/cbo9781139061285

Panzner, M. (2007). *Financial Armageddon: Protecting your future from four impending catastrophes.* New York, NY: Kaplan Publishing.

Pareto analysis. (2018). Retrieved from https://en.wikipedia.org/wiki/Vilfredo_Pareto

Perkins, J. (2008). *The secret history of American empire.* New York, NY: The Penguin Group.

Perloff, J. (2013). *Truth is a lonely warrior: Unmasking the forces behind global destruction.* Burlington, MA: Refuge Books.

Peterson, P. (2004). *How the democratic and republican parties are bankrupting our future and what Americans can do about it.* New York, NY: Farrar, Strauss, and Giroux.

Pigou, A. (1943). The classical stationary state. *Economics Journal,* 53(212). doi:10.2307/2226394

Pikety, T. (2014). *Capitalism in the 21st century.* Cambridge, MA: Harvard University Press.

Rand, A. (1957). *Atlas shrugged.* New York, NY: Random House.

Reagan, R. (1986). I'm from the government and I'm here to help. *Journeyman. The Daily Kos.* Retrieved from https://www.dailykos.com/stories/2011/4/30/971741/

Reich, R. (2007). *Supercapitalism: The transformation of business, democracy, and everyday life* (5th ed.). New York, NY: Knopf.

Roberts, C. (2015). *Craig Roberts Global on derivatives: The $1.5 quadrillion time bomb.* Retrieved from http://thesbocc.com/blog/?p=1396

Rodrick, D. (2011). *The globalization paradox: Democracy and the future of the world economy.* New York, NY: W. W. Norton.

Rothbard, M. (2005). *A history of money and banking in the united states.* Auburn, AL: Van Mises Press.

Rothschild, M. (1813). *Permit me to control the money of a nation and I care not about its standing armies.* Retrieved from https://quotes.yourdictionary.com/author/quote/594454

Saez, E., & Pikety, T. (2006). The evolution of top incomes: A historical and international perspective. NBER Working Paper No. 11955, Issued January 2006NBER Programs: Public Economics. doi:10.3386/w11955

Saez, M., & Zucman, G. (2014a). Wealth inequality in the United States: Capitalized income tax data. *National Bureau of Economic Research,* Washington, DC NBER Working Paper No. 20625 October 2014. No. H2N32 p.6. doi:10.3386/w20625

Saez, M., & Zucman, G. (2014b). Exploding wealth inequality in the United States. *VOX Cepr Policy Portal.* Retrieved from https://voxeu.org/article/exploding-wealth-inequality-united-states

Schere, B. (2018). Deficits don't matter so why are Democrats complaining? *Politico Magazine.* Retrieved from http://www.politico.com/magazine/story/2018/02/07/deficits-dont-matter-so why-are-democrats-complaining-about-them-216946

Schinasi, G. (2005). *Safeguarding financial stability: Theory and practice.* Washington, DC: International Monetary Fund Publication Services. doi:10.1108/1765680910932513

Schumpeter, J. (1950). *Capitalism, socialism, and democracy.* New York, NY: Harper Brothers.

Schwartz, N. (2018). As debt rises the government will soon spend more in interest than on the military. *The New York Times.* Retrieved from https://www.nytimes.com/2018/09/25/business/economy/us-government-debt-imterest.html

Seth, S. (2018). Why currencies collapse. *Investopedia.* Retrieved from http://www.investopedia.com/slide-show/5-failed-currencies-why-they-crashed/

Sherman, E. (2018). U.S. healthcare costs skyrocketed to $3.65 trillion in 2018. *Fortune Magazine.* Retrieved from https://fortune.com/2019/02/21/us-health-care-costs-2/

SOI Tax Facts. (2002). *The Internal Revenue Service.* Retrieved from https://www.irs.gov/statistics/soi-tax-stats-irs-data-book

Spring, A., & Friedberg, L. (1994). The future of American power. *Political Science Quarterly,* 4, 2021. doi:10.2307/2151658

Stone, S. (2020). A guide to statistics in historical trends in income inequality. *The Center on Budget and Policy Priorities.* Retrieved from file:///C/Users/17034/AppData/LocalMicrosoft/WindowsINetCasch/IE/C4JW4K-JR/11–28–11pov.pdf

Stone, C, Trisi, D., Sherman, A., & Beltran, J. (2020, January). *Center on budget and policy priorities: Guide to statistics on historical trends in income inequality.* Retrieved from https://www.chop.org/research/poverty-and-in-equality/a-guide-to-statistics-on-historical-trends-in-income-inequality

Storm, L. (2017). *The new normal: Secular stagnation and the vanishing middle class.* Working Paper No. 55, May 17, 2017. doi:10.1080/08911916.2 017.1407742

Story, L. (2010). A secret banking elite rules trading in derivatives. CNBC. *The New York Times.* Retrieved from https://www.cnbc.com/id/40628316

Summers, L. (2013). U.S. economic prospects: Secular stagnation and the hero power round. *Business Economics, 49*(2), 49, 65—73. doi:10.1057/be.2014.13m

Szmigiera, M. (2019). Most severe threats of economic damage worldwide in 2019 by Amount of GDP at risk. *Statista.* Retrieved from https://www.statista.com/statistics/995457/most-severe-threats-of-economic-damage-worldwide/

Taibbi, M. (2010). The great American bubble machine. *Rolling Stone Magazine.* Retrieved from https://www.rollingstone.com/politics/politics-news/the-great-american-bubble-machine-195229/

Tax facts. (2020). Retrieved from https://www.irs.gov/statistics/soi-tax-stats-irs-data-book

Temin, P. (2017). *The American dual economy: Race, globalization, and the politics of exclusion.* Working Paper No. 26 November 2015. doi:10.1080/0 8911916.2016.1185311

Temin, P. (2017). *The vanishing middle class: Prejudice and power in a dual economy.* Cambridge, MA: MIT Press.

The Economist. (2017). *The history of central banks.* Retrieved from https://www.economist.com/briefing/2017/04/27/the-history-of-central-banks

The Federal Reserve Website. (2018). *About the Federal Reserve.* Retrieved from https://www.federalreserve.gov/aboutthefed/section7.html

Tobin, J. (1978). A proposal for international monetary reform. *Eastern Economics Journal, 4*(3), 159. Retrieved from https://www.jstor.org/stable/20642317

Transparency International. (2018). *Global Corruption Perceptions Index.* Retrieved from https://www.transparancy.org/en/cpi/2018/results

U.S Debt Clock. (2019). Retrieved from https://www.usdebtclock.org/

U.S. Government Spending. (2018). *Monthly deficit spending/deficit charts.* Retrieved from https://usgovernmentspending.com

Semega, J., Fontenot, K., & Kollar, M. (2016). Income and Poverty in the United States. U.S. Census. (Average Income). *September 13, 2016.* *Retrieved from:* https://www.census.gov/library/publications/2017/demo/p60–259.html

Vanderbilt, C. (1882). The public be damned. *Dictionary.com.* Retrieved from https://www.dictionary.com/browse/the-public-be-damned

Vidal, G. (2001). *The last empire: Essays.* New York, NY: Avalon Publishing.

Vidal, G. (2002). *Perpetual war for perpetual peace.* New York, NY: Avalon / Nation Books.

Vidal, G. (2004). *Imperial America: Reflections on the United States of America.* New York, NY: Avalon Publishing Group.

Vine, D. (2015). Where in the world is the U.S. Military? *Politico.* Retrieved from https://www.politico.com/magazine/story/2015/06/us-military-bases-aroud-the-world-119321

Voltair, F. (1729). Paper money always returns to its intrinsic value-zero. Retrieved from http://libertytree.ca/Voltaie.Wuote.2BC6

Weil, D. (2014). *The fissured workplace,: Why work became so bad for so many and what can be done about it.* Cambridge, MA: Harvard University Press.

Weil, F., Katz, A., & Knueger, B. (2016). *The rise and nature of alternative work Arrangements in the United States labor market, 1995–2015.* NBER Working Paper 22667. September 2016. doi:10.3386/w22667

Weiss, G. (2006). *Wall Street versus America.* New York, NY: Penguin Group.

Williamson, J. (2004, September). *A short history of the Washington consensus.* Washington, DC: Peterson Institute for International Economics. Retrieved from http://www.iie.com/publications/papers/williamson00904–2pdf

Willie, J. (2005). Inflation: The hat trick letter. Retrieved from https://www.kitco.com/ind/Willie/printerfriendly//dec212006p.html

Wilson, W. (1913). I have unwittingly ruined my country. *The American Mercury Periodical: Encyclopedia Britannica.* George Jean Nathan, Henry Louis Mencken, 1924, 56, Speech.

Witko, C. (2016). How Wall Street became such a large chunk of the U.S. economy and when Democrats signed on. *Monkey Cage*. Retrieved from https://www.washington.com/news

Wolfe, E. (2017). *Household wealth trends in the United States, 1962–2016: Has middle class wealth recovered?* NBER Working Paper No. 24085. Issued in November 2017. doi:10:3386/w24085

World Bank. (2019) 15 of the world's most productive countries. Retrieved from https://collectivehub.com/2018/15-of-the-worlds-most-productive-countries/

World Economic Forum. (2018). *These are the worlds happiest countries.* Retrieved from https://www.weforum.org/agenda/2018/03/these-are-the-happiest-countries-in-the-world

World Economic Forum. (2019). *These are the world's healthiest countries.* Retrieved from https://www.weforum.org/agenda/2019/02/these-are-the-the-worlds-healthiest-nations/

World Health Organization (WHO). (2019). Measuring overall health system performance for 191 countries. GPE Discussion Paper Series No. 30 EIP/GPE/EQC/ World Health Organization. Retrieved from https://www.who.int/healthinfo/paper30.pdf

Zuchhi, C. (2018). Derivatives 101. *The Hill*. Retrieved from https://www.investopedia.com/articles/optioninvestor/10/derivatives-101.asp

About the Author

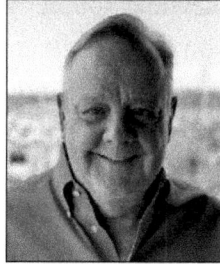

James Glenn grew up in the Washington D.C. metropolitan area and attended American University in Washington D.C. where he earned a BSBA in finance.

Upon graduation from American University, he spent over 15 years in the brokerage business as an investment adviser with Merrill Lynch, Prudential-Bache securities, and others. He spent 10 years in the banking business as a financial specialist, commercial lender, and underwriter for Wachovia bank, among others.

He has worked since 2004 in academia, both as a full-time business chair, full-time educator, curriculum developer, education consultant, dissertation mentor, advising, teaching and mentoring students at the doctoral, MBA, and undergraduate levels in business, finance, economics, accounting, management, statistics, and research.

His education also includes a Doctorate in Finance from Nova Southeastern University, Davie, Florida, and an MBA in finance from Palm Beach Atlantic University, in West Palm Beach, Florida.

Dr. Glenn has been writing on financial, economic, and political matters for over 20 years. He has written for numerous websites including financialsense.com, and Retirement USA, and has been a keynote speaker at George Washington University in Washington D.C. on financial and economic subjects. Dr. Glenn has a keen interest in promoting and working towards a more socially just and economically fair society.

He currently resides in Northern Virginia with his wife and two cats.

www.ingramcontent.com/pod-product-compliance
Lightning Source LLC
Chambersburg PA
CBHW071337210326
41597CB00015B/1481